Restructuring National Security

Restructuring National Security

Lt. Gen. Ashok Joshi (Retd.)
PVSM, AVSM

Manas Publications
New Delhi-110 002 (India)

MANAS PUBLICATIONS
(We Convert Fighters into Writers)
(Publishers, Library Suppliers, Importers & Exporters)
4402/5-A, Ansari Road (Opp. HDFC Bank)
Darya Ganj, New Delhi-110 002 (India)
Off. ✆ 23260783, 23265523; Fax: 011-23272766
E-mail: manaspublications@vsnl.com
manaspublications@yahoo.com
manaspublications@gmail.com

ISBN 81-7049-100-2
₹ 495/-

Designed at
Manas Publications

Printed in India at
Harmain Offsets, Delhi
and published by Mrs Suman Lata for
Manas Publications, 4402/5-A, Ansari Road
(Opp. HDFC Bank),
Darya Ganj, New Delhi-110 002 (INDIA)

Preface

"Restructuring National Security" in its scope and reach is extensive, and admits a variety of interpretations and treatment. Focus on purely military activities by the armed forces would have narrowed the field to their possible role, tasking, structuring, organizations, and so on. Further zooming in on to the operational art, tactics, and weapon systems, and so on, would have been perfectly natural. This would also have had the advantage of defining a narrower field, and studying it in greater depth. I decided, instead, to pan, and to enlarge the scope to examine the nature of conflict in its wider connotation :why does conflict emerge or is brought about ; by whom, for what purpose, and how. Armed force are important, and perhaps, principal actors in major conflicts. But often they are not the prime movers in bringing about conflicts, or in their resolution. Operational strategies, tactics, motivation, and actual performance of the armed forces is predicated upon the higher organizational inspirations, structures, and mechanisms. Those are at least as important, if not more, as the organizations and operations of the armed forces themselves, for the simple reason that they virtually predetermine and may even pre-ordain the performance of the armed forces in the field.

I decided to explore the larger field, rather than turn to matters such as size and number of formations, their logistics and so on.

Strategy deals with utilizing the consequences of battles to achieve the political objective. Strategy is as much the concern of the professional soldier as it is of the political master. Without political direction and objectives, strategy would have little meaning. This book is primarily concerned with policy and strategy.

The reader that I have had in mind, is the middle-piece officer of Indian Armed Forces in general, but in particular, that of the Army. With his numerous commitments on active duty, mostly under demanding and difficult conditions, he may not have time, energy, or opportunity to think of matters discussed here, much less to read about them. Though these matters are relevant to soldiering, admittedly at one or two removes, they tend not to attract attention. Indian armed forces do not tire of introspection, or shy away from critiques. They carry out frequent appraisals and studies with a view to improving efficiency, economy and effectiveness. But generally they do not move beyond tactics and the operational art. The broader and more general considerations that go into the evolution of policies and strategies, and their implementation, either do not attract adequate scrutiny, or prevailing ideas are accepted without questioning.

One of the difficulties experienced in exploring basic ideas and concepts connected with the matter at hand is the absence of standard terminology, but for which common understanding is difficult to arrive at. Terms like consciousness, power, security, strength, conflict, strategy and so on, cannot be depended upon to convey precise meaning. In order to avoid vagueness, working definitions of even commonly used words have had to be attempted. This could not be avoided even at the cost of attracting the odium of pedantry.

Lt.Gen. Ashok Joshi (Retd.)

Acknowledgements

I wish to place on record the kindness and understanding of all those who proffered friendship, help, and advice — Dr. V. R. Gowarikar, Vice Chancellor of the University of Pune, for facilitating the ideas; Professor Gautam Sen, Head of the Department of Defence and Strategic Studies, for his sharing of experiences, and helping me with his personal books and journals. Shri Bhagwan Joshi, former Financial Adviser to the Ministry of Defence, Major General K S Pendse(Retd.), and Professor Sohan Modak of the Botany Department of the University showed great patience in listening to whatever I was brimming with at the moment, during our leisurely conversations. They responded with candour, and I found my interaction with them highly enjoyable and educative.

I have benefitted from discussions that I have had with Professor A. S. Kolaskar, Professor S. L. Joshi, Dr. V. V. Bhate, Professor M. B. Konnur, Dr. M. H. Hirani, Dr. K. S. Nair, Dr. S. B. Paranjpe, Dr. A. S. Dalvi, and Dr. A. K. Taj The Staff of the Department of Defence and Strategic Studies, led by Shri Ravindra Nalawade have been most courteous and helpful.

Shri Anirudha Joshi assisted me in my research and was of great help. His enthusiasm is infectious.

I would not have undertaken this Study but for the insistence of Arundhati, my wife, Shashikant [Dr. S. S. Joshi], my brother. and Commodure Dhamdhere(Retd.). All of them reposed greater faith and confidence in my ability.

General Officer Commanding-in-Chief Southern Command extended to me the facility of working in Headquarters Southern Command Library. I am most grateful to him. Colonel P S Bhatnagar and his library staff were most courteous and helpful.

I take this opportunity to thank them all.

Contents

1

Collective Identities and Associations

Individuals turn to collective endeavour because individual effort and capability may be unequal to the task at hand and inadequate in many ways. Unequal because forces of nature, and many of the challenges and threats cannot be faced or countered individually, and inadequate because many individuals find themselves incomplete except in groups. A group may be short lived, or enduring ; impetus to form the group may owe its existence to history, pure chance or accident, or it may have been purposefully put together, with or without the consent of constituents. Individuals comprising that group may share perceptions in large or small measure ; it may be goal oriented mainly on an individual, or collective plane, or both ; or it may have no collective goal at all, and individuals may be seeking no more than company. It is obvious that this variety must be reduced to manageable proportions to enable exploration of collective behaviour dealing with struggle for survival and betterment, and/or conflict.

In a well publicised incident, a group of air-travellers, (Indian Airlines), most of whom were strangers, protested collectively against the abnormal delay before take-off, after the aircraft had been boarded. They became aware that the delay was due to the non-arrival of a VIP. Eventually, the VIP arrived, but refused to countenance the condition set by the irate passengers that he should apologise. They in turn would not allow the aircraft to proceed. The stand-off was resolved when one of the travellers pleaded with the rest that he was bereaved and could not brook the delay any longer because some one's death rites were delayed, pending his arrival at the destination[1]. The group of travellers, apparently, became a collective 'entity' when they became aware that their fortunes were linked for the duration of the flight. Till then, of course, most of them were perhaps strangers, with individual goals and purposes, and so would they have emerged, no sooner than leaving the arrival lounge at the destination. The collective entity turned gradually into an 'association', when many travellers felt that unjust treatment was being meted out to them, and thought of collective action with a limited aim. Soon enough, some rudimentary organization and makeshift leadership, in the form of spokes-persons and action group of protestors, emerged. Or, perhaps,it was an individual who took the lead and found support. They accepted some individual inconvenience — after all everyone was getting delayed — in return for individual satisfaction of having done the right thing, till requirement of one individual overpowered the collective purpose — of extracting an apology from the VIP. The association had a brief existence and it dissolved into an entity as soon as the protest ended. The entity itself evaporated as the travellers filed out of the aircraft at the destination. Nothing enduring or permanent of that group remained, but for a short duration, consciousness of every individual in the group had coalesced in some manner, to give rise to a collective will. Collective entity emerges when there is an awareness amongst individuals comprising that group of shared fate, opportunity, wants, or apprehensions, or in general, a commonality of at least some perceptions.

Collective identities is an outcome and product of virtual merging of individual identities, more or less. Collective identities can lose need, purpose and potency to revert to associations, just as associations can become entities or totally dissolve when individual wants in question and aspirations are no longer in need of being collectively addressed, or when individuals become or feel so very self sufficient that a particular collective endeavour seems superfluous.

It is believed that the concept of identity — whether individual or collective — is a derivative of consciousness.

'I and you', 'we and they' separations are a matter of common and every day experience. An individual defines his identity with reference to a periphery, or a boundary which includes him and his — or her, and hers — and excludes everyone else. An individual constituent of a group, could similarly conceive of a periphery beyond which lie they and theirs. To start with whatever it is that resides within and makes an individual aware of peripheries or boundaries that separate him from the rest of the environment could be called consciousness.

Consciousness[2] could also be taken to be that which determines, within a very broad range, a person's predisposition to likes, dislikes, preferences, acts, and abstentions to cover the entire spectrum of thoughts, emotions, reactions, and responses that a person is endowed with. Since there is no changelessness or immutable constancy in this respect, and individuals are seen to react differently in similar or comparable circumstances from day to day, consciousness could well be construed as a process, or even more appropriately, a set of processes of decision making , since lack of constancy and consistency in decision making is indeed a matter of common experience. Changes in decision making could then be viewed as naturally altered responses to changes in environment. It is often seen that some individuals are more prone to react or respond in a particular or predictable manner in a given set of situations than some others and, therefore, they are said to have a character. Others show more variations, but even their behaviour shows some 'traits' or evidence of predisposition. If a number of individual constituents of a group respond, feel, act, or abstain in a similar manner, generally, two conclusions could be drawn : (1)there is a collective consciousness[3] that informs the responses and actions of the group; and (2)there are shared traits in decision making processes. The commonality of traits could certainly be a contributory factor but may not be the sole determinant of their collective consciousness, since individual responses are likely to vary considerably depending upon the situation. The collective identity of the group could then be taken to be a derivative of the more enduring aspects of collective consciousness, on the analogy of individual identity being a derivative of the individual's consciousness.Carving out of Pakistan from the sub-continent was an assertion of an independent political identity by a sizeable number of Muslims of undivided India who felt that - "there [lived] in India another nation, with another language, a new culture, a new way of thinking and this nation [had] as much right ...[4]." as the rest to bid for independence.

Bid for independence itself was fuelled by a desire to define and assert a new collective identity in political terms. Pakistanis see the partition as - "culmination point of the long struggle of the Muslims to establish their identity as a separate nation, the struggle itself grew out of the larger freedom movement..[5]"

The larger freedom movement itself was an assertion of Indian identity in political terms.

The genesis of a collective identity could just as easily take another route. It does happen in some instances that the boundary or peripheral conditions that define and contain a group get established in the first instance, and collective consciousness emerges as a natural sequel thereafter. Prisoners, who may have had very little in common in their earlier lives, have a collective identity imposed upon them when they are made to live and work together. Collective consciousness emerges soon enough. Numerous jail riots in which the collective purpose — say, a jail-break — so overpowers the concerns of individuals for their own well being that many of them give up their lives in the ensuing fight. Collective identities need not necessarily draw upon loftiness of ideas or nobility of individuals comprising them. Collective identities emerge when collective enterprise subsumes individual concerns.

An individual's physical identity is fully autonomous, and neatly etched at a point of time. Other dimensions of an individual's identity may be inherited, or derived from social or situational context: an individual could acknowledge being a husband or wife, or be aware of being someone's son or daughter, or may belong to one of the professions. At a point of time an individual may not be aware of all the dimensions of his identity in a comprehensive manner, and therefore he may not be certain about their relevance or relative importance. Some of the dimensions may be transitory or elusive even to his own self — a person might have considered himself a communist in his student days, but may have moved away later; during that period he may have denounced his caste by birth, only to embrace it later when he got married within his own caste. Every dimension is a bond or a link that ties the individual to the world outside. Every dimension has the potential to cast the individual as a member of a collective entity, association, or identity. Birth and inheritance confer on an individual memberships of several collective entities : gender, religion, caste, class, citizenship, nationality, etc. A few of them may emerge as associations or identities. An individual may choose to, ignore, or renounce his inheritance, and may opt out of one or more of them. Yet other collective associations and identities may be sought and acquired. At a particular point of time, an individual may be forced to, or have reasons to, or may choose to, emphasise a particular dimension of his individual identity as a consequence of which his dominant collective identity might emerge. It is the natural inclinations — traits — and prevailing motivation of an individual that primarily determine his collective identity.

Perceptions of own collective identity are crucial in determining how an individual in a given situation or context acts or reacts, thinks, and more particularly, feels. One could come to such a conclusion even without taking an extreme position that our collective identities determine the totality of our feelings and responses. Our views of art and beauty, science, technology, some of the ethical and moral precepts and so on may not be related to the group identity, not always, and not ineluctably. But when it comes to achievements by a person or persons from another group, particularly a rival group, even in scientific or technological fields, the judgement may be swayed by considerations of group or collective identity. Two well meaning, balanced, informed and otherwise objective individuals may take contrary views of the same event, object, or person, mainly because of their identity, or who they perceive they are.

The idealism that hopes to improve the human condition by extending collective consciousness of common man to make him a citizen of the world is likely to encounter the hurdle of collective identity — several collective identities, actually — which it may not be able to cross[6].

So far collective consciousness has been merely as a 'vector resultant' of consciousness of several individuals in a group. That is to say, that very similar or comparable traits that influence decision making processes are shared by most individuals in the group, and on that basis, they tend to arrive at very similar or comparable conclusions regarding the issue at hand. But collective consciousness is more than that : it also includes the relationships that exist or develop among individuals — and among groups that they constitute — on account of their awareness of shared decision making traits and other deterministic or imposed circumstances. Individuals who not only 'think' alike, but also believe that they share chances of securing prizes and avoiding penalties, show an inclination to act together, and bonds grow among individuals. These bonds —involving obligations, expectations, commitment — create cohesion in the group as also reinforce the extension of individual consciousness to include other members of the group. It is the large content of commonality in perceptions and not necessarily their totality, or total congruence, that contributes to emergence of collective consciousness. Collective consciousness may extend or contract boundaries or peripheries that define collective identities, to include new member or exclude some present members. Since the collective consciousness and identity are derivatives of personal attributes, the changes and swings in the one are not without an impact on the other. If an individual's consciousness and dominant dimensions of his identity as perceived by himself is in a state of flux, its perception by others must be even more so. That which is more enduring and constant, is absorbed by the group to acquire group character. Some individuals, more than others, because of their capability, and sense of obligation and commitment that the group feels toward them, may exert such influence over it that it acquires characteristics over and above those which are commonly shared. An enduring group with a characteristic collective consciousness yields a collective identity.

A feeling, or conviction, of collective destiny and necessity for collective endeavour on the part of a group — a belief that the individual is not likely to fare as well as the group — contribute to determining the nature of the dominant collective identity. Asking of an individual that he should voluntarily subordinate his self interest to some other, or that he should supersede his own purpose by another is asking for too much. There is always a nagging doubt that this fanciful demand is, disingenuous. In ordinary circumstances, it contradicts essence of personal experience and common sense. And yet, such demands are made commonly enough and they do not always go begging. This inversion — subordination of self interest or purpose — can perhaps be construed not by doubting the essentially self serving nature of man but by conceding that an individual may decide, under certain conditions and in a given state of mind, to give precedence to the long term considerations over the immediate, and to subsume purely personal interest to that of his extended self — group. An internal struggle of some kind within a collective identity for a greater share of prize gained through collective effort of the group is only to be expected, except when the more compelling needs dominate, and cause the individual constituents to defer considerations of individual profit and loss. Considerations of how the group actually fares, what contributions individuals are expected to and actually make, what returns are expected by individuals, what they actually get, to what extent they acknowledge having received the returns, what proportion of returns are to be reserved for collective purpose, who is to take related decisions, and so on, impinge upon the collective consciousness. If individual constituents feel that they are being exploited, that is, their returns or satisfaction is not commensurate with their contribution, or that decision making is faulty, or that only a few benefit at the expense of other constituents, maladjustment within a collective identity is likely to take place. This maladjustment within a group may well lead to assertion by individuals or sub-groups, consequent internal struggle, and eventual break-up of the collective identity. Ideally, cooperation is an antidote to conflict, but cooperation without merging of identities in some ways; or some adjustments among them, is a non starter, and by merely emphasising the need for cooperation, genesis of internal struggle is not inquired into or addressed.

Struggle for and assertion of leadership is the most fundamental cause of internal conflict in a collective identity, possibly because assertion of pre-eminence in perpetuity in the chosen field is the most attractive of all prizes that the talented individuals seek. Leadership without a committed following is unthinkable. It cannot even emerge, much less survive, without support of a collective identity. But, paradoxically, it threatens that very collective identity with internal conflict. This built in contradiction is never really resolved, and for that very reason, struggle for leadership constitutes a pre-eminent factor that leads to internecine feuds, quarrels, and splintering of the collective identity. Apart from the struggle for leadership, the interplay of individual aspirations for the greater share of prizes, and mutual likes and dislikes also contributes to the internal struggle. Internal struggle within a collective identity is controlled partly through the loyalty[7] route, and partly through the 'strategic' cooperation route — a euphemism for sharing of leadership and other prizes on best available terms till diminution or elimination of rivals, and their inseparable adherents, becomes possible. Accumulated loyalties have the potential to protect group cohesion and identity, provided of course that other factors like lack of competence, means, and the like, do not produce an adverse impact. But the loyalty route to the resolution of the internal conflict does not wholly resolve matters, any more than it renders them less complicated. Loyalty route does not seem to help much in eliminating the possibility of internal struggle due to claims for the leadership of the group. Precept of loyalty, though not a panacea for curing all ills that afflict group cohesion, is employed effectively in creating the nation-state[8] structure so that it successfully accommodates numerous collective identities.

On the basis of the pre-eminent dimension, strand or element of one's identity at a given moment, an individual may lend more or less of himself to a number of collective identities, associations, and entities that constitute the nation. Some entities turn themselves into associations and start making collective demands, as in the case of transporters strike against the newly introduced service tax in the Union Budget of India for the year 1997-98. Some associations are in the process of turning into identities and putting up a violent struggle as happened in language related riots by Telugu speaking people in 1950s. Till then, fervour for language had not reached a state that individuals were willing to throw away their lives for what they considered to be the rightful place for the Telugu language. An 'Andhra' collective identity was emerging. It placed demands on the loyalty of Telugu speaking people and created a confrontation with the Union Government. This happened in many other places subsequently. The number of collective identities and associations seeking individual constituents are numerous, and even if all of them were to be compatible, the individual would still have to make a difficult choice about how he is going to divide his time and contribution amongst many collective identities and associations that he has either himself selected, or those which have laid successful claims on him. This problem can become magnified and unmanageable when it is compounded by an antagonism or incompatibility between collective identities themselves. What should be the priority in which a person should respond to demands made upon him by his family, profession, religion, language or trade association, or a humanitarian cause like human rights? Even in purely ethical terms, it is a difficult question to answer. But when it is overlaid with personal preferences and weaknesses, it seems to defy an answer that can satisfy most individuals. The problem, in purely theoretical terms, has part of an answer in the very concept of the nation: nation is the repository of all loyalties, that is loyalty to every other individual, collective identity, and association; and other causes must take a lower precedence. If an individual were to be subjected to demands on his loyalty which 'nest' together, somewhat like the 'Matrushka' dolls — a smaller doll being enclosed in the larger —, with each next larger collective identity completely enclosing the former, the problem will become somewhat tractable. In other words, an individual constituent should be required to be in the hierarchy of the nesting collective identities at a point of time. Demands that other associations make on him and those which he makes on them must not be incompatible with demands for loyalty that the presiding collective identity — the nation-state — makes.

Even if this precept were to be accepted unquestioningly, it gives no clear indication about whether there is a need for specifying for all times a hierarchy of collective identities, associations, and loyalties with a relative precedence; if anyone would succeed in doing so, and circumstances in which most individuals would abide by it. In traditional, homogeneous, or totalitarian systems such prescriptive regimes are naturally accepted or enforced.[9]

Collective identities are meaningful to the extent that they actually attract commitment of the individuals and groups that they comprise. Commitment calls for focusing on the totality of collective interest, contribution of individual effort, some times without recognition, willingness of individuals and groups to suffer for the collective good, and tolerance. It goes without saying, that the collective good is a matter of opinion, and there may be no agreement on it, also that the claims for and demands by leadership may cause confusion about the right course as well as the ultimate object of loyalty: leader, or cause? Notwithstanding these real issues, without the basic commitment to the collective identity, there is no possibility of success in crisis situations.

Collective identities which underpin the nation, which subsume all others, and which must be sustained and nourished by invoking loyalty of all individuals and associations have to emerge out of consensus on the following:

(1) Enduring aspirations, which if given up, will make the nation unrecognizable.

(2) Irreducible minimum assets and attributes which,if compromised, have the potential to dissolve the nation.

Invoking loyalty of individuals for lesser reasons is unlikely to succeed. Only a few collective identities are totally predicated upon loyalty, amongst them the armed forces. Profit motive — maximising share of prize — relies on creating collective associations rather than identities by relating the compensation to the extent of contribution and efficiency on the one hand, and the willingness to take risk on the other. Commitment and liability are limited and well defined. Collective identities derived from loyalties tend to be more enduring and autonomous, whereas collective associations based on profit motives tend to rely on the rule of law for cohesion and survival, and can be dissolved without bitterness. Loyalty and profit motive both are facets of struggle for survival and betterment. Ultimately, both are essential for nourishing and strengthening collective identities. Stability and equilibrium in a collective identity is predicated upon the intrinsic capacity of the prevailing order to minimise and manage internal tensions so that they do not develop into a consuming internal conflict. When an order cannot contain rebels, they may well begin by asserting a separate identity, for which purpose they need a new system, a new book of rules, and help and assistance from 'aliens' - those who subscribe to another vision, and another order. The aliens may make common cause and help rebels, or other break-away groups, to subserve their own purpose.

An individual, or a group, which is so situated that it remains on the fringes of collective identities, with which it finds itself incompatible, is constrained to negotiate life on very unfavourable terms, being forced to be a victim or a participant in conflicts not necessarily of its own choosing. Such situations bedevil Serbs, Croats, Bosnians, Kurds, and Palestinians to mention the more unfortunate examples. In India, in the midst of communal riots, polarisation on Hindu or Muslim planes may become the dominant factor and cause individuals to act on that basis; on the other hand, during the language riots, the religion may be subsumed. Collective identities are also prone to swells and shifts in prevailing moods. It is the ability to create a presiding loyalty, which has the potential to absorb and subsume the subaltern groups and cultures, and dissolve their incompatibilities, that holds the promise of reducing causes of conflict.

Collective associations — associations — are motivated by the desire of the constituents — individuals or collective identities themselves — to secure the greatest share of prize at an acceptable cost. Constituents of associations look upon collective effort, and the associations themselves, as means to an end, and with no particular sense of commitment. Associations cease to survive when they become ineffective , that is, when individual constituents do not feel satisfied with the share of prize that they can secure. Leadership may be claimed on the basis of efficiency, competence, and effectiveness. Considerations of loyalty do not bind constituents to commitments beyond those which are well defined, and already made. It is interdependence and hope of a reasonable share of prize that cements the association. Leadership has to be claimed and justified by virtue of greater contribution and effectiveness. Competence and competition are encouraged in the interest of productivity. Constituents are not willing to take any punishment and show great reluctance to continuation of leadership which brings punishment. Associations represent an evolutionary development of the basic collective identity model. Collective identities can survive with an internal order, but associations need, additionally, an orderly and well regulated environment or order which allows them to combine or cooperate with other associations. Associations have a comparatively more liberal regime for the constituents who have a greater freedom to make a choice as compared to a collective identity where the code of conduct of the 'pack' or the 'tribe' is binding. Associations demand less of the individual — by way of contribution, sacrifice, commitment, and conformity —and promise him some gains, with hopes of more, and that too, at a minimum of risk. Associations can survive for so long as the incidence of hazard and risk is minimal, and the possibility of gains is substantial.

If the institution of sovereign and hereditary king was a logical development of the tribal collective identity, the nation state was a further refinement : it replaced an individual family by institutions that represented the state to which unlimited loyalty was to be owed, and created a concept of territorial boundary. Both became symbols of the collective identity of the nation state leaving citizens in no doubt about either the location of the 'we and they' divide, or what constituted the ultimate repository of all loyalties. Citizens no longer considered themselves mere subjects. Within the periphery, it liberated them from servility to an individual or a family ; without, it created opportunities for exploitation by constituent associations and identities. This commonly acknowledged sovereignty within borders of nation states created conditions in which 'balance of power' concept could emerge. Nation states could create an international order, admittedly restricted and somewhat transactional, In which associations — alliances — could be formed. These associations could enter into strategic cooperation, for as long as necessary or required, and act like collective identities for the duration of actual campaigns. They were made conscious that a change could be brought about without losing the essence of the collective identity.

The East India Company established by the Royal Charter was an association, that is, the share holders and the directors were in it for profits for so long as their interests were served. In India the Company got opportunities to acquire territory by force, and perforce had also to defend it by force. The use of force in those times meant very great hazards and risks, and an army with its own values and stakes in mission, rather than own survival had to be raised. Such an army soon came into being, and virtually acquired the whole of the sub-continent for the Company which had only commercial interests at heart. Directors of the Company, and England in turn, were fattening on the profits made till the whole enterprise went up in flames following the uprising in 1857. At this stage England found it convenient to wind up the

Company, and take over the administration under the control of the Crown and India became a part of the Empire. Company had no collective identity; it had nothing to preserve, or to fight for once the Directors got their compensation. But the units of the Army they had created had a collective identity . Obviously, the British very wisely decided to absorb the British and Indian Units into the imperial system and Army in India came into being. They would have had a very hazardous and messy problem of disbanding, if not of fighting against the former units of the East India Company on their hands, otherwise. So, an enterprise started by an association, ended up by creating assets for the collective identity of which they had been a part of. Once again, Britain formed an association with British India, to be retained as long as profitable. British India was never a part of the British collective identity.

Nationalism was a refinement of the tribal culture when it came into being. It was further refined when it created scope for collective identities and associations to coexist within its structure, and utilize whichever mode was more beneficial. And beyond that, nation states themselves could combine into more complex and profitable organizations to get into and out of alliances and treaties. Collective identities lost some of their rigidity to avoid being brittle on the one hand, and acquired skills in evolving higher organizational structures which would be more productive and better suited to cope up with the unavoidable change.

With the coming of liberal age, nation states themselves are beginning to function more and more like associations : globalization is meant to eliminate all barriers to trade, communication, and movement. Understandably, entrepreneurs have the opportunity to combine with their counterparts in all parts of the globe in associations to create assets, and secure their parts of the prizes, with minimal political interference. But the basic building block of the international system, the nation state has not changed. It is striving to create supra-national institutions which will support an international order in which more and more complex organizations in the nature of associations can function and prosper for so long as they are effective and efficient. Nation states, within, cannot do without collective identities for the fear that when survival is at-stake, associations may not take the stress; even associations have to harden into collective identities when necessary.

But what happens to gains made, assets created, and prizes secured by associations. They get reinvested into collective identities so that those may be perpetuated. Though associations may be formed with anyone, where productivity is the dominating concern, those associations which have the potential to act as collective identities in difficult situations attract special support and care. Collective identities to whom the assets are bequeathed certainly happen to be those which are based on affinities of common race or racial mix, civilization, culture, religion, geography, and history. There is a feeling that associations formed by European nations may harden into collective identities the core of which would be the European civilization. Notice the ex-patriate Chinese who are returning to China with skills and capital acquired in the West. Perhaps they wish to invest in China so that the Chinese identity may be perpetuated.

The merging of collective identities — those which have a firmly etched periphery or set of border conditions which mark 'we and they' divides across which commitment for caring and sharing does not travel without major changes or transformation — is a comparatively rare phenomenon. It does happen now and then though: for example, federation of independent states into the United States of America and in our own times, the union of Hawaii with the United States. But generally, this is difficult to bring about because the protection of boundaries may have demanded too great sacrifice in the past and the periphery may have become hallowed and overloaded with an unremovable burden of history. Notice the resistance to giving up the vestiges of collective identity in the European Union where new patterns of collective associations are emerging — the very continent where the concept of the nation state was born. In spite of the resistance, with no threat from within, and with assured security, possibly because of the dissolution of the Soviet

Empire, as also continuation of Eastward looking NATO, there has been a gradual shift to primacy of associations in which individual and collective goals are aligned, but returns sought are in proportion to the inputs. The state is making room for individuals and associations to be in the forefront for prosperity. Though at present trans-national associations are arching over borders, and the idea of unstinted loyalty and sacrifice for the nation state appears to take a back seat, there is no guarantee that the nation state collective identity has been erased. Perhaps, there is a need to distinguish between survival related border, and prosperity related frontier. British and French nuclear capability contimues to be in place to take care of the survival related border. Frontiers of prosperity can keep expanding. We do not know if the pooled prosperity of individuals and associations will be used by the state, in times to come, to assert itself, as in times gone by.

An association, if it hardens into a collective identity, may want to opt out of presiding collective identity, and join another one or remain independent, asserting its own separate domain and new boundary conditions. Happenings in Sri Lanka may be seen in this light. LTTE want their own Tamil Eelam. As to why would associations want to opt out of a collective identity, to what extent they succeed, the means they adopt, and justification they give deserve scrutiny. The nature of boundary conditions — we and they divides — are significant. If they create not only differing but essentially incompatible view points, seceding association may be seen as a potential adversary. On the contrary, collective identities which were torn asunder show willingness to merge, even after a brief spell of adversarial relationship provided the basic self definition and world view largely overlap. Merger of two Germanies — FRG and GDR — after nearly 44 years of independent existence signifies this.

Collective identities, because of the claims that they make on individual's loyalty, have the ability to pool and employ resources on a substantial scale. They seem to be the principal players in the struggle for survival, prosperity, and conflict. The nature of conflict is essentially determined by how and why collective identities assert themselves, and the means that they have at their disposal. Most conflicts seem to fall into one of the four categories stated below. It is to be seen that they are related more or less directly to preservation, perpetuation, and or prosperity of collective identities or emergence of new identities:

Secession and civil war which may lead to splintering and emergence of new collective identities.

Expansion to acquire new territory, colonies, or wealth so that 'out-siders' can be exploited.

Forming associations and alliances to create opportunity for pushing forward frontiers of prosperity, from which collective identities derive strength and sustenance.

Diminution/elimination of alien identities, values, and influences, which are considered hostile or incompatible.

NOTES

1. The anecdote is not apocryphal. Details about the incident such as the name of the VIP are excluded because they are redundant.

2. William J. Calvin, in ' The Cerebral Harmony', (Bantam Books, 1990), quotes observations of the neurobiologist J. Z. Young who describes consciousness with reference to conscious mind : " The 'conscious mind' relates to dealings with the outside world, which requires elaborate analysis in the light of the past, and preparations for the future course of action."

   Calvin further quotes the psychologist Barton Perry to caution the unwary about 'consciousness' : " There is no term [consciousness] at once so popular and so devoid of standard meaning."

3. The term collective consciousness is used in both the senses: as the summation of the traits of the individuals as well as the resultant of the decision-making process of the group.

"What is true is that individuals and their properties and relations are the indications and references for collective terms; there is no other way by which meanings can be empirically specified." Abraham Kaplan, `The Conduct of Inquiry', Sachin Publications, Jaipur, 1980.(p.81.)

4.M. H. Askari, 'Thought: Let's celebrate the end of Raj too', Asian Age, Mumbai, (By arrangement with Dawn), May 5, 1997. He quotes G Allana from, 'Our Freedom Fighters'.

5.ibid.

6. Aron observes : "Humanity does not constitute politico-military entity", Raymond Aron, `Clausewitz, Philosopher of War, Routledge & Kegan Paul, London 1976,(p.374).

7. Working definition of loyalty . an attribute of an individual — or that of a constituent of a larger collective identity — that causes him to accept that he ought to contribute a little more towards the collective endeavour than what he expects in return, be prepared to accept a little more of disadvantage than the next man, and allow the group leadership to take decisions for the group. It is not used in the sense of old fashioned loyalty to the person of sovereign which can only travel upwards.

8. Bertrand Russell emphasises that " A nation, unlike a class, has a definition that is not economic. It is, we may say, a geographical group possessed of solidarity. Psychologically, it is analogous to a school of porpoises, a flock of crows, or a herd of cattle. The sentiment of solidarity may be due to a common language, a supposed common descent, a common culture, or common interests and common dangers. As a rule all these play a part in producing national sentiment, however produced, is the only essential to the existence of a nation." Bertrand Russell, `Freedom and Organization—1814-1914', George Allen and Unwin, London, 1934,(pp.394-395)

9. Bertrand Russell observes : " The characteristic doctrines of German nationalism are all to be found in Carlyle : belief in the importance of will rather than knowledge, faith rather

than reason, and duty rather than happiness; worship of the state and admiration of vigorous despotism; emphasis on race and on heroic individuals; dislike of industrialism disguised as a pity for industrial proletariat." Bertrand Russell, Freedom and Organization — 1814-1914', George Allen and Unwin, London, 1934. (p.399)

2

Strength and Power

Power holds such fascination because it promises results and satisfaction. Power-politics, power-tennis, international power-play, power-steering, power-brakes, and the like are a testimony to the fascination that 'power' holds. Physicists have defined it neatly and in a manner that admits of no disagreement. But social scientists who deal with matters that involve human beings have a more complex subject matter to deal with and have not found the task easy. There is little agreement amongst them[1]. Power, is considered here in the context of conflict and/or cooperation, that is, from the point of view of social scientist, because war is a cultural and social phenomenon. Here we are mainly concerned with power that individuals and groups generate and exercise to achieve results, so that, answers to questions such as —what is power, what are its sources, how is it generated, how is it employed, what results are hoped to be achieved, how is power projected, resisted or countered, and other allied questions can be found. But to start with, it is worthwhile to sample some of the definitions of power that social scientists and thinkers have to offer.

According to Voltaire -

"Power consists of making others act as I choose".

The emphasis is, clearly, on compulsion. Bertrand de Jouvenel has in mind the relationship born of authority, when he observes that

"To command and to be obeyed : without that there is no power".

""Power is the possibility of imposing one's will upon the behaviour of other persons", is the definition of power according to Max Weber[2].

The thread that runs through all these definitions is one of compulsion, imposition, or authority with some variations in emphasis on inter-relationships. At the other end of the spectrum we have the definition of power by Hannah Arendt who views power from a totally different perspective :

"Power corresponds to the human ability not just to act but to act in concert. Power is never the property of an individual; it belongs to a group and remains in existence only so long as the group keeps together[3]."

This definition of power views it not so much as a facet of authority or compulsion, but as that of cooperation.

Bertrand Russell defines power as - " The production of intended effects". Dennis H. Wrong finds the definition satisfying except for one rider : " Power is the capacity of some persons to produce intended and foreseen effects on others.[4]" These definitions do not tell us as to why someone would want to impose one's will on others. In some way, they get separated from the purpose, unless exercise of power itself is the purpose. Bertrand Russell does actually emphasise that at least exercise of some of the political power may have no other purpose :

"Since power over human beings is shown in making them do what they would rather not do, the man who is actuated by love of power is more apt to inflict pain than to permit pleasure[5].

Unless power is linked with purpose, it would soon become a-rational, in that it would no longer remain an instrument, and turn into a loose cannon that may hurt someone or the other, without serving anyone's purpose. About the only agreement that exists about power is that it is meant to achieve results that bring satisfaction. Chanakya, perhaps, makes the point by juxtaposing power and success, and further by defining success as happiness[6].

Now, the purpose may be as compelling as mere survival, or it may be as grand as conferring human rights and democracy on mankind, or spreading communism to liberate mankind from shackles of capitalism, or saving the world from state control over economy. Purpose needs no justification; not any more than that required for wanting to acquire power as an instrument for fulfilling that purpose. Raymond Aron quotes Morgenthau to stress that the need for power is a basic urge and does not stand in need of justification :

"International politics, like all politics, is a struggle for power. Whatever the ultimate aims of international politics, power is always the immediate aim. Statesmen and people may ultimately seek freedom, security, prosperity, or power itself. They may define their goals in terms of a religious, philosophic, economic, or social ideal. They may hope that this ideal will materialize through its own inner force, through divine intervention, or through the natural development of human affairs. But wherever they strive to realise their goal by means of international politics, they do so by striving for power. The crusaders wanted to free the holy places from domination by the Infidels; Woodrow Wilson wanted to make the world safe for democracy; the National Socialists wanted to open Eastern Europe to German Colonization, to dominate Europe and to conquer the world. Since they chose power to achieve these ends, they were actors on the scene of international politics[7]."

Perhaps, a working, if not generally satisfying, definition may be devised by making an effort to reconcile some of the apparent contradictions in views cited above and by concentrating on the insights no matter how varied. Steven Lukes thinks otherwise,

"Perhaps, but I doubt it. It is more likely that the very search for such a definition is a mistake[8]."

In spite of this caveat, it would still be necessary to start with a working definition so as to avoid confusion; additionally, the field of current inquiry will stand clearly delineated. Such a working definition could be: Power should be regarded as the totality of instruments that secures prizes. Power is the capacity to cause others to cooperate, and/or impose compliance on them, more or less, so that such cooperation and/or compliance assist in securing of prizes; power also incudes capacity to punish or reward.

Power manifests when it is developed by realising the power- potential. Power potential may be described as strength, without making an effort to define strength at this stage. Raymond Aron distinguishes between 'puissance' — potential — and 'pouvoir' as realised potential. Difference between strength and power is analogous[9]. Some of the salient aspects of strength and power that need to be taken into consideration are their genesis, manifestation, and operation : how do they come into being, or how are they generated; how do they manifest, or how are they seen or perceived; and lastly, how do they operate. Surprisingly, much of the apparent disagreement about what constitutes strength or power, or how should they be viewed or defined, seems to narrow down when separate aspects of strength and power are considered, as will be seen later.

Raw sources of strength may be traced to fundamentals like land, people, their characteristics and attitudes, knowledge, cohesiveness, institutions, education, state of development and so on. Some individuals in a group may be better endowed and developed than others: they may have better intelligence, vision, public concern and spirit, ability to persuade others, skills and knowledge. The following quotation from Laswell includes eight human attributes that are basic sources of power:

"Laswell has constructed a comprehensive scheme of eight base values which, although not necessarily exhaustive, are certainly inclusive; power(which can serve as a base for more power), respect, rectitude or moral standing, affection, well-being, wealth, skill, and enlightenment[10]."

Individuals with such or similar attributes may, therefore, constitute the leadership of the group. Such leadership through persuasion, fear, or incentives may cause the group to accept collective endeavour as a means of solving some problem, or attaining some goal that is generally accepted by all the members of the group. In this way, 'power' of the leadership may have tapped the fundamental sources to create group-strength. Group-strength, in turn can be developed to yield power, to create a bigger group with larger strength, or to subdue another group. The argument can be extended to include the nation state. Attributes of leaders are sources of their strength, but leadership itself is 'power', in that it is an instrument that is employed to achieve the desired results. Strength and power cannot exist separately, but they are quite different. Together they have the capacity to rise in a spiral, the one drawing on the other. The need to treat strength and power as two separate concepts will shortly become apparent.

Strength manifests in a nation state in a number of ways :

Politically,

> it leads to a stable collective identity that creates the right balance between competition and cooperation within the borders; there is a common desire to bring about an evolutionary change in prevailing order, and reinforce pride in collective assets and values; it shows an innate ability to reconcile the demands of democracy, or aspirations of common man with requirements of excellence and productivity; it makes it possible to reward talent without placing the handicapped at a positive disadvantage; it tempers idealism with pragmatism; and it reduces the level of violence in society.

Economically,

> it produces a net surplus; reduces consumption and encourages savings; achieves self sufficiency in essentials, self reliance and inter-dependence through production of quality goods and investments abroad; and ensures investment for growth.

In the Social Sector

it leads to improvements in health care and education and elimination of unfounded prejudices.

Taken together, strength manifests as stability and growth. Strength is an end in itself. Strength can be drawn upon and converted into power, but not without opportunity costs. Strength, in a sense, does not operate at all. But it exerts an influence, that resists alien or hostile power-projection. Strength, by itself, cannot counter hostile power, but it reduces its effectiveness and acts as a disincentive to adventurism. Strength is, also, potential power, and therefore, acts like power at one remove. Potential for strength enters all political calculations about the future.

Power operates by fulfilling or denying wants of the victim or object; additionally, power also brings about changes in the receptivity and perceptions of the object (victim) so much so that object's out-look about his needs, wants, desires, and dislikes undergoes changes which are desired by the subject. The results achieved may never be total, complete, final, or even enduring. Application of power may not be enough or sufficient to achieve such results, or perhaps, human spirit is not wholly conquerable by power. But generally, the desired results or obtained by operating power in the manner stated. Power also operates by creating consensus, sometimes amongst those who are not even aware that there is some common ground or shared interest in respect of which their views converge, and therefore there is a need for cooperation, and further, that such cooperation would secure for them prizes that they seek, if not in entirety, and for all the times to come, then at least for the time being and for a sufficiently long time thereafter. Such an example was on hand when the Secretary General of the United Nations created consensus during his visit to Iraq in February 1998, and resolved tensions in and around the Gulf which were threatening to get out of hand, what with the United States wanting to strike and Iraq not willing to blink.

When power so operates, to create awareness of common concerns amongst the deprived and the under-privileged, and a genuine possibility of cooperation, on the basis of consensus and an agreed minimum programme emerges, there is an upsurge of a feeling of solidarity and strength in that group. Such a group creates its own instruments of power and either cooperates with larger groups, or confronts others till their demands are conceded. The euphemism for compromises so reached is 'empowerment'. The point to note is that power can and does operate to create cooperation or confrontation, or both. Arguments are often put forward in defence of common man, that he wants to cooperate, and it is only the leadership that pushes him into confrontation, for its own end. This may or may not be true. The relevant point here is that operative power can and does create consensus and cooperation, and 'empowers' groups to fulfil their own wants, instead of an outside agency being in control, and either fulfilling or denying wants by keeping the object on a leash.

Power manifests as capacity to deny or fulfil wants, and to influence mind and spirit. The manifest power may be viewed as consisting of three components:--

(1) ability to meet own needs, directly or indirectly, by fulfilling wants of others by providing goods or services in exchange — named 'e' for economic;

(2) ability to deny wants and impose deprivation on others and thereby prevailing upon them to comply — named 'c' for coercive ; and -

(3) ability to influence others into consenting or complying without actually making a significant direct use either of 'e' or 'c'— named 'i' for influence.

Component 'e' is the quintessential economic power that depends upon mutual consent for carrying out exchanges. What matters is the attractiveness of prevailing exchange values, and offerings at hand that more or less meet mutual needs. Component 'e' is negotiable , or largely negotiable rather than assertive in nature. If the need is intense, and provider has a virtual monopoly, the difference between 'e', and 'c' gets narrowed. Component 'c' — coercion —, perhaps, covers a wider spectrum. It relies on denying basic essentials like food and other necessities, or minimal freedom from pain and discomfort without which life becomes unbearable, or it may deprive a person or a population of every possession, or life itself. It is obvious that deprival of life cannot be construed as 'c', except as an example to others of what they can expect if they fail to comply. The whole range of physical force, and other instruments of coercion are covered by 'c'. Component 'i' — influence — undoubtedly derives in large part from the other two components which already invest a person or a group with power, and 'i' is, then, the bonus that is derived from the attendant prestige. That apart, 'i' can also be traced to non-material human strengths and traits such as leadership and character qualities, or ingenuity, and to organizational strength. As an instrument of power 'i' component can best be described as 'political.'

An individual by virtue of his total inability and need may evoke compassion or pity in those who are well endowed; perhaps, he exercises some negative influence. Cynically, it could be said that, the most deprived and handicapped are also not without power. They may well exercise 'i' component of power by making the rich and healthy feel insecure in their good fortune and, 'blackmail' them into parting with some alms or assistance. These examples may not be far-fetched in analytical or abstract terms; but even in real life, we do see that help is rushed to refugees, half way across the globe, to satisfy requirements which are as much of the donor as they are of the receiver. Denial of approbation, or approval and praise can also be construed as components of power lying in undefined areas. There is hardly any individual who is totally powerless. In this interpretation of power, what is worth noting is that, accrual or manifestation of power takes place only through interaction. Manifestation of power does not take place without interaction because power has to be 'applied' to fulfil or deny wants, and influence has to be 'used' to achieve a purpose. Otherwise it remains a potential. In some of the definitions of power it is presumed that unless an individual is made to act against his will, power is not employed. This view of power detracts from power being a complete instrument for achieving results. In the event of there being two groups with largely divergent views and desires, if an area of agreement is found and made operative, no matter how small, and divergence reduced to that extent, power would have been generated and employed, if the desired purpose — which may be the gaining of a breather by lowering of tension — were to be achieved. Influence may have been used by leaders of one of the contesting parties, or by a mediator. What is significant here is clubbing together of all means or instruments, no matter how different they are, and disregarding the nature of means themselves, or the agents who operate them.

The relationship between strength and power is not of simple causality, though the latter without the former is not thinkable. How strength is generated also depends on the nature of collective identity to a great extent. All the sources of potential power remain embedded in strength. Power is a particular realisation of strength. Intrinsically, sources of strength and power are the same, but the manifestations of strength and that of power are very different from each other. In economic terms, manifestation of strength may be production, but the instrument of power may be export, or even better, a monopoly. Educated and motivated manpower is a manifestation of strength, whereas a trained soldier is a part of 'c' component of power. Strength creates many possibilities for realisation of power. Unrealized power is retained as strength, giving rise to many possibilities. Without strength, there will be no generation of power. Power cannot grow on its own. It remains an instrumentality. As an instrument, power may be employed by individuals — leaders — to bring about awareness of collective strength. Greater power yield can only be had from greater strength. Strength is available for conversion to power for projection as also, for resisting and countering hostile power.

Power projection, if it results in deleterious effect on the strength of the nation, proves disastrous. Call it 'over reach' or otherwise, it spells doom. Because the loss is twice over: actual losses and waste, plus the opportunity costs. There was a time that power projection with 'c' component in the lead could win overseas possessions. Thereafter the victor's order was established, and through now well known colonisation techniques, the projected power was converted into strength, and there was unprecedented growth of the imperial power. Power projection in Vietnam failed because it wore down instead of adding on to the US strength. As of now power projection with 'e' component in the lead can be used to bleed the adversary's strength effectively; besides, power projection with 'c' component in the lead is always fraught with risks.

Collective identities owe their existence to their ability to secure prizes which are beyond the reach of individuals. A collective identity would not survive but for its ability to generate power and apply it in a manner that collective and individual needs are generally met; and even more, that distribution of prizes and power is conducive to a stable equilibrium. The totality of power and prizes ultimately get distributed amongst constituents unequally, possibly in conformity with the phenomenon of normal distribution, that is the top one sixth of the population commands a disproportionately large quantum of power and prizes, the bottom one sixth are deprived abnormally, and remaining one third of the population occupies the middle. Even amongst the top one sixth, the same pattern of distribution oncc again emerges. The pyramid, so to say, narrows rather steeply. With some exceptions here and there, the pattern is almost universal. Collective identities have to survive in spite of this lopsided distribution. If the lopsided distribution were to correspond to the equally lopsided, and equally natural, distribution of actual talent and ability that individuals have, some stability may still be achieved in spite of ongoing turbulence occasioned by assertion of claims to even more power by the talented. But in the real world, the unequal distribution of power and prizes is a product of many factors, including inheritance, and the talent and ability both often go begging for want of opportunity. And in any case, ambition and ability are not necessarily correlated. Collective identities create and retain their ability to generate and employ power in spite of the natural handicaps and hindrances mentioned. It is not only because of the institutions and apparatus of governance that collective endeavour — power generation and application — becomes possible, but it is because of the prevailing order that holds out the promise not only of collective and individual survival but also of prosperity. An element of coercive power has necessarily to be employed to retain the existence of a collective identity like a nation state. If it is used in accordance with the law of the land to maintain order, the use of coercive components including force may not expose the collective identity to the breaking strain. It is obvious that if 'c' component of power is not made inaccessible to a large proportion of population, coercion required for governance will increase proportionately. This will also detract from the overall productivity, because denial of goods and services by one section of population to the other must have an adverse impact on 'e' component. Power that is used up in governance is not available for 'power projection'. Power projection requires an out look that relies upon minimising domestic 'power in use'— which would also include consumption, but not saving and productive investment — and exporting goods and services to secure prizes, which may also include import of essential goods and services. Contrast this with 'self-containment' approach which would aim at self sufficiency. Self sufficiency may give a feeling of lack of vulnerability and autonomy, but it preempts possible use of 'e' component for power projection. The use of 'c' component for power projection is more readily appreciated, and that too only of force. Without exporting and causing dependence to develop, the possibility of denying goods and services as a part of the 'c' component of power does not arise. Conversely, a sizeable importer can stop imports completely, or the threat of such action can be used as a coercive instrument

Influence does spring from two other components of power, but not necessarily. Influence can also be an outcome of engineered misperception, or illusion. A suitable mix of reality and illusion can influence the behaviour of friend and foe alike. What is new is the totally unprecedented ability to create and transmit images that produce the desired result. Reality can be bent and twisted to order without stretching the viewer's or listener's credulity, and that too in a short span of time. Ability to influence or the 'i' component of power has gained in importance in a totally unprecedented manner. It now rides the sky wave and cannot be kept out. Self isolation as a protective mechanism is no longer a possible option. Power component 'i' from now onwards will always contain a mix of the real and the unreal, honest information as easily as disinformation, and has the potential of producing an impact totally out of proportion to the resources used. Component 'i' in the past was directed principally at the decision makers, and marginally at the population. Now the population and the decision makers can be subjected concurrently to the same influence, and thereby the decision makers can be robbed of time that is available for decision making, and freedom to take unpopular decisions. Equally, leaders and the rest of the population can be subjected to subtly different influences so that the process of decision making itself can show leadership in poor light. Instant results can be produced. It may take days for the actual impact of a strike or an embargo, or an oil price rise to be felt by the sections of the population not directly affected, but the 'i' derivative of power can perhaps be more potent because it can magnify the actual effects and project them virtually with the speed of light.

When power-differential is favourable, a stable equilibrium may be created by actually deploying power in such a way that the disadvantaged get a feeling that they can somehow put up or live with transactions and exchanges that are actually 'offered' to them — unequal though they may be in real terms — and keep away from trials of will. This may be brought about by minimising 'power in use'— that is, power actually brought to bear to secure prizes — in relation to overall power that could possibly be employed in the event of need. It is the awareness of the unused power potential that drags the disadvantaged into acquiescence in transactions and exchanges which are unequal. An odd trial of wills may not be avoided, and may indeed be sought — to make an example — but not too often. Unused power potential can be brought to bear notionally to secure advantageous transaction on a continuing basis. Its actual utility increasing in proportion to its non-use. Much less satisfaction would be forthcoming were the power to be actually employed to obtain favourable results in trial of wills. Greater the power-differential, greater is the benefit of non-use. Power-differential can also be increased by splitting or reducing the overall size of individual transactions or exchanges on which the same unused power potential can be effectively brought to bear. Unused power potential substantially contributes to the 'i' component. Creation of great power potential confers substantial advantages provided a stable equilibrium is created, and frequent trials of will are avoided. If done purposefully and consistently, this can lead to augmentation of the exploiter's strength which may be harnessed to generate even more power. This, of course, is not a practical proposition except when the prevailing order is controlled by the exploiter, and the force-in-use is kept to the minimum through adroit management. If the prevailing order is disturbed, and its restoration without the use of substantial force becomes impractical, the edifice collapses and exploiter may choose to pull out rather than end up by losing every thing . If governance is made impossible through non-cooperation, and order cannot be restored at all, not even by force, the result for the exploiter may still be the same. He would have the choice of using his superior power to destroy what he cannot exploit, but he would still not be able to exploit. The movement, launched by the Indian National Congress on August 9, 1942, dissolved the order, till then maintained by the British in the sub-continent with minimal force, by causing the individual to break out of his mind-set that, heretofore, had found the exploitive dispensation livable, possibly because of the vast power-differential in favour of the British. On the one hand, World War II had weakened the British, and on the other hand, their unused power potential derived from the obedience and reliability of the British Indian Armed Forces had become suspect. With the virtual dissolution of order that the British had enforced in the sub-continent, the political space that they had created and occupied also disappeared. British India had no residual strength. New political space had to emerge, and it had to be occupied by new collective identities, and order of their choice. This is an interpretation of the 'Quit-India' movement in terms of strength and power. This interpretation does not wholly explain the entire movement, or its consequences, and certainly discounts the nature of British democracy and other institutions which may have cast a liberal influence in favour of pulling out. Power actually employed for securing of prizes out side the nation may be called power projection. Power projection, to be advantageous, must create conditions in which the secured prizes eventually contribute to accretion of strength, and growth is not sacrificed.

Development and prosperity is often equated with strength, if not directly, then by implication. Development is expected to sort out the problems of nation building. Improved conditions of living may contribute and help, but they will not necessarily augment strength. In fact uneven development can induce tensions which can threaten strength. If talk and promises of development give rise to expectations which remain unfulfilled, investment in development may not contribute much to national strength. Insurgency in Punjab cannot be wholly explained by lack of development. Peaks of prosperity that have resulted from uneven development in China may also pose a threat to the strength of China. When the Soviet Union broke up, the per capita income and the state of development was of a higher order, in all its constituents, in comparison with those obtaining in many developing countries. Nation state is a mental construct and the strength ultimately lies in the minds of the people. Structural strength of a nation lies in its collective identity which supports and maintains the political space. Economic well being is essential, but it cannot replace the structural strength. The Japanese performance when measured against all economic and development indices is so high that it possibly masks their extra-ordinary national consciousness which is at the root of their intrinsic strength. Loss of strength manifests as shrinking and eventual disappearance of political space, and its displacement by violence, disorder, and chaos. It is not to be forgotten that the habit of creating disorder and denying governance, cultivated during the freedom struggle, has persisted in India much after the exit of the imperial power. It is a powerful tool which most political parties, when out of power, have not felt shy of using. The disorder and chaos that is created in the name of political agitation saps the strength more effectively than lack of development.

The purpose of collective endeavour can only be served provided all the sources of strength are tapped and strength is nurtured with care. Without development, strength is likely to ebb away, but development by itself does not bring strength in its tow. Faith in the collective identities and loyalty inspired by them is essential if uneven and unequal development is to be coped with. Not only must there be an overall economic development, it must also not be at the cost of national cohesion. Growth without strength can spell doom for any country, and particularly so for a large country like India. Realization of strength into the right components of power, in right proportion and mix, creates conditions for not only sustainable development, but also for growth of strength itself. A suitable mix of power components creates possibilities for fulfilment of collective endeavour.

Force is the core of the 'c' component of power. The next chapter explores the nature of force and its application.

NOTES

1. "Of all concepts used by sociologists, few are the source of more confusion and misunderstanding than power", Michael Foucault, 'Disciplinary power and subjection', Steven Lukes(edited), 'Power', Oxford, England, 1986, (p.243).

2. These definitions are extracted from 'Power', edited by Steven Luke.

3. Dennis H. Wrong, 'Power', Basil Blackwell, Oxford, 1988,(p.p.2-21).

4. Bertrand Russell,'Human Society in Ethics and Politics', Routledge,London,1954, (p.164).

5. Bertrand Russell, 'Human Society in Ethics and Politics', Routledge, London, 1954, (p.164).

6. R.P.Kangle(translator), 'The Kautilya Arthasastra, Part II', Motilal Banarasidass, Delhi, 1992,(p.166).

7. Raymond Aron, 'Macht, Power, Puissance', Steven Lukes(Edited), 'Power', Oxford, London, 1986,(p.263-64), H.

J. Morgenthau, 'Politics among nations', New York, 1949,(p.13)."

8.op. cit., (p.4).

9.Raymond Aron, 'Macht, Power Puissance', Steven Lukes (Edited), 'Power',Oxford, England,1986, (p.257).

10.Robert Dahl, 'Power as the control of behaviour', Steven Lukes,(Edited), 'Power', Oxford, London, 1986, (p.44).

3

Force and Threats

War, the most intense form of conflict, is mainly about application of force to achieve the policy objectives. War[1] is also about standing up to and overcoming force, and ultimately prevailing, so that adopted policies can be pursued. What is under consideration here is the use of force in the context of clash of wills that occurs when competitors or rivals wish to obtain and secure for themselves prizes of their choice. Physical force that may be employed to secure or obtain prizes which are uncontested, or destruction or devastation that result from release of natural forces are to be excluded. What concerns us here is purposeful employment of force. It is customary to describe the use of force as violence. Two connotations of violence can be readily accepted. First, from the point of view of the perpetrator or the subject : it implies the breaking of existing or prevailing bonds and/or continuities in a sudden, swift, vigorous, or abrupt manner; and second, from the point of view of the victim: for him violence appears as gestures or acts that frighten, hurt, displace, damage or destroy. Schelling describes violence as " pure pain and damage[2]." No great difficulty is encountered in understanding or describing overt violence. Difficulties are experienced while understanding, acknowledging, or dealing with violence that has remained sub-surface or 'latent' till it erupts like the violence associated with race riots in the USA in 1960s, or communal riots in Mumbai in 1993. Were the riots a mere response to immediate events, or were they the release of violence held back or contained till then by the system, needs careful consideration. If it was the release of latent violence, where did the latent violence reside; in those who retaliated or in the system of constraints which involved violations of some of the self evident rights and natural aspirations. It would appear that a large number of constraints are perceived by the victims as violations, particularly when the cost of stepping out is exorbitant and the reasons for constraints themselves are exploitive. Constraints so imposed could well be described as violations or latent violence, because they are a precursor to violence. If the underlying layer, namely, the circumstances or causes of imposition of constraints were to become the subject of inquiry, the reasoning may well lead to the basic iniquity in nature, and arguments could be advanced about latent violence being pervasive and immanent even in apparently stable and peaceful societies. It is not intended to describe iniquitous social and legal constraints in societies as force, while acknowledging that violation often leads to violence. The reason for doing so is that the constraints are not mostly physical in nature. Latent violence or repression does lead to conflict and use of force. Reduction of sub-surface violence could lead to elimination of some of the causes of conflict. Violence can just be an expression of frustration and/or anger; or, violence can have a purpose and it may be well directed to achieve it. It is in the latter sense that the term force is used hereafter. According to Thomas C Schelling "violence that can still be withheld or inflicted, or that a victim believes can be withheld or inflicted " is latent violence.[3] Totally different interpretations of violence are possible as will be seen from the following observations of Hannah Arendt:

> "Violence, finally, as I have said, is distinguished by its instrumental character. Phenomenologically, it is close to strength, since the implements of violence, like all other tools, are designed and used for the purpose of multiplying natural strength until, in the last stage of their development, they can substitute for it .

At the point of contact, the object or the victim of force may experience grave discomfort, pain, injury, constraint, captivity, deprivation, and a range of emotions. The victim may also witness death, maiming, and mutilation of others.

The emotions experienced may cover a wide range from anger to fright, to grief, to vengeance. Responses, similarly, could vary widely from flight to fight, but they are likely to be a product as much of immediate physical and emotional experience, as of the basic nature, antecedents, and preparedness of the victim. Generalising, it could be said, that destruction or damage, pain — physical and psychological both —, constraint, and deprivation are the main 'agents' of force that the victim comes in contact with.

Dennis H. Wrong defines force as follows:

"Force refers most commonly to physical or biological force: the creation of physical obstacles restricting the freedom of another, the infliction of bodily pain or injury including the destruction of life itself, and the frustration of basic biological needs ... Force involves treating a human subject as if he were no more than a physical object, or at most a biological organism vulnerable to pain and the impairment of its life-precesses. The ultimate form of force is violence: direct assault upon the body of another in order to inflict pain, injury or death.[5]"

Force include employment against humans, and or animals, of one or more of the following, to physically exhaust or overburden senses, to cause pain, injury, or disease, or to render body dysfunctional, and/or to cause mutilation or death.

Kinetic, chemical, electromagnetic, sonic, thermal, or radioactive energy.

Poisons, toxins, gases, harmful chemicals, and living organisms, singly or in combinations.

Total or partial denial to humans, and/or animals,of food, water, and other life sustaining substances and systems through their destruction, contamination, or physical interception also comes under the ambit of force.

Physical imposition of constraints and restraints on humans with a view to denying them liberty and basic human rights is a less violent form of force.

Unlike other instruments of power, force is very nearly autonomous, in that it can be employed against a victim unilaterally. There has to be a willing recipient to enable the use of 'compensatory power', just as there has to be a an observer or listener to create the possibility of mind being conditioned. Therefore, there necessarily has to be an exchange or interaction for these two instruments of power to be employed. Force, on the other hand, can be used against a totally unwary victim for reasons or motivations which the victim may not at all be able to comprehend, much less divine. Justifiably or otherwise, indian political leadership in 1962 showed total and uncomprehending surprise when Chinese launched major attacks in Ladakh and NEFA. Major General Palit describes the attitude of decision makers of the Government of India in the wake of the disaster at Namka-Chu in NEFA in October 1962 when a brigade had been run over by the Chinese.

> "Looking back across the years, it seems to me that within a few days reality was successfully exchanged as fantasy. The whole border episode was misinterpreted in the light of self-serving interests : a treacherous neighbour had taken advantage of the peace loving Indians by launching a surprise attack on the its border posts...[6]".

There was a feeling, shared by the nation at large, that the Chinese had stabbed India in the back, and the country was swept by a wave of self pity and regret.. Whether the Chinese used force unilaterally in 1962 is not as relevant as the fact that they could well have done it. The victim of force is not required to 'co-operate' with the perpetrator. It is the capability and the preparation by the attacker that matter, and if these are not interpreted realistically, a nasty surprise may be inevitable. Striking the unwary is a force multiplier, which the attacker is unlikely to abjure unless the cost benefit considerations indicate otherwise to him.

Through physical injury and pain, force has the potential to completely empty the victim's mind of everything other than concerns of obtaining relief on the one hand, and of fears that worse could follow, on the other hand. By so dictating the agenda, the attacker tries to push the victim in a reactive mode, and thus deprives him of many of the choices which he could exercise. In depriving life, and inflicting irredeemable or lasting damage, force has a finality about it which no other instrument of power has.

Force can be used or employed to great effect by an attacker, way down in the hierarchy of power, against the powerful, provided the attacker is willing to take the consequences, and has the skill and ability to locate and exploit the vulnerabilities of his victim. It is for this reason that terrorism at personal and national level often succeeds when other instruments of power are not accessible to the weak. Physical force is insensible of human attributes and values. It is just as effective against the guilty as against the innocent. It has the capacity to set back human civilization unlike other instruments of power.

Efficacy of force, as an instrument within the ambit of power, is attributable as much to the punishment — destruction and damage — that it actually inflicts, as it is to the fear that it induces, alike in the victims and witnesses. It is the latter, far more than the former, which gives rise to possibilities from which the attacker benefits. Initially, fear can be used to compel the victim under duress, and subsequently, to obtain compliance; the ultimate purpose, of course, being the conditioning of the mind of the victim to bring about the desired change in attitudes, so that the attacker and aggressor is viewed by the victim, at least for the duration that matters, as a benefactor; and the need to comply is interpreted by the victim as a divine dispensation. Admittedly, force and its concomitant, fear, cannot by themselves produce such effect, but they do play a major role. It is only when force is retained and employed as an instrument — a means to an end — that the full vista of possibilities opens up.

Overcoming of hostile force has three facets: protection, with a view to stopping or dissipating force before it reaches the target so that punishment is minimized or averted ; riposte, with a view to inflicting punishment on the attacker so that his ability to use force is impaired; renewal, with a view to repairing or replacing damage so that the contest continues till the hostile force attenuates and disappears, or till such time as the attacker no longer finds it expedient to use force. Absence of protection increases vulnerabilities and causes a shift in emphasis towards riposte. Riposte leads us back into the domain of using force. But even protection, may imply use of some force, and this in itself may have to be done by facing up to punishment.In any case, protection, no matter how strong or complete, can never be anything more than a part of response to force. In essence, force can only be countered by force, but unless it is backed by a capacity for renewal, it is unequal to the task of overcoming force. Out of the triad, it is only renewal which is qualitatively different, in that it does not involve active use of force. Capacity for renewal is more an aspect of 'strength', rather than that of 'power'. Capacity for renewal at a rate that exceeds the rate of destruction may prolong the trial of wills, and may give rise to doubts in the mind of the attacker about the efficacy of force as an instrument. Ability of Mahatma Gandhi's organization to replace a 'satyagrahi' , no sooner than he was flattened by blows to his head, was a method of overcoming force through renewal.

If combat is defined as direct application of force, ("In combat force is objective reality in action[7]"), prizes which are amenable to being secured in direct combat are comparatively few, but not insignificant on that account. Seizure of adversary's assets, scattering of his armed forces and/or their disarming, destruction of his principal sources of strength and/or power, and so on, are goals attainable by combat. The whole philosophy of first strike — destruction of all strategic nuclear weapons in a preemptive attack — centres around disarming of the adversary, which is a prime prize. Many thinkers fear that the idea may gather strength if and when the technologies being developed under the SDI programme can provide a fool-proof shield against the residual missiles which might have escaped the first strike.

As an extension or part of combat is the manipulation of victim brought under physical duress. Sieges or blockades — but not sanctions by themselves — are part of physical duress in so far as the victim is concerned. Victim's freedom is physically curtailed, and his choices are bound to get more and more limited with passage of time. Under physical duress, he may feel compelled to abide with the wishes of the subject or attacker. Alternatively, disarmed victim(s) may be given or allowed freedom just sufficient for them to do the subject's bidding on pain of more punishment. Galley slaves with enough slack in their chains — so that they were not restrained while rowing — exemplifies the victim under physical duress. A victim could be allowed even more freedom and compelled to abide by the dictates of the subject or the perpetrator. An anecdote recorded by Lt Gen Sir George MacMunn from the days of 'The Sepoy Mutiny[8]' illustrates the point very satisfactorily.

> "This story ..was told to me by an old lady...The old master gunner[from the army of the East India Company] who was put to such trial was her father...Delhaney, driving back ir buggy from visiting his daughter, had been seized by the mutineers and dragged before Ressaldar Major Ramzan khan of the irregular Horse..Delhaney's fame as a gunner was well known. It was therefore, proposed to him that he, for untold gold, should join the rebels and train their gunners under commission from Padishah.. Delahaney's refusal had been direct... He was then and there tied up to the wheel [of the gun] and flogged till even his spirit gave away and he became insensible...
>
> " Will you now fire the guns?", he was asked, and on refusing, flogging continued.
>
> "Take me down ," he cried, "and I will fire your blasted guns!" But he laid the round well off the gate and the first shot took no effect.
>
> Ramazan Khan ordered: "Flog him another fifty, till he can remember to shoot straight. "Fifty more lashes were laid on. [He was told] that "every bad shot you make will mean fifty more."

Once he had given up struggle he had worked his guns steadily and accurately."

Physical duress, to be effective, must leave no room for the victim to act in other than the desired manner. Subsequent grudging compliance would still call for physical duress, but much less. Willing compliance could well follow under certain conditions. The matrix on the next page shows the responses of a victim who has been subjected to intense physical force ,to start with. Although his will to resist is intact, physical conditions do not allow him to resist meaningfully. This response is shown in the matrix as C1. Over a period of time his will to resists gets eroded, and even when physical constraints are of a lower order he begins by lowering his physical resistance although grudgingly C2 and C3. C4 Indicates the state when he has virtually capitulated: the operative force is minimal, freedom that is available to him to resist has increased in the sense that the operative physical force has attenuated. Were he to decide to act, disregarding costs, the opportunity would be there. It is not being suggested that freedom in purely mechanical or physical terms is all that is required to put up resistance; the will by far is the more important factor. Even so, some minimal freedom from physical restraint is necessary to act. Then, freedom and limited means can be used to assert the will. Incidentally, that is what audacity is about: it is about not counting the costs, and disregarding fear. Some succeed, others succumb. Incidentally, 'order', a state of comparatively stable equilibrium, maintained by minimal force-in-use, is quite outside the 'area' that this particular matrix covers. This aspect will be pursued in a later Chapter.

Physical duress cannot be created except through destruction and damage, and yet, if the damage and destruction exceed certain limits, the whole purpose may be lost. No movies showing a bank hold-up seem to miss on this: the leader of the gang invariably admonishes the enthusiastic young crook for killing the cashier before he had disclosed the combination, or handed over the keys to the safe, or some such faux pas. To obtain compliance, under duress, grudging, or otherwise, requires proximity with the victim, if

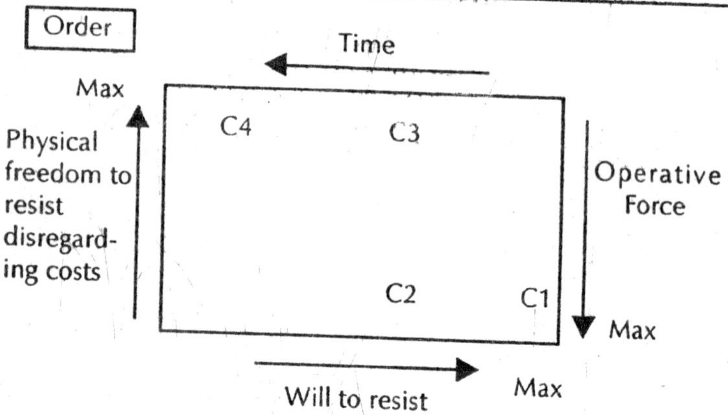

C1: Behaviour under extreme physical duress.
C2 & C3 Behaviour under some physical duress, and in fear. Evidence of some residual resistance.
C4: Behaviour under minimal duress: grudging compliance; and eventual capitulation.

Responses of a victim subjected to intense force.

the destruction is to be restricted so that it may not prove counter-productive. Although technology has made it possible to get many things done by remote control, obtaining compliance without undue destruction from great distances does not seem to be one of them. The attacker has to close in at some stage, and proximity exposes the attacker to the risk of punishment. It is the ability to restrain and constrain without excessive resort to destruction that gives substantial advantages to the attacker.

Even in combat, physical force is cleverly mixed with physical duress and threats with a view to deriving maximum benefit. Central to the use of force is the ability to inflict and/or take punishment without suffering irremediable damage in fulfilment of the desired purpose. It is punishment that is instrumental incompelling victims, under physical duress, to ineluctably act in the manner required by the attacker, even when they can clearly see that the compliance can yield no more than partial and momentary relief, or even worsen the situation over a period of time. Troops in trenches are forced to keep their heads down when exposed to unremitting fire even as they are aware that the attacker is moving towards them under its cover. Eventually, he will close in with larger numbers and either kill or take them prisoners. Heavy volume of artillery, aircraft, and mortar fire may exercise such deleterious influence on their minds that they might come to believe that the only choice available to them is to keep their heads down and save themselves from certain death.

Threat of force by itself, as distinct from combat or physical duress, is employed to advantage. Dissuasion is a method of posing and articulating a threat in which the adversary is made aware of acts or actions, which will attract penalties. Thus the onus of triggering actions that release force against him is transferred on the adversary's shoulders. The subject, or the 'defender' in this case, makes the object aware of the preparations and readiness for combat and its inevitability when the 'trigger' is activated by the victim. Dissuasion is an age old idea of posing threat. Land mines are a form of dissuasion. Land mines are there to keep away the attacker. He endangers his life or limb when he steps forward and chances stepping on buried mines. The choice debilitates. The same can be said of sea mines laid in entrances to harbours or in sea-lanes. The adversary has merely to refrain from venturing forward and avoid the hazard.

Luttwak regards, dissuasion as the negative half of 'suasion', the positive half being called persuasion. The term dissuasion has been used in this study to indicate what Luttwak calls dissuasion by actual or physical denial, as against dissuasion by fear of retaliation or punishment.[9] The distinction is relevant and significant. It is the certainty of promised combat that makes dissuasion effective, as against deterrence — particularly nuclear deterrence — which relies on increasing the risk by posing yet more fearsome threats.

The subject is fully aware of the game and he retaliates in a similar manner, that is by posing some threats himself. The denouement could well be the threat of infliction of fearsome punishment after the act — that is, retaliation — , or mutual accommodation as it happened in October 62 in the Cuban Missile crisis. According to Schelling -

> " The Cuban crisis raised the prospect of a very different species of limited war. More than just raising the prospect, probably it should be construed as an actual instance of the new species, one in which no shots were actually fired. This new species is the competition in risk- taking, a military-diplomatic manoeuvre with or without military engagement but with the outcome determined more by manipulation of risk than by actual contest of force."[10]

The Cuban Missile crisis proved that deterrence when operative, was no more than risk management and/or manipulation. Greater and greater threats were posed. Deterrence can stop someone but it cannot get the other to act in the desired manner.

The Indian Army was successfully deterred by the Chinese. In the wake of the Chinese unilateral withdrawal from some of the occupied territory of India, the top hierarchy of the Indian Army, according to General Palit, showed reluctance to reoccupy the vacated areas although the Government was keen to do so, perhaps because they did not want to provoke the Chinese.[11]

If there is a grave mismatch, the victim may either give in to the threat, or walk into the opposite camp. India in 1971 found it very opportune to sign a treaty of friendship and cooperation with the Soviet Union to escape some rough handling at the hands of the United States who were firm on backing Pakistan at all costs because it facilitated the access of the United States to the Chinese. Hindsight vindicated the prudence that India showed. The crisis was serious enough for the US to consider the nuclear option in December 1971 according to Luttwak.[12]

There is an essential difference between dissuasion and deterrence. Dissuasion is predicated upon the use of force, or combat when the adversary attacks or advances disregarding the costs or penalties. When dissuasion is rendered ineffective, defender resorts to combat. Deterrence is meant to be no more than a threat — a part of diplomacy. It is never meant to release the ultimate strategic nuclear weapons. 'Deterrence' as a concept has materialised due to a number of developments in technology : ability to inflict very severe punishment with a degree of certainty, satellite surveillance and target seeking capability, and precision guidance. The stakes were raised to unacceptable level — one or both the parties could end up with unacceptable punishment — without discovering any countervailing prizes which were worth the risk.

'Compellence' is another technique of posing a threat which, theoretically, aims at getting the victim to perform in response to the subject's bidding by transferring the onus of triggering combat on the shoulders of the victim. What caused Delhaney to perform as well as he could was compellence. Schelling coined the term. He explains the main characteristics : " Compellence, to be successful, involves an action that must be brought to successful closure. The pay-off comes at the end, as does the disaster if the project fails.[13]" This strategy was nearly put into effect by the US in January and February 98 by informing Iraq that they must allow the UN inspections-teams full access; and failure to do so would unleash force against Iraq for which Iraq itself would be responsible. Compellence requires positive compliance by the victim; deterrence calls for no more than some specified inactions. As Schelling has observed,

> " Compellence is the business that the United States got into in North Vietnam. It was trying to make the North Vietnamese regime to do something (even if only to stop something it was doing) and that is different from deterrence. Compellence helps to explain why the coercion took the form of delivered damage, not just verbal threats of damage; the Americans communicated the threat by progressive fulfilment, because the first step was up to the Americans.[14]"

Compellence calls for infliction of punishment and to that extent, dissuasion and compellence make up a pair.

Compellence is a real possibility as an extension of combat, either before or after the event.

The ultimate prize sought through the use of force and threats is willing compliance, something that lies in the domain of 'order'. Thomas C. Schelling quotes H. L. Nieburg as follows:

"The 'rational' goal of the threat of violence is an accommodation of interests, not the provocation of actual violence. Similarly the 'rational' goal of actual violence is demonstration of the will and capability of action, establishing a measure of the credibility of future threats, not the exhaustion of that capability in unlimited conflict.[15]"

The physical use of force or combat by it self has been rendered somewhat less attractive than the combined use of combat and threat of combat.

The use of force is not always guided by rational processes which distinguish clearly between ends and means and try to establish linkages between them. Force is often a medium to express intense emotions born of hatred, anger, frustration, vendetta, or contempt. And emotions need not always be negative: a bomb cast in the Legislative Assembly almost in self abnegation by Bhagat Singh was an act of courage and valour. Cathartic use of force itself brings satisfaction: means and ends fuse. There may be awareness of but no great rational concern with effects or consequences. There may not always be a clear demarcation between force that is employed in a rational manner — as means to an end — and that which is impelled by strong emotions. Decisions to use force are rarely taken only at the behest of reason except within an established order, and if then. Reason may help to guide and regulate the use of force if and when, and to the extent that, it is permitted to operate and perform. Reason may well help to rationalize and justify the use of force. The stated 'cause' is not the prime motivator or mover many of the times. Why, when, and how force is used may have more to do with availability of means, opportunity, and considerations of prizes and penalties rather than with ethics, morality, and justness of cause. Such is the fascination that the use of force holds for mankind — more so in some cultures than in others — that it may even be accepted as an arbiter of justness of claims. What else does resolution of a dispute through a duel indicate ? Even when it is directed rationally from the top, force cannot actually be brought to bear on the opponent or the victim, at the business end, without substantial emotional content on the part of those who actually use force, that is, fight; even more so when their own survival is at stake. Use of force is a domain in which reason and emotion mingle to often produce the unexpected, and even the unthinkable. Therefore it is appropriate to rule out nothing when it comes to the likely use of force. Actual capability is most significant and the possibilities of its rational and effective use should be considered without ruling out its 'irrational' employment. Known and stated intentions of those who have the capability must be viewed in this context.

Following or comparable conditions may have to be fulfilled before a decision to employ force is considered 'reasoned', or rational : (1) There are expectations, on the basis of expert opinion, past happenings and performances, current trends, and cause and effect linkages, that give rise to beliefs that policy objectives are wholly or in part amenable to being achieved through the use of force by itself, or in conjunction with other means. (2) The use of force is not expected to prove counter productive, i.e. it is not expected to give rise to undesirable consequences which cannot be coped up with. The remedy ought not to prove worse than the disease that it is meant to cure. (3) The cost benefit calculus is favourable in those situations where a choice is available; and the penalties by way of losses and punishment are not unbearable, in those situations where no real choice is available.

The use of force to quell insurgency brings into focus the validity of all of the above considerations. At least some of the implacable hard-core insurgents have to be held in captivity, a process which cannot be carried out without the use of force. When force is used, there is always a spill over that hurts and alienates those who might not have been sympathetic to the cause of the insurgents. If force is spared, insurgents represent it as a sign of weakness. If force is used strictly in accordance with the letter of the law, insurgents make use of devious means to get better of the government, thus turning the protection granted to the law-abiding citizens to their advantage. That apart, force becomes inefficient, in terms of the number of security persons actively involved in counter-insurgency per hard-core guerilla. The point at which the force becomes counter-productive through excessive destruction and/or inefficiency has to be watched with care. If the use of force does not lead to the creation of a better order, it is counter-productive. Clausewitz has highlighted this inherent contradiction in the use of force by styling it " heterogeneity of materials and product, of colours and pictures, of violence and its political end.[16]"

This is not to say either that decisions to use force are or should be taken only when the above conditions are fulfilled, or that all the relevant information, data, and the expertise to arrive at the right conclusion are likely to be available to the decision makers. Had this been the case, Neither the Japanese, nor the Germans would ever have launched on the adventures which ended in disasters for them, nor would England have stood up alone to the Nazi Germany and fought it out in the sky during the Battle of Britain. Complete and total inputs are rarely available, and the imponderables make accurate predictions rather difficult, if not impossible. But if reasoning alone were in the driving seat, decisions to use force would have to be tested in the manner indicated.

Force may well be employed for one or more of the following 'reasoned' intents : (1) To create and impose national, regional, or international order in conformity with a grand global design or hegemony.(2) For a bigger niche in the national, regional, or international order, but without challenging the global design or script.(3) To resist the creation or imposition of global order with a view to eventually re-ordering the global arrangement. (4) With a view to disrupting order, or creating disorder so that prizes sought by adversaries are denied to them. (5) To clear portions of land, sea, or slots in space which are required to be appropriated, perhaps for alternative use, or because there is a requirement to get rid of plagues or pestilence that pollute — that is, for the purpose of cleansing or extirpation.

Some force is decidedly required to maintain order — termed 'force-in-use'—because the state does not seem to wither away, having become superfluous.. But there are natural limitations on the use of force. Force-in-use has to be restraint or regulation, rather than destruction or violence oriented ;otherwise it is likely to be counter-productive. It is quite likely that those pursuing intents (1) and (2) above may not opt for indiscriminate destruction, whereas those bent on any of the intents (3) to (5) may heavily rely on destruction. Weapons of Mass Destruction, or their diminutive or garden variety versions, are most likely to be used in pursuit of such intents.

In the past too, force has been employed to achieve comparable ends. Prima facie, the concept of international or global script and order may appear to be the creation of contemporary times. But perhaps, not so. In Europe, before the advent of nationalism and nation states, crusaders aspired for a universal christendom. In India, Kautilya fired the imagination of his would be conqueror disciple with the vision of a kingdom that occupied the entire sub-continent. Force in isolation is hardly ever adequate to achieve the kind of purpose set out above, and other instruments of power would have to come into play, but without the use of force, the purpose is likely to be ill served, because force has the capability to overwhelm as few other instruments of power have. Element of uncertainty and possibility of suffering punishment in riposte oriented encounters is substantial. The strong and the powerful, when unprepared, or unwilling to take any punishment whatsoever, resort to the application of force from 'stand-off' distances, employment of proxies , mercenaries, or agents and the like, who use force on their behalf in hazardous situations, and deter the adversary with threats of total destruction. The use of force from stand-off distances has to rely on the blanket effect and cannot but increase the scale of destruction.

A case is often made out that certain instruments of force are more undesirable than some others. The creation of criteria for evaluating the undesirability of weapons systems, and then placing particular weapon systems on a scale of undesirability is a formidable task. Since it is not possible to consider 'humane' any particular method of causing pain, injury, or death, the scale of undesirability cannot be constructed or calibrated without taking into consideration several factors, inter alia, the potential attackers and the victims, the context in which the weapon systems have been, or are likely to be employed, and so on. Even the use of nuclear weapons is not ruled out in self defence by the International Court of Justice. Are the after effects of nuclear strikes less harmful than the after effects of a chemical strike ? It is very obvious that these are the factors which will evoke highly subjective responses and reactions. On the other hand there are some factors which can be better guides for objectively determining the relative undesirability of the weapon systems: degree of destruction produced; pervasiveness, persistence, and intensity of the after effects produced by the strike or the use of the system, its amenability to retrieval, its easy accessibility, and so on. The magnitude of destruction and the residual hazard could be used to construct and calibrate a scale of undesirability. On this basis, chemical weapons will figure well below the nuclear. Land mines may figure well below many of the air and missile delivered weapons, or may not figure at all. The campaign against the chemical weapons and the land mines seems to lack justification rooted in transparent logic. Perhaps it has more to do with the divide between those considered mature and responsible, and the rest. The aim seems to be to facilitate unhindered policing by the mature nations.

Combat, physical duress, dissuasion, deterrence, and compellence are the labels attached to the combinations and modes of combining and employing physical force and threats in the desired proportion. Thought processes that have gone into their evolution are fundamental to tactics and strategy both, that is winning of battles and wars.

Significant use of power in general, and force in particular, have an impact on national and inter-national order. Force may be employed to enforce or disrupt order, or to create a new order. There is a strong linkage between order and the use of force.

NOTES

1. "Clausewitz defined war as the use of physical violence , particularly by the armed forces." Raymond Aron, 'Clausewitz, Philosopher of War, Routledge & Kegan Paul, London 1976, (p.375).

2 .Thomas C. Schelling,' Arms And Influence',Yale University Press, New Haven, Connecticut,1966. ,(p.9).

3.This is not the sense in which the term has been used here. Schelling, op. cit., (p.3).

4.Hannah Arendt,'Communicative Power', Steven Lukes (Edited), 'Power',Oxford, England,1986, (p.p.64-65)

5.Dennis H. Wrong, 'Power', Basil Blackwell, Oxford, 1988, (p.24).

6.Major General D. K. Palit Vrc, 'War in High Himalaya', Lancer, (p.276).

7.Edward Luttwak, 'Strategy : The Logic of War and Peace, Harvard University Press, Cambridge, Massachusetts, 1987, (p.191)

8.Lt Gen Sir George MacMunn, 'Vignettes From indian Wars', Sampson Law, Marston & Co., London, (p.p. 172-178).

9.Edward Luttwak, 'Strategy : The Logic of War and Peace, Harvard University Press, Cambridge, Massachusetts, 1987, (p.198).

10.Schelling, op.cit., (p.166).

11.Palit, op. cit., (p.p. 407-420).

12.Palit, op.cit.,(p.201).

13.Schelling, op. cit., (p.75).

14.Schelling, op. cit., (p.174).

15.Schelling, op. cit., (p.13.).

16.Raymond Aron, 'Clausewitz, Philosopher of War' Routeledge and Kegan Paul, London, 1976, (p.345).

4

Order

Public order has been defined by the Supreme Court, and differentiated from law and order[1], the international order or the world order is commented on, and explained by its authors, but order by itself does not, seem to attract much attention. All that one can make out from the Supreme Court ruling is that order is affected when law is contravened. Therefore one would surmise that the domain of order extends beyond the rule of law. Inspiration for order seems to have come from nature. Predictability and changelessness of some of the natural phenomena, its amenability to the 'laws' understood and interpreted by man, harmony and beauty that is visible in nature notwithstanding the diversity, the life cycle that goes on uninterrupted with predators feeding on their preys who in turn draw their sustenance from the earth, adjustments among living things and so on, offers a paradigm for human affairs, on the assumption that there is order in nature, and mankind could emulate it. There is also an assumption that power that controls nature also controls mankind and order in conformity with the divine will can be maintained by those who have the capacity to understand and interpret it. No wonder that religions have been instrumental in evolving order.

> "Religion was man's first attempt to control his environment. The creation of imaginary supernatural beings behind natural phenomenon was not, as might appear at first thought, a vain duplication of these phenomena : it reduced them to a system and seemed to make them indirectly amenable to human control [2]."

In India the cosmic order has always been considered inseparable from truth, and man was encouraged to be in harmony with the cosmic order.

"For nearly 3000 years Hinduism has believed in stratified social system as a divinely ordained feature of the cosmos and its teachings has given full religious sanctions to the four classes (varna) and the innumerable castes (jati)[3]"

Order is movement away from anarchy and chaos. This conclusion, of course, presumes collective consciousness that not only differentiates between personal and collective domains but also gives precedence to collective concerns on the basis of a common understanding about (1) what is essentially required by way of institutions and organizations for carrying on the daily business of making a living and improving quality of life, and, (2) commonly accepted values. Order is about reconciling contradictions that are inherent in a group, or in a constellation of groups that share collective consciousness and constitute a collective entity.

Many of the prizes that men aspire to are not very different, and therefore, they set out to contend and claim prizes with unequal means, that is, on an unequal footing. The share of prizes that individuals acquire is bound to be unequal, not only on account of unequal talent, but also due to vagaries of fortune or chance, even if all other cultural factors were to be excluded. It would also appear that general satisfaction with some sort of equity, rather than insistence on equality bears testimony to the 'natural' acceptance of unequal distribution of talent, wealth and good fortune. Even if nature were to abhor equality, she may not necessarily also abhor 'equity'. This problem of 'equity' — creation of an equilibrium and stability in a group in which individuals with unequal capability to acquire prizes have to share them equitably, for common good —, is central to any order. Lord Charnwood, in his biography of President Lincoln, remarks that equity or justice springs from accepting that even an 'unequal' person may have to be treated as an equal in some respects.

"It should not be necessary to explain as Lincoln did long after, that Jefferson did not suppose all men to be of equal height or weight or equally wise or equally good. He did, however contend for a principle of which one elementary application is the law which makes murder the same crime whatever be the relative position of the murderer and the murdered man[4]."

In the natural state the share of the prize is most likely to be determined, primarily, by 'power' that an individual can bring to bear in pursuit of his needs and desires : how far he is able either to satisfy or deny wants of other contenders, after, of course, satisfying those of his own wants which he cannot —or chooses not to — suppress. Arguably, power may also manifest in collective enterprise, but that would only mean that the essential problem would get magnified. The surplus of power at the disposal of the individual, or a group for that matter, yields three sets of instruments : viz inducement, coercion, and influence. Inducement relies on fulfilling wants of other contenders in return for an advantageous exchange. Coercion also aims at obtaining an attractive exchange in return for sparing confinement, hardship, pain or punishment to which the victim can be subjected to at the will of the 'powerful'. Influence is on hand to create consensus, or confrontation, or to condition minds. Suitable instruments from the three sets can be used to obtain exchanges which are essentially iniquitous. Therefore, such an adjustment may lie in the periphery of the region of tolerance of the victim, and may prove to be unstable. Therein lie the seeds of conflict. Equilibrium is retained, essentially, by conditioning the minds of both, the powerful and the weak. That seems to be one of the main purposes in establishing or modifying order: to create a web of rights and duties, expectations and obligations, liberties and taboos, conventions and codes, rewards and punishment that, through general acceptability of the strong and acceptance by the weak, keeps the incipient conflict in check and within manageable limits : to create conditions in which the group as a whole does not have to proceed against individuals often or severely ; to create mutual trust, and enlarge upon areas of individual freedom and opportunity.

Prevailing order is determined by the substance and totality of obligations that most individuals and institutions generally accept and actually abide by on most occasions.

Order is indeed essential for any kind of individual or collective activity or interaction within and among groups. A certain minimal trust and a reasonable certainty that it will be fulfilled are a product of order. It is a precondition for any kind of social or economic activity. It has this utility value for which it is prized and 'paid for'. The payment — whether willingly made imposed, or exacted — is in the form of submission and tribute to collective endeavour, and authority that codifies, and upholds order i.e. government. The concept of the 'social contract' — payment of tribute and submission to authority, in return for security and good order — has been well understood since ancient times.:

"When people were oppressed by the law of the fishes (matsya nyaya), according to which the bigger fish swallows the smaller one), they made Manu, the sun of Vivasvat, the king. They fixed one-sixth part of the grains and one-tenth of their goods and money as his share. Kings who receive this share are able to ensure the well-being of their subjects[5]."

Governments, inter alia, make laws which are , by definition, enforceable. But the social requirement is for the day to-day business of life being carried on without outside intervention or intrusion, efficiently and properly, and to the advantage of groups and individuals alike. The secular law merely defines the minimum expectations of conduct and behaviour, and touches upon those areas of life which are in need of regulation, that is, it lays down bounds which must not be transgressed. Recourse to law is unproductive and messy and a great deal of legislation and litigation signifies that the prevailing order is under strain. The law of the land can be enforced by the government; it can also make use of the law to maintain public order, but beyond that, the government cannot enforce order as such. Rule of law itself appears, prima facie, a very wholesome idea that frees the disadvantaged of many of the handicaps. But the laws themselves are based on the prevailing order which they reinforce. Laws indicate the paths that can be traversed, grounds that cannot be trespassed, or commons that are there for everyone's use. But laws do not create a level field, as claimed.

"Since legal statutes are stated in general and impersonal terms, they appear to support abstract principles of justice rather than the special interests of particular men or classes of men....Anatole France saw this clearly when he wrote , " The law in its majestic equality forbids the rich and as well as the poor to sleep under bridges, to beg in street, and to steal bread [6]."

It is through order that a group copes up with the consequences and effects of unequal individual talent and capability on the one hand, and the expectations of the disadvantaged for at least equitable, if not equal, share on the other. It is very obvious that both — unequal capability, and expectations of equitable rewards — are natural. Nature does not seem to throw up individuals with equal or even comparable capability. It would appear that talent amongst individual conforms to normal distribution. The bulk of mankind - that is the two thirds - excludes the highly talented and the less endowed. Even within the bulk of population the variation is not inconsiderable. It is not as if a group seeking order creates a power centre or authority to fulfil its purpose —although that may also happen sometime—but it is the other way round more often than not : the natural urge and talent for leadership seeks authority — ability to obtain conformity and compliance. Authority is to be had through power which is acquired either by fulfilling some commonly felt and persistent needs of the group or by denying it conditionally, that is, till the desired outcome is arrived at. In creating, maintaining, or improving upon prevailing order, leadership fulfils one of the most basic requirements and thereby acquires power. On the other hand, a group or a people have within their gift to accept leadership of a person or an institution, and this ability translates itself into power when the gift can also be withheld or denied. It is the most basic balance of power that obtains : between the leader and the led. This balance is crucial to a stable order.

Status quo leadership, most of the time, does not want significant changes in the prevailing order because it protects its sources of strength. This is exemplified in the titles of many of the heads of the state who are described as the defenders of faith or the constitution. What they are promising to do, really, is to uphold the prevailing order, which includes serving of their own cause. This, of course, does not mean that they resist evolutionary change. They may introduce even radical changes provided it serves their political cause. Nationalization of banks in India by Prime Minister Indira Gandhi is so viewed by many in retrospect.

Order has to be supported by good governance ; if it were not so, there would be little need for authority. On the other hand, order that needs frequent governmental intervention for its maintenance — in nature of things, with ever increasing rigour — is unlikely to endure. The relationship between governance, which must necessarily draw upon legitimate authority, and order is such that if the former is not firmly embedded in prevailing order, it gradually loses potency. Governance essentially implies support to, and upholding of, an acceptable order and avoidance of situations in which public order has to be enforced frequently, and by brutal force at that. Most practitioners of the political art, find it beneficial to bring about shifts in prevailing order through persuasion, rather than through imposed legislation. Changes in prevailing order without undue turbulence or violence are brought about by modifying and transforming ideas about legitimacy and fair play.

Political order is the sovereign or all-dominating order that determines and governs power distribution : It deals with questions such as who will be at the pinnacle, who will support the pinnacle and hold it in place, how will other claimants be dealt with, what will they be allowed to get away with, and what will be denied to them, how will the system be made acceptable to the people at large, and so on. Political order subsumes other orders — social, economic, religious, and so on — and generally decides upon their relative autonomy and importance.

Economic order and institutions are allowed a space in which to operate. Notice the trade between India and Pakistan after partition in 1947. It dropped significantly, because political order in Pakistan viewed it as a threat to the newly emerging Pakistan. Both countries had been — and continue to be -- parts of natural economic zone. But the natural economic zone could not cause the flow of trade across the international border. It is not as if the economic forces can operate against the political will. They can occasionally bypass or subvert political will. It is believed that indirect trade between India and Pakistan takes place through Dubai, or some other ports in the Gulf region, and it is far in excess of the volume of direct bilateral trade. King Henry VIII of England came forward with an innovative approach to subsume order prescribed by Catholic Church so that the prevailing political order was not compromised.

A harmonious structure includes checks and balances , and rewards and compensations that create stability on the one hand, and — perhaps, because of it — promote enterprise on the other. Mere transfer of power from one individual to another — whether it is through 'the king is dead,long live the king' mechanism,or through elections — without significant changes in, or modifications to, the prevailing order does not produce turbulence. Put it in another way, a 'political space' or a polity has an 'order' associated with it. In fact, if the prevailing order is seriously impaired, the political space shrinks and eventually disappears. Happenings in Afghanistan after the Soviet ingress in 1979 are a testimony to this. The mujahdins matched violence for violence till the prevailing order was debilitated. Eventually, the Taliban did the rest, and destroyed it completely. Chaos prevails, and so it will, till a political space is created and order is reestablished by some charismatic leadership. Destruction of prevailing order is the chosen method of revolution.

A political order promotes some collective identities, and permits some kind of associations, just as it deprecates some others. Those collective identities which are likely to threaten either the existing order, or the political structure, or the ruling elite, are manipulated and controlled whenever that is possible; otherwise, they are divided and eventually discounted. Creation of a new political space, with a view to occupying it, requires creation of a new order, which is invariably accompanied by turbulence which is minimised to the extent that the old order is either not interfered with, or gently modified over a period of time. If the existing order is modified and changed as a result of a controlled movement, the political space is gradually reshaped even as it is taken away from the ruling elite. On the other hand, use of force may facilitate or allow creation and occupation of new political space, eventually to be filled with the desired order.

Different models of orders have emerged - with wide variations, depending upon the civilizations and cultures that they belong to — not only to create a stable and balanced whole out of virtually warring parts, but also to create conditions in which the whole will progress and benefit.

Every order has its biases : the collective identities and associations that it supports, a distribution of power that it approves of, opportunities for seeking power and recognition that it considers just and adequate, autonomies, freedoms and enterprises that it allows on the one hand, and curtails on the other, the values, beliefs, and faiths that it promotes, the methods and means of coercion and rewards that it prefers, and concepts of justice and fair play that it considers beyond doubt and challenge. Order determines the script writers, who in turn, allocate roles, preside over the performance, and judge merits. Understandably, the script writers also determine who the ruling elite will be. It is obvious, that the script writers cannot think of every thing, cannot predict the future, go wrong in their calculus, under-estimate human ingenuity and element of chance, and attempt to create an order which, unknown to its makers, may be flawed in its design — as may be revealed later. That apart, the 'actors', may not perform their role to perfection, or others may take over the roles. It is not as if history runs the course that is ordained by the script-writers, but that is not for lack of such desire on their part.

Order within a political space, controls internal conflict through effective regulation, that is by laying down the rules for competition, and thereby bringing it within the domain of the rule of law. It also indicates areas in which competition in any form is not permitted. This is done by specifying the exclusive domain of the government : for example, private parties may not maintain armed forces, or jails to compete with the apparatus of the state.

Enlargement of political space beyond the nation state invariably calls for a world order that is predicated upon agreed conventions and practices, if not upon a universal law.

By virtue of prevailing order, at any point of time, there is a distribution of power within collective identities and nations. Ambitious individuals and groups may make a bid to get into positions of power, and if the system does not necessarily guard particular individuals in power, but merely positions of power, the stability of prevailing order per se may not be challenged : succession does not threaten stability. It is only when there is dissatisfaction with the prevailing distribution of power, and redistribution of power with new centres of power is desired that order is threatened. This threat is posed by assertion of collective identities in political terms : new collective identities may emerge, or existing collective identities may reconstitute or rearrange themselves for the purpose. If the prevailing order lacks stability — ability to contain demands for redistribution of power through operation of checks and balances, or by accepting marginal adjustments, or by use of force — newly assertive collective identities are likely to intensify the struggle which may eventually lead to a clash.

Order can also be viewed as a cumulative effect of conditioning power. Galbraith observes that conditioned power is a continuum from objective and visible persuasion to what an individual has been brought up to believe[7]. Effect of conditioning power manifests, at the level of the individual, in the form of attitude(s) that generally predispose him to a set of actions, reactions, and responses. The scope is very large and includes all matters: from material to spiritual; from mundane to esoteric. It is not as if the individual will invariably act as 'programmed. He may not only show individuality, but also inconsistency in his choice. Even so, when not particularly applying himself, he will be more likely to willingly accept certain things, just as he will turn away from certain choices without much thought. Collectively, a group also shows similar traits. Analogy of the effect that terrain produces on the flow of water may perhaps be appropriate. The grain and natural rise and fall of the terrain determine the course that surface water takes. Terrain can be modified, and water courses trained or changed, or new ones made for that matter, but at a given point of time, every drop of rain that falls on the surface is predisposed to flow or seep in a particular manner. Similarly, at a point of time, prevailing order causes certain occurrences, actions and reactions to appear more appropriate and natural than others. Conditioning power is operative the entire time, and the cumulative effect does undergo a change, sometimes revolutionary, but more often evolutionary.

If prevailing order cannot create institutions and organizations that reconcile conflicting demands and competition, most of the vital energy may be consumed in internal strife; if it boxes in its disadvantaged in ghettos, they will survive on sufferance, but not contribute to collective wellbeing; if it curbs innovation and enterprise, it would soon run out of its material resources. A regressive and suppressive order will give rise to latent violence waiting to break out. In such a situation, the strength of the polity will be minimal and the polity itself may be ready to fall apart. This is a reasonable description of conditions as they obtained in India at the time of the advent of the British.

"In all their [British] onward progress they had the assent and support of the population who desired to maintain law and order. The decadence of the Mughal rule was proceeding rapidly when Clive first landed in Bengal. Then the buffalo was to the man who held the bludgeon. These pages show, how under the English rule, the buffalo is the property of man, woman, or child who had the legal right to possess it[8]."

Because of the social structure in India, the sub-stratum on which order rests, many of the productive and regulatory occupations had got associated with a few castes or caste groups. There have been some changes, over a period of time, but the situation has not greatly changed. Further, because there has been an irrevocable linkage between occupation and castes, areas of professional and occupational interests, such as problem identification and resolution, remained confined to particular caste groups and classes. Organizations, and institutions which came into being — associations or guilds — drew their sustenance from the parent caste groups. Manual labour was never married with knowledge, or only rarely, with the result that although crafts came into being, the art and science of production lagged behind. Green and white revolutions had to wait till the intellectuals, scientists, and management experts addressed what had, till then, been the concerns of only those whose assets were no more than the inherited practices of farming, and a capacity to labour and last. Availability of technology, hither to unknown, was of course significant. The trust and expectations of one class were matched by those of another in a synergic effect to produce lasting benefits for the whole society.

Undivided India accounted for 24.5 percent of the world's manufacturing out-put in 1750. In the year 1913, it dropped to 1.4 percent[9]. This of course is true and much blame is rightly apportioned to the British rulers. But another possible explanation is that this was possible only during a period when agriculture was a prominent part of the total production. During those times, manual labour accounted for much of production, and farmer's and artisan's knowledge, skills, and labour sufficed to produce some surplus. Industrial revolution changed all that, but the revolution itself could come about because, on the one hand, the skills and judgement of the artisan was 'intellectualised' and theories were propounded, and mathematical models were produced to interpret the practice or phenomenon; and on the other hand, the products of intellectual labour were applied to real life problems. Obviously, organizations and institutions then in existence in Europe allowed this intercourse of ideas across the classes. The prevailing order in Europe supported such interaction, and in India, perhaps, it did not.

A curious explanation of the defeat of the Indian King Porus by Alexander in the Battle of Hydaspes has been quoted by Rosen. Referring to Alexander's battle with Porus, he observes that when Indian charioteers found Alexander's troops wading out of Hydaspes (Jhelum) river, they did not attempt to stop them because they felt that this was an infantry task below them :

"As a result, the coordination among the various components of the Indian army that were drawn from different strata was poor, with charioteers refusing to fight as infantry[10]."

Rosen raises questions regarding correlation between social structure and strategic [military] behaviour. He implies that if a unit is composed of caste groups, who share mutual hatred, they are not likely to cohere, nor cooperate with units composed of other classes. Rosen has no first hand experience of the Indian Army today, and his extrapolation of an interpretation of a lost battle may not be valid. Even so, the point that he makes has relevance, in that, the prevailing order has an impact on institutional and organization strength and weakness.

Elites, whose only forte is winning of elections, are unlikely to add to the strength of the nation because they would themselves have no faith in institutions or professionalism. Order which does not respect (professional) competence or merit, is unlikely to add to the strength. Order must indeed support the elitism of the professional because if competence, competition and innovation, are not harnessed, productivity and material well being is likely to suffer, and but for it, the question of generating power just does not arise. Without equity, prevailing order becomes unstable; without elitism, it cannot compete and generate power. Without institutions and organizations that support both, equity and excellence, prevailing order can get fossilized.

A profound aspect of culture, order is a major determinant of strength that a nation can generate, growth that it actually achieves, and power that it generates. Changes that are being brought about in (internal) order should be carefully examined to determine who the script-writers are, and what their purpose is, because -

"Ruling classes do not justify their power exclusively by de facto possession of it, but try to find a moral and legal basis for representing it as the logical and necessary consequences of doctrines and beliefs that are generally recognized and accepted[11]."

Sudden shifts and changes in prevailing order, whether caused by emergence of new centres of power, or calling for a re-distribution of power to bring it conformity with changed circumstances, create instability. The collective response may contain elements of conflict, cooperation, or both. Inability of a fossilized order to cope up with changed circumstances can also lead to turbulence and turmoil.

NOTES

1. "The distinction between 'law and order' and 'public order' has been explained by this court time and again...'Law and order' is wider in scope in as much as contravention of law always affects order, while public order would be affected by only such contravention which affects community at large. It is the length, magnitude, and the intensity of the terror wave unleashed by a particular eruption of disorder that helps distinguish it as an act affecting public order from that concerning 'law and order'. The question to be asked is : does it lead to disturbance of the current life of the community so as to amount to a disturbance of the public order or does it affect merely an individual leaving the tranquillity of the society undisturbed.", All India Reporter 1992, Supreme Court Section, AIR Ltd, Nagpur,(AIR 1992, Supreme Court 687)

2. Harry Elmer Barnes, 'An Intellectual and Cultural History of the Western World, Volume Three, Dover Publications Inc., New York, 1965,(p.1316).

3.Encyclopedia Britannica, Volume 11, 1964, (p.55).

4.Lord Charnwood,'Abraham Lincoln', Pocket Books, USA, 1948.

5.R. P. Kangle (translator), 'The Kautiliya Arthasastra', Motilal Banarasidass, Delhi, 1992, (p. 116).

6.Gerhard Lenski,'Power and Privilege', Steven Lukes (Edited), 'Power',Oxford, England,1986, (p.p.245-246).

7.John Kenneth Galbraith, ' The Anatomy of Power', Hamish Hamilton, 1984, (p.4).

8.Colonel G.B. Malleson, ' The Decisive Battles of India', Sagar Publication, New Delhi, 1969, [first published in 1883], (excerpt from preface to the second edition).

9.Samuel P. Huntington, 'The Clash of Civilizations, and the Remaking of the World Order, Viking, New Delhi,1996 (p.86).

10.Stephen Peter Rosen, 'Societies and Military Power — India and Its Armies', Oxford University Press, Oxford, 1996. (p.p.77-82)

11.Michael Foucault, ' Disciplinary Power and Subjugation', Steven Lukes (Editor), 'Power', Oxford, London, 1986, (p.247).

5

Conflict and Cooperation

Conflict is a clash, or a collision, or a trial of wills that absorbs energies and resources to yield an outcome, which is not always predictable, not entirely or wholly in conformity with the expectations or preferences of any of the — willing or unwilling — participants, and which is invariably accompanied by some damage or irretrievable losses, which are rarely shared equally, but in some measure by all participants. Conflicts occur amongst men, groups of men, and animals. Conflict is very rarely free of violence, although the scale of violence in some conflicts may be very low. Edward N. Luttwak can think of conflict in which overt military force is not employed. He defines Cold War in such terms[1]. Since he does not exclude 'covert' military force, it could be inferred that he does not necessarily exclude the use of force in some form or the other, from conflict. It is indeed possible to think of a clash of ideologies or values taking place without violence, but in real life, such clashes are invariably accompanied by violence.

Margareta Sollenberg and Peter Wallensteen define a 'major armed conflict' as " prolonged combat between the military forces of two or more governments, or of one government and at least one organized armed group, and incurring the battle related deaths of at least 1,000 people during the entire conflict[2] ". This definition emphasises that violence—'incurring' of deaths — and conflict are inseparable, but also that conflict other than armed conflict is conceivable.

Perhaps the ground that extends beyond armed conflict and yet lies within the domain of conflict in general —clash or collision amongst men, or groups of men, or nations, with some content of violence — needs to be explored.

Edward D.Bono equates conflict with clash of" interests, values, actions, or directions[3]." `Interest' is scarcely distinguishable from pursuit of tangible and intangible goals. Bono`s concept of interests, perhaps, excludes values.

> "A conflict rises when two or more people or groups endeavour to pursue goals which are mutually inconsistent[4]."

Individuals and groups, or nations for that matter, are in search of 'prizes' - anything and everything that, minimally, fulfils basic wants, and beyond that, brings satisfaction and holds out the promise of even greater satisfaction preferably for all times to come. The list of prizes can be unending and there may be no common agreement on it, but it is likely to include many of the following:-

* Material resources that sustain and adorn life includin precious, scarce, and nonrenewable items.

* Land, and access to high seas and space. Land holds a unique attraction for man because it fulfils three of his main needs which, in their order of importance, could be summarized as sustenance, habitation, and locomotion. Land can be possessed and held, or occupied indefinitely, and denied to others. Seas yield limited sustenance, but are not habitable — excluding some floating colonies off the coast —, and therefore, they cannot be occupied. Seas can be used to draw sustenance from, and they are an incomparable medium for travel and transportation. Space at present remains only a medium for manned and unmanned travel and exploration. Seas and space can be dominated and denied to others to some extent, but unlike land, neither can be occupied. Technological advances make access to seas and space very attractive prizes. But, for so long as seas and space do not become habitable, even limited expanses of them would not be amenable to being possessed, or retained for exclusive use. Unlike land, seas and space are prizes more amenable to condominium arrangement. For agrarian civilizations, land is the prime prize, but that does not mean

that land loses its charm as a prize for the second and third wave civilizations. Dwindling populations in the third wave civilizations, and their present capacity to command pretty much what they like from lands populated by first and second wave civilizations, may create a false impression that land has lost its attractiveness as the prime prize[5].

* Skills, knowledge, ideas, and technology that are relevant and promising in contemporary times ; capital and infra-structure for efficient production.
* Energy and its sources.
* Cheap labour, and preferably an underclass.
* Power and sources of power .
* Pre-eminence in chosen fields.
* Invulnerability.
* Autonomy.
* Leadership.

The quest for prizes is not necessarily driven by greed, though very often it is, and it may include an element of common good, well being, and a grand vision which promises something for everyone, or some other kind of utopia, always distant and beyond reach, and for that very reason all the more attractive because it keeps distant hopes alive, and discounts set-backs which are a part of real experience of everyday life.

Where do values and ideology figure in the prizes that individuals and groups seek? Ethical i.e. secular or moral values restrain an individual from pursuing his interests and fancies in disregard of concerns of others, and to a certain extent, even at the cost of his own long term interests. Values that are derived from, upheld or directly prescribed, by religion or other ideologies, rely more on faith than reason. Ethical values are easily accessible and more comprehensible because they are amenable to reason, they do not purport to derive their strength from metaphysical matters and/or convictions, which can neither be proved nor disproved. They generally seem to emanate from considerations of prudence, and greatest good for greatest number of people and so on. Religious or ideological values on the other hand, in many instances, but not always, can also be interpreted in rational terms. No matter what their origin, in general, value-based conduct makes very heavy demands on an individual. He is required to often act in direct contradiction to his immediate self interest. Values impose a regime of restraint or sacrifice on the adherents and exact a commitment in return for satisfaction or fulfilment that may be derived from considerations of common or greater good which may be realised here and now, or in the future, or even in the next world(?). Restraint or forbearance require holding back or inaction, just as voluntary service in the cause of community or nation may call for action. Demand for value based conduct, for so long as it falls within the realm of 'reason', invites circumspection and prudence from followers who may be expected to remain within limits set by contemporary mores. On the other hand, values born of ideology or religion seem to reach deep within and access emotion. Therefore ideological or religious 'zeal'[6] often seems to culminate in strife. Action or inaction born of reason is unlikely to have the white hot heat that is born of emotion. Bertrand Russell has emphatically stated that it is emotion or desire that leads to action, and reason does no more than to regulate.

> 'Desires, emotions , passions (you can choose whichever word you will), are the only possible causes of action. Reason is not a cause of action but only a regulator[7]."

Presumably , inactions or actions implied in regulatory functions are within the domain of reason. Acts of great courage and sacrifice are, perhaps, in pursuit of values on a visceral plane. Fanaticism is a pejorative basically used not so much to denigrate acts themselves - which in another context may well be described as heroism -as to condemn the causes which are not approved of. Barbarous behaviour, particularly in war, may well be at the behest of 'reasonable' men presiding over and representing nations, and not always by fanatics. Ends and means both, when they are derived from fully reasoned and truly universal values may also not prevent conflict but may succeed in minimising it. On the other hand, when emotion drives ends and means both, the intensity of 'heroics' is likely to increase.

In the international arena, it would appear, that values get upheld mainly when they are fused with national interests to yield a highly useful alloy from which instruments of the state can be forged. Indeed, which of the values are immune to being trumped by raison d'etat? Henry Kissinger says as much:

> "Universal values are defined by their perception and not in need of constant reinterpretation; indeed they are inconsistent with it [raison d'etat][8]."

Values are generally employed or 'used' selectively to further national interests i.e. to inspire own population or to cover the ugly face of the foreign policy. And that is not the only 'use' to which values can be put to. But, for the present, it is sufficient to say that clash of values per se may not necessarily lead to conflict.

Christianity had not been conceived of as a religion of a particular group any more than Communism had been devised as the national ideology for the Soviet Union. They were not meant to subserve particular nations. But in due course Christianity was exploited by Spain, as was done by other European powers, to support her Empire.

> "De Soto , who has been called the best of the conquistadors is one example of the Spanish methods and state of mind.... Side by side with his butcheries, incidentally, De Soto introduced religion; the words gold and God were linked in his vocabulary[9] ."

Communism could not and did not prevent the rupture in relationship between the Soviet Union and the Peoples Republic of China as a result of animosity that began to accumulate from the time that China felt let down by the Soviet Union during the Korean War even though

> "Lenin's original programme called for the communization of the world after benefits of the true faith had come to Russia[10] ."

Interests of the nation state obviously supersede most other values. Incompatibility in values and ideology is more likely to sharpen rather than cause irreconcilability of interests among nations. The Gulf War was not caused by the distaste of Western democracies for the totalitarian regime in Iraq. Since the Gulf War, Iraq's population is made aware that much of their continued misery — because of the sanctions — is attributable to their support of a totalitarian regime.

Coblentz, in his survey of warfare has surmised the power that the prizes exercise over the seekers:

> "The Europeans were attracted to other lands in the first place by the hope of finding gold and other treasures ; and secondly by anticipation of free land to be exploited by slave labour...Throughout most of the vital eighteenth century , Europe was dominated by the economic creed known as mercantilism. It was this cult core than economic necessity that underlay much of thrusting and grasping, the shoving of nation against nation ... and exploitation of colonies[11]."

It is appropriate to describe the struggle for prizes amongst the seekers as competition in some instances such as sports and adventure, but perhaps not always. The convention to so describe the inter-action amongst the groups owes its origin to the winners who wish to proclaim that they have 'walked away' with the prize in a 'fair' manner. Competition invokes the images of equal opportunity, a comprehensive and agreed book of rules, and impartial referees who not only decide fairly, but also enforce their rulings. Genuine competition does indeed confer legitimacy on the winner, and perhaps that explains the reason for describing a host of interactions as competition.

Competition begins by eliminating the weak and the unprepared. When competition reaches a certain level of intensity and becomes a 'zero sum game', that is, the gain of one results in the loss to the other(s), competition as a determinant of who should get or share the prize becomes less and less attractive, and even the 'competent' join the 'incompetent' in avoiding or getting round the competition by other means. We are aware that cartels are formed to subserve the interest of the bidders who do not wish to 'quote' competitively but merely desire to give such an appearance, and thereby profit collectively at the cost of the government or some other public institution. Some other stratagems may also be used, but we will come to them presently. There is little likelihood of genuine competition without a moral or ethical commitment on the part of the competitors; even more, without a commonly understood, acknowledged, and accepted structure of rules and conventions, and an impartial authority which will enforce them. Competition survives more because of the latter than the former. A total preoccupation with moral and ethical considerations, may even cause a movement in the direction of cooperation and away from competition, as we understand commonly, i.e. securing of the largest possible share of the prize after prevailing over rivals. One could think of competition in cooperation but the seekers of those 'prizes' are indeed rare.

Since the essence of competition is prevailing over rivals—and emphasis on the fair means more a requirement of the order or system —competition can easily lead to a desire to weaken, incapacitate,or even eliminate rivals. Edward Bono acknowledges as much when he concludes that no matter what the form of competition, it contains some elements of conflict[12].

> "In fact all conflict can be seen as competition. Conflict is only one way of carrying out this competition."

The dividing line between competition and conflict appears to be the desire to hurt and eliminate rivals i.e. looking upon rivals as adversaries. Inconsistent goals are an essential precondition to conflict. Inconsistency in goals occurs when one or more competitors aspire to secure the same prize without any desire to share it with others, or desire to secure a disproportionately large share of the prize which others are not willing to concede to them. When combined with adversarial relationship among rivals, inconsistency in goals gives rise to potential conflict.

Since major conflicts are waged between groups, it is the consideration of their collective identity that is significant. Unless prizes that are sought are collectively desired, consistently, and for a length of time, the drive to pursue them is unlikely to be meaningful. At a point of time, the sum total of practical considerations must appeal to most individuals in the group so that there is a substantial congruence between their individual and group interests. They must be convinced that in pursuing prizes for the group, their individual requirements will also be met, if not in a large measure, then at least at an acceptable level. This may be the main precondition that supports the edifice of collective identity. Admittedly, it is the leadership that picks the prizes that will have the necessary appeal, and makes individuals aware of how their individual and collective destinies intermingle and intertwine to re-affirm or create collective identities. It is the leadership that emphasises the values that inspire individuals to place a premium upon collective prizes. Every collective identity is ultimately defined by a series of 'we' and 'they' divides. These divides, together create the periphery, or the pale, beyond which lie those with whom collective 'interaction' takes place: some times co-operation, at other times competition, or even conflict. Collective identities — their strengths and vigour, as also their weaknesses and handicaps — not only create drive to seek prizes, but they have the potential to determine who the rivals and competitors will be. This interaction between collective identities, within the frame-work of a prevailing order — and there would always be one — to seek prizes of choice, and a larger share of prizes, is the stuff that is scarcely distinguishable from the struggle for survival and betterment in which all living creatures must naturally participate. Conflict, it would appear, is a sub-set of the much larger struggle for survival. An increase in intensity of the struggle for survival — which often appears indistinguishable from a desire for betterment — crystallises into conflict.

Struggle for survival — and betterment — is a causality of conflict, and perhaps, a part of human condition.

Cooperation, may be the antonym of conflict — if there is one — and perhaps lies as the opposite pole within the totality of the field of struggle for survival and betterment[13]. Cooperation, ideally, presumes coincidence and compatibility both of ends and means. When there is a total compatibility of ends and means both, there is a virtual merging of identities, that is, the satisfaction — the ultimate prize — is so completely shared, that it is virtually indivisible. Common experience, with rare exceptions — like mother nursing her child — makes us aware that a total and lasting congruence of ends and means among human beings is not to be found. M.B.Nicholson observes:

> "Man is a purely self seeking animal who derives no satisfaction whatever from the contentment of others. This may conceivably be true in international relations[14] ."

Sharing of ends and means does lead to the possibility of cooperation, without necessarily reducing the likelihood of conflict. The outcome is determined chiefly by the calculus of where the advantage lies, and several other practical considerations associated with actually bringing about cooperation which calls for trust and generosity, at least to start with.

The observation of M.B.Nicholson, quoted above,no matter how much it reflects reality, does contain an apparent contradiction in need of resolution: how does the selfish human being reconcile its self interest with national interest, so much so that nations derive their collective strength from individuals and groups which make them up. It would appear that enduring collective identities have within them the ability to create a sense of loyalty and obligation which requires individuals, or constituents, to invert the natural calculus of seeking maximum advantage, and to cooperate. We will revert to this later.

The antithesis of conflict is cooperation. The pivotal idea that informs cooperation viz a viz competition or conflict, is the perceived need or compulsion to participate in a common and collective endeavour. Collective endeavour is not looked upon merely as an enabling expedient or device

— for seeking of some other prizes, but a prize in itself. Willingness to share the fruits of collective endeavour — prizes — is a natural outcome of the cooperative attitude. Interdependence is not looked upon as an unavoidable evil, something to be lived with and endured only because self reliance is not achievable, but as a wholly natural and desirable byproduct of shared life. Cooperation is predicated upon a desire to subsume individual and collective identities for common joy and benefit. Cooperation does not dispense with the need to secure prizes, but stresses equity and common goals as the motive force. Cooperation of this kind is not difficult to conceive of but somewhat difficult to find in real life, like the pure and simple goodness. Cooperation can only result from a consensus or agreement to which a large number of individuals and groups remain committed. It is worthwhile to analyze the major factors which govern interaction between groups and what impact they tend to have on the possibility of cooperation. It would appear that there are five major of factors — each one a cluster of several sub-factors — that determine nature of interaction between groups :

(1) Collective identities, and associations, that large groups or nations form;
(2) prizes they seek;
(3) means that they can, or choose to adopt;
(4) the prevailing situation; and
(5) the time-frame that they look at.

Collective associations may get energised to emerge as collective identities, or tend to dissolve into collective entities. They may expand to admit new constituents, or shrink to shed those who wish to separate. Thirteen sovereign states merged to create the United States which eventually expanded into its present form. The Soviet Union splintered to reemerge as CIS. Pakistan split to yield Bangladesh. There is speculation about whether distinct civilizations will coalesce into collective identities, eventually to clash with other civilizations. The size and commitment of collective identities determine the scale and intensity of collective effort, therefore, they raise the stakes. Collective identities also tend to define adversaries on account of perceived incompatibilities. Collective identities define the outside limits of fair competition on 'level fields'; beyond those limits, the concept of the level playing field is to be argued. But when the outside boundary of major collective associations which the presiding collective identity supports, for example, trade blocks, is also crossed, it could be war with other names. Therefore, views on who are to be denied prizes outright, or substantial share of prizes in any case, get determined in the light of what constitutes the limits of collective identities and associations.

Agreement about which prizes are to be sought, in what order, in which time frame, and how are they to be appropriated, rotated, or shared is at once the stuff of ideologies on the one hand, and hard headed national and business strategies on the other hand. Much of national and international politics revolves around it. During India's struggle for Independence from the British, those who felt that social and structural reforms of the Indian Society should have precedence over self-rule clashed with those who felt that the home-rule had to have the pride of place. At least some of the discord between Mahatma Gandhi and Dr. Ambedkar is to be seen in this light, as also that between Mr. Agarkar and Lokmanya Tilak. Discord that arises from the 'loaves and fishes' is proverbial. Towards the end of the Second World War, the United States wanted to deny the residual empire to the United Kingdom, whereas the British Prime Minister was very keen to deny to the Russians Eastern Europe. The consequences of this discord — purely prize related — led to the consolidation of the Soviet Union. Britons and Americans made common cause with the Soviets till the defeat of Germany. Thereafter there was stand off between the former allies and two camps emerged till the end of the Cold War. This shows movements between poles of conflict and cooperation. Even among Allies in the Second World War, cooperation was by no means total : it was restricted to meet a particular purpose. Americans did not share the secrets of Project Manhattan with other allies; they also showed keen interest in winding up of the British Empire.

Ends — prizes — can hardly be thought of without reference to means. Agreement or discord about means is no less common. Many a division in the ranks of those who sought freedom from the British yoke was about the means : Mr. Gokhale and the 'moderates' opted for the constitutional means , but Lokmanya Tilak and the 'extremists' chose the approach of agitation. The 'revolutionaries' took to bombs, even as Gandhi embraced non-violence. Later, Netaji Bose collaborated with the Japanese and raised the Indian National Army to 'liberate' India, but Pandit Nehru said that he would resist his advent in India because of his collaboration with Japan which was a part of the Axis Powers led by the Nazi Germany. None of these discord was mock or superficial. It prevented cooperation amongst patriots with the same goal, and reduced the intensity of struggle against the British rule on the one hand, and brought about a change in its nature, on the other hand. The relationship between diverse streams was far from symbiotic. Agreement about the freedom from British rule got submerged under the discord about priorities and means. In our own times, the debate about centrally controlled versus market economy was also about means, although it concealed some other issues.

Situations and circumstances create opportunities which need to be grabbed, just as they give rise to hazards which need to be averted. For so long as the no-war pact between Nazi Germany and the Soviet Union led by Stalin held out during World War II, the Indian Communists opposed the Imperialists, only to turn around and attack the Indian National Congress for their anti-British stance, because by then, according to the wisdom of the Communists in India, British deserved the Indian support in their fight against the Nazis and fascists, who had attacked Russia. India who criticized the policies of the United States, had to seek help from them to stave off food shortage in India. In the wake of the Russian advent in Afghanistan, the United States were reduced to seeking the support of Pakistan at any cost, even if it meant turning a blind eye to the development of the nuclear bombs by Pakistan. The above examples have not been quoted with a view to denigrating any particular nation for lack of consistency or 'principles'. The only purpose is to show that the circumstances and situations are very dominant factors, and that reversals of polarities or agreements is nothing uncommon.

The time perspective is, perhaps, even more important in determining the nature and valency of compulsions. It is not so much the certainty, but it is the imminence of an unavoidable and important event or development that pushes people into action — it would appear that, in case of India, even imminence of grave hazards or adverse developments have not always produced an appropriate response. Indian population, at the present rate of increase, will defy development after another quarter century is common knowledge, but that does not seem to produce compulsion to act at present. Come 2020, India will be forced to take drastic measures — perhaps not, if the population growth is controlled by then. Under the compulsion of that development, when imminent, all the consensus and agreements reached within and without may have to undergo drastic changes. Similarly, to borrow time to correct acts of omissions and commissions, totally unexpected developments take place including changes in alliances and attitudes : when Stalin-Hitler pact was signed, both knew that they were gaining time, each one hoping to derive greater advantage from the temporary reprieve. Uncertainty, that passage of time brings, does not invest long term agreements with the same degree of expectations, commitment or seriousness. Experience shows that imposed reparations may not be paid, and bail out packages may appear. Defeated Germany owed to the Allies 6 billion pounds sterling in 1921 as reparations. In 1922, Germany defaulted on payment of reparations, and the German currency lost its worth. Ultimately 750 million pounds worth of foreign loans had to be extended to Germany. Reparations imposed on Germany made it revanchist, and extension of loan at a later date did not buy any advantage to the Allies[15]. Future is invested with hopes and fears both, so much so, that likely dates for the process of nuclear disarmament to be completed are pushed beyond near time-horizon. In short, plenty of allowances are made, and abundant margins are left, while arriving at agreements and commitments effects of which may be expected to materialize after a generation or so.

More commonly, we come across 'strategic cooperation' driven by some commonality of purpose, or congruence of interests on the one hand, and interdependence on the other. Under such conditions even adversaries cooperate.

When there is a realization among several aspirants seeking a set of prizes, that prizes can only be secured by arriving at an understanding, but for which not only that the prizes will be forfeited, but additionally, unacceptable penalties will accrue, that some kind of interdependence emerges. For so long as the circumstances and conditions remain unchanged, and interdependence endures, cooperation to the extent agreed upon, may ensue. Adversarial feelings and relationships may be subsumed in the interest of expediency or survival, but since 'strategic cooperation' lacks a genuine willingness to share prizes, and even more, a desire to act together in unison, it cannot but be a transient phenomenon. Given that a workable model or plan for securing of prizes by and for all aspirants is feasible and exists, even for strategic cooperation to endure, there is a need for a continued agreement that fulfils the following three conditions :

(1) Perceptions of and about interdependence must be fully shared collectively and severally by all aspirants.

(2) Expected prizes and shares of prizes must exceed the minimum requirements of each aspirant; in other words, no aspirant must feel short changed because of the ongoing strategic cooperation.

(3) Contributions sought from each aspirant must not be withheld by them.

The formation of the United Front government in India in 1996, instability experienced by it as a result of the threats of withdrawal of support by one of its allies, and its final collapse leading to early General Elections in February 1998, serve to illustrate the validity of conditions for strategic cooperation stated above.

Cooperation that we experience in everyday life, and there is quite a lot of it, is perhaps an exercise in value maximization — where total returns from competition are not expected to be appreciably more, or in the long run, may be even fewer, that is, after taking into account the vagaries of fortune. Even so, it is to be seen that cooperation is restricted to those amongst whom interdependence is natural or unavoidable. Cooperation is, often, no more than a prudent investment, the more circumspect or timid being a little more cooperative than the strong and the wilful. But cooperation, by far and large, proves to be the small change of life, all big transactions being carried out in competition or conflict 'mode'. Where prizes are substantive, competition replaces cooperation, and to prevail, all the faculties and resources are brought to bear on the enterprise by all the competitors. The results are often determined by efficiency, although chance and extraneous factors may also matter. In contrast, cooperation emphasizes mutual goodwill and well being, often at the cost of efficiency, except in rare circumstances when stakes are so very high, or bonds amongst cooperators so very strong that symbiosis produces good results. But otherwise, in the general run of things, there is neither the desire, nor the incentive to excel. Competition leads to elitism, and cooperation to equity. Uncontrolled competition may sow seeds of discord and disintegration. Cooperation may contribute to lack of discord, though not to positive cohesion. Competition brings out the best, but there is always the danger that it will get out of control and degenerate into conflict that creates resentment or hatred in the losers ; cooperation keeps the pot from boiling over, but results at best may turn out to be mediocre. In the best of systems, the right balance between competition and cooperation is to be struck.

Collective identities, and larger architectures comprising them, like nation states, depend upon internal cooperation. This yields one of the constituents of strength, viz cohesion, but one of the likely by-products of cooperation, viz inefficiency, has to be kept in check, otherwise cooperation may lead to debility. Collective associations, within collective identities — or with their support — create immense scope for competition by defining limits of risks and commitment, and by shifting emphasis on effectiveness and gains.

Relationship between the effective emergence or resurgence of collective identities in political terms in the sub continent, since the advent of the British, on the one hand, and the incidence or occurrence of conflict on the other is very relevant. The British fought the Mughals, their satraps and governors, the Marathas, the Sikhs, and numerous other chiefs and potentates for the mastery of India. Although some springs of the emerging Indian national identity were visible in the violent out break of 1857, largely it was a struggle waged by sepoys and chiefs of states who had felt robbed of their inheritance, power, and privilege. A very large number of people in the sub continent remained unmoved during the uprising, although later, when many experienced British 'pacification' first hand, and even more when the stories of atrocities by both the sides spread far and wide, British seem to have defined their collective identity separately from and in opposition to the 'natives'. They were no longer the colonisers who had come to stay — as in America, Australia, or New Zealand, but a separate people who were in India for a finite time. Churchill says as much :

> "The scale of Indian Mutiny should not be exaggerated. Three quarters of the troops remained loyal. It was in no sense a national movement .... But terrible atrocities had been committed by both sides. From now on there was an increasing gulf between the rulers and the ruled. The English no longer looked on India as "home", or themselves as crusaders called to redeem and uplift great multitudes[16]. "

Many believe that Indian patriotism was thus born: in reaction. What is significant is that assertion of collective identity by the British created ground for reactive emergence of Indian collective identity within the geographical borders of British India. Assertion of collective identity, as distinct from its mere existence, would imply not only an emphasis on the 'we and they divides' to bring out contradistinction in bold relief, but also a determination to pursue exclusively those goals which strengthen own collective identity while showing particular disregard for those who lie outside the pale. Struggle against the British was seen by many Muslims to have had a pronounced Hindu character. Muslims, for, whatever reason, saw it rather as a ploy to subjugate the Muslims than a way of getting rid of the British.

> "[I]n first two decades of the twentieth century in Bengal, where, owing to the influence of Bankim Chandra Chatterji and Swami Vivekananda, there was a fusion of religion and nationalism, so that the nationalist feeling had a pronounced Hindu complexion and Hinduism a pronounced political character[17]."

Irrespective of whether emergence of Muslim collective identity was a reaction to 'Hindu' nationalist movement or not, its assertion in political terms by leaders of the Muslim community by claiming equal share of political power with the more populous Hindu community did sharpen the divide between the two communities. Other collective identities emerged, as a ripple effect, and began to assert themselves by opposing each other on the one hand, and sometimes opposing the British on the other. Sikhs, the Backward classes, the Communists, and so on did perceive 'we' and 'they' divides differently and jockeyed for power by casting themselves in cooperative or competitive roles with the British. But these collective identities could not cast themselves effectively in an adversarial role with respect to the main stream nationalist movement. Ultimately, it was the ability of a substantial number of the Muslims in the sub continent to create and assert an enduring collective identity, perhaps because it suited the imperial interests, that led to Pakistan. Two nation theory can be construed simply as an unwillingness on the part of two collective identities to cooperate or to share a prize. Adversarial relationship does not merely stop at unwillingness to share a prize; it goes beyond, by wanting to deny it to the rival.

As long as there was stability in Pax-Britannica, assertion of collective identities was contained and controlled.

Weakening and exhaustion of British power in India, at the end of the Great War, created instability when a little push could have created imbalance. At least so it seemed at the time. It seems that many of the Indian nationals and Amir Amanulla of Afghanistan thought so at the time. When a similar or worse situation arose at the end of World War II, assertion of collective identities, by nationalists and the Muslim League brought about the partition.

It would appear that emergence or resurgence in collective consciousness, brought about by compelling and effective leadership, leads to emergence and strengthening of collective identity, and its assertion in political terms has a potential to lead to conflict.

The matrix on the next page depicts the interplay of factors, and their outcome with regard to the independence movement in India. The southwest quadrant represents the lassitude born of years of slavery on the one hand, and the faith in the British Raj, on the other hand. Most professions, guilds, and caste-groups offered loyalty to the British in return for rewards for themselves. These were collective associations in which individuals participated for so long as it fulfilled individual goals. Collective identities remained dormant.

The northwest quadrant depicts the heightening of collective consciousness and emergence of a set of identities which formed an association to assert themselves. This was combined with rising disaffection with the colonial order on the one hand, and a willingness to submerge internal divides like Hindu-Muslim differences, on the other. Dominion status was the goal, and getting rid of the imperial yoke was the prize sought most of the time by many dominant groups comprising the movement for Indian independence. There were flashes which showed emergence of an Indian identity, but otherwise, all the assertive collective identities were not brought under a single overarching presiding identity.

The northeast quadrant depicts the situation and the operative forces which led to the splintering of the incipient presiding identity. In February 1947, the British declared their decision to leave the sub-continent in June, 1948. Now the moves and counter-moves for the securing of prizes on the one hand, and denying them to the adversary, on the other hand, commenced in earnest. Assertion of Muslim identity was part of the Muslim movement against the British, the other part being, the denial of power to the Hindus. Mr. Jinnah, the founder of Pakistan is quoted by Mr. Woodrow Wyatt, [former MP] as follows :

> " Together with the British they [Muslims] would rule India indefinitely... " Stop all the nonsense about independence." [18]

The obvious banter is not without serious undertones.

There was a desire to seek support of the rulers for partisan ends by one group or the other, and collective identities seemed to clash amongst themselves.

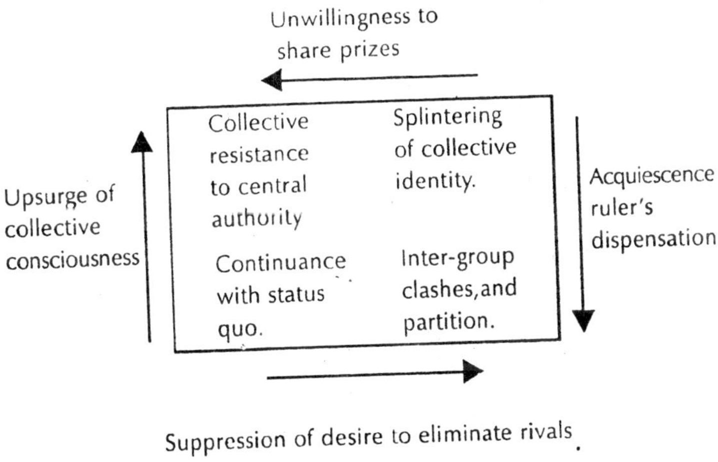

Eventually, this adversarial feeling resulted into total unwillingness to share power, on the one hand, and a desire to deny it to the rival group, on the other.

The Southeastern quadrant depicts communal conflagration, partition, and the ultimate acquiescence in the British dispensation. It was a dissolution of pre-partition Indian consciousness, such as it was, and a failure to forge a presiding Indian identity.

Most conflicts in the sub-continent have been amongst unequals. aggressors with good organizational and political strength, derived from a sense of strong identity, have prevailed against nominally more numerous opponents showing utter lack of collective consciousness. Indian cultural inheritance did not find exclusiveness of any kind at all attractive, and did not support coalescence of groups into collective identities with clearly delineated peripheries, and organizational strength. Inability to knit identities into organizations which can acquire and exercise political power has been a major weakness, with the result that some seek a solution by denying the very existence of divides, and collective identities.

The matrix on the preceding page can also explain in many ways the splintering that India seemed to face during the language agitations of the sixties, as also the insurgencies and separatist movements in the Northeast. Emergence of a collective identity does seem to create a wave effect, and subaltern identities also come to the fore to compete for a larger share of the prize, or in order to assert themselves. For so long as the prevailing order holds out and there is no desire to diminish or eliminate a rival group or subgroup, a competition ensues, and the anger is vented against the central or federal authority, and its dispensation is challenged. The Southwest quadrant should not always be seen as stasis — although, so it was under the foreign yoke — but as absence of identity related rivalry, competition, or conflict.

Conflict is viewed, essentially, as perception, creation, and assertion of collective identities: the boundary condition of collective identity being determined primarily by two main parameters:

(1) All those who share ideas on what constitutes inalienable assets, values, and a vision of an internal order, including those who are willing to give it a try, or live with it, are in; others are out.

(2) All those who are willing and committed to share prizes and penalties equitably and fairly — that is, on the basis of accepted values and envisioned internal order — are in; the others are out.

Conflicts occur because there is a general unwillingness to share prizes with outsiders , particularly with those who are perceived to be so very different that they cause annoyance or irritation, invite contempt and/or anger, constitute an immediate or potential threat, or perhaps, because of differences which are perceived to be irreconcilable. Civilizations may well prove to be one of the determinants of boundary conditions, and fault lines may well run along civilizational divides as suggested by Professor Samuel P. Huntington. Or will they ? Or will members of G 7 plus club successfully straddle divides of civilizations to avoid internecine conflict?

Edward Luttwak explains three rival conceptions of war in following terms: Marxists-Leninists see "it as a projection of class struggle"; pacifists view it as "unnecessary" and avoidable; and peace-researchers view it "as an event...and an outcome of political forces and structural facts...rather than result of conscious decisions[19]." The Marxist-Leninist perception of war — major conflict — casts it as an extension of class struggle which is not very different from struggle for survival and betterment. When the peace-researcher ascribes it to `political forces and structural facts', perhaps he intends to convey that nation states are organized at present in a manner that they hold themselves in readiness for conflict. Their attitudes and postures create conditions in which conflicts tend to occur. That is another way of saying that the world is predisposed towards conflicts unless active measures are taken to prevent them. The peace researcher canvasses for understanding and `cooperation' so that accidental wars may be prevented at any rate. He wishes not to tackle just yet the causality of political forces and structures that make the undesirable events — unintended conflicts — possible. Perhaps, there is an effort here to acknowledge that resolution of factors that create struggle and conflict may not be a practical proposition. The pacifist, however, holds the view that it is possible to avoid conflict — causes for conflict as well as accidental occurrences. Absolute and total cooperation amongst all, were it possible, could indeed achieve such a state. If conflict is caused by inability or unwillingness among aspirants to adjust, it is minimised, controlled, or even avoided when adjustments take place, or cooperation occurs. Peace cannot be defined merely as lack of overt violence or conflict. Only total cooperation — that can eliminate the causes for conflict and conflicts themselves — can lead to peace. Marxists saw such a dream — when the state itself would become redundant — but only at the end of an almost indefinite class war. If conflict implies destruction, pain and misery, it also appears as means to the disadvantaged to escape from exploitation, humiliation, and sub-human conditions. If a desire on the part of the disadvantaged to cooperate were to be of any help, they might not want to resort to conflict; if prizes that can be secured through cooperation were to satisfy the talented and the competent, they would not resort to conflict either. And what if it were possible to dissipate adversarial feelings without resorting to conflict?

Individual and groups alike face up to and accept hazards, or turn away from them and accept compromises in the name of security. Some may undertake big spending on armament even as they stint on welfare programmes. Security, as a concept, is perplexing and full of paradoxes. Chapter 6 examines it.

NOTES

1. Luttwak, Edward, N.,'A Dictionary of Modern War',Allen Lane The Penguin Press,London,1972 reprint. His definition of Cold War:"International conflict in which all means other than overt military force are used; a description of the state of East-West relations in the late-1940s-mid-50s period . The use of a combination of economic warfare, propaganda, subversion and covert operations is now sometimes described as confrontation",(p.53-54)

2.SIPRI YEAR BOOK 1995, Stockholm International Peace Research Institute, (p.21) .

3.Edward D. Bono,Conflicts: A Better Way to Resolve Them, Penguin Books, London, 1985, (p. 5).

4.M. B. Nicholson,'The Resolution of Conflict', Oran R. Young (Editor), 'Bargaining, Formal Theories of Negotiations', University of Illinois Press, 1975, (p 231).

5."Third Wave 'postnations' form the newest tier of global system. Unlike agrarian states, they have no great need for additional territory. Unlike industrial states, they have no need for vast natural resources of their own. .. (Third Wave Japan , by contrast, has grown immeasurably richer without either colonies or raw materials of its own.)"
Alvin and Heidi Toffler, 'War and Anti-War,Survival at the Dawn of the 21st Century', Warner Books, London, 1993, (pp. 328-329).

6.Genuine religious experience is not likely to incite passions or anti-social or harmful behaviour. 'Zeal' is intended here to convey passions incited in the name of religion or an ideology.

7. Bertrand Russell, 'Human Society in Ethics and Politics',Routledge, London,1954,(p.8).

8.Henry Kissinger, 'Diplomacy', Simon and Schuster, London, 1995, (p.63).

9.Coblentz, 'Arrow to Atom Bomb', Peter Owen, London, (p.283)

10.Ibid.,p.451.

11.Ibid., p.282.

12.Edward D. Bono, op.cit., (p.142).

13.This description of cooperation may be found offensive by some. Presumably, genuine cooperation without any thought or consideration for exclusive advantages for individual or collective self does exist. But its incidence is so rare, that cooperation in the present context is taken to mean , merely, as one of the options in pursuit of prizes.

14.Nicholson, op.cit., (p.231).

15.Major-General J.F.C. Fuller, ' The Conduct of War, 1789 - 1961', Eyre and Spottiswoode, London, 1961, (p.p.232 - 233).

16.Churchill Winston S.,'A History of English Speaking Peoples, Volume IV, Casell and Company, London, 1957, (p.70).

17.Chaudhuri, Nirad, C., 'Thy Hand, Great Anarch' ,Chatto & Windus, London, 1987, (p. 502).

18.Mr. Woodrow Wyatt, 'Two Fathers with a Mission', The Asian Age, Mumbai, August 14, 1997.

19.Luttwak, op. cit.,(p.p.212-214).

6

Security

The term security is perhaps intended to convey an innocuous image of the minimal, least objectionable, and therefore legitimate safety to which every nation ought naturally to be entitled; some kind of 'self evident truth'. Safety is included in it , but it does not occupy the entire domain of security, which stretches well beyond safety. Even safety cannot be defined in purely objective terms, since it extends beyond mere survival. National security cannot be defined in purely objective terms, nor by a single nation in isolation.

" So long as international politics is anarchic in the sense that there is no government above the independent states, security will depend on the interaction of states policies[1]."

But we do know that the security is a label that covers numerous beliefs, attitudes, capabilities, functions, and processes that deal with identification and pursuit of interests. Although, theoretically, a seamless global security that allows all nations to pursue their interests is conceivable, in reality, incompatibility of many of the prizes and interests that nations seek, gives a lie to such a possibility. The totality of global security concerns of super powers, instead, led to Cold War and alliances which stretched the security frontiers of super powers as far as they wanted to and gave rise to numerous conflicts including those in Vietnam and Afghanistan. These were waged in the name of security.

"The concept of collective security and alliances are diametrically opposed...The casus belli of collective security is the violation of the principles of peaceful settlement of disputes in which all peoples of the world are assumed to have a common interest[2]."

There is, therefore, a need to look at the concept of security with some care, to find out if it has any real meaning and utility, or does it merely represent Orwell's 'doublethink' and 'doublespeak'.

A people with collective consciousness, born of common interests and shared values, constitute a collective identity. They may or may not even own a piece of land. The Zionist movement began when they had no land which they could call their own. The Palestinians did not have consolidated land assets for many years. A sizeable proportion of Muslims in the sub-continent became a collective identity much before they secured from the British parts of undivided India to create Pakistan. The East wing of Pakistan ceased to be that even when the Pakistan Army had the possession of land, because East Pakistan, as a collective identity, had evaporated much before December, 1971. The prime national asset does seem to be the collective identity — or a set of adjusted, well aligned and 'nesting' collective identities presided over by the national collective identity. Perhaps, national integrity is associated with a minimum of prime assets; if and when they get further depleted, the national collective identity becomes untenable. Presiding collective identities can change without grave turbulence provided the constituents can adjust well under the umbrella of another collective identity. This can happen only when there are no major changes in either the value system and or prevailing order. The birth of autonomous Chinese region of Hong Kong in place of the Crown Colony did not cause grave turbulence. The Chinese presiding collective identity had replaced, on July 1, 1997, the British Empire. Allegiance to the British Crown was no longer considered a cherished value in so far as the people of Hong Kong were concerned, but prevailing order with many of the institutions continued with minimal changes, with the blessings of the PRC. This turning over of power by the British was in marked contrast to the turbulence in the sub-continent in August, 1947, in the wake of the British withdrawal, because new collective identities — with theocratic and secular values — came into being, and no overarching collective identity could contain them. But the bureaucratic structure and the prevailing order remained unchanged, or changed only superficially. Perhaps that is the reason why things were not any the worse, and the kind of upheaval that follows major revolutions did not take place.

Strength could be thought of as consequence and outcome of positive and productive utilization of all national and available sources that leads to growth — savings, investment, and further growth. The growth, in turn, can be depended upon to yield a steady surplus which can be employed to guard and protect own vulnerabilities on the one hand, and on the other hand, to exploit those of the adversaries — and potential adversaries — with a view to preempting threats. Development is readily admitted as the most major security concern of the developing societies or nations. Undoubtedly so, but there is little point in equating development with security.

"In a modernizing society, security means development...A developing nation that does not, in fact, develop simply cannot remain secure... If security implies anything, it implies minimum measure of order and stability...Human nature cannot be frustrated indefinitely. It reacts because it must; that is what we do not always understand and what governments of modernizing nations do not always understand[3]."

Development by itself cannot counter threats, although without development strength may be jeopardised, and even internal collapse may be possible.

National assets, tangible and intangible both, could be considered under two heads: those, which are so intrinsically important or highly regarded, that their diminution or abridgement would inflict a lasting and crippling injury, unlikely ever to be forgotten by constituents, and therefore, capable of threatening the collective being with unacceptable mutation or extinction ; and those others, which contribute significantly to guarding, protecting and nurturing the primary assets. It would be tempting to use the analogy of the field and fence to differentiate between the two. But that would be misleading, because the distinction between them — the field on the one hand, and the fence on the other — is stark and clear, and the relationship is inorganic : together, they do not constitute a collective whole. The relationship between the prime and other assets of a collective identity, like a nation state, is more comparable to that which subsists within sub-systems of an organism : although there is interdependence amongst sub-systems, it is not based on direct reciprocity. Exchanges between, say, the skin, which guards and protects all the organs and the tissues of the body, and other vital sub-systems, e.g. the cardio-vascular or the central nervous system, are not governed by considerations of reciprocity. A healthy collective being is an indivisible continuum of assets. And though the being acknowledges the vital, without neglecting other assets, it does not hesitate in 'discriminating' in favour of the vital in an emergency — scarce resources are jealously conserved by the body so that the brain and heart do not get famished; the nourishment is 'smartly' distributed, in good and bad times. Security begins from concerns for developing organic relationships between assets which are to be protected and the means which are required for protecting them. The collective identity which creates and holds together the nation state, and the associated strengths are the prime assets.

Vulnerabilities could be seen as openings or access corridors that allow adverse capability or influence to seep through into the body politic to injure and/or neutralize assets including sources of strength and power. Without the minimal strength that is associated with 'integrity' of the nation, there would neither be growth, nor any possibility of guarding vulnerabilities. Exploitation of adversary's vulnerabilities is so very attractive because it gives good 'returns', that is, exploitation yields either substantial mechanical advantage or leverage to undertake those ventures which otherwise may seem impossible, or offers prospects of substantial gains for limited risks and efforts. Simmering discontentment and disaffection in Indian Punjab, was a vulnerability waiting to be exploited by Pakistan. Angry Sikh youths in Punjab gave access to Pak to diminish cohesiveness in the border state, and reduce industrial and other economic activity which constitutes the source of national strength. Loss of strength — or emergence of weakness to give it another name — by it self may only be half the problem. Natural calamities and disasters can also bring that about. The subcontinent is certainly familiar with earthquakes, bad monsoons, and typhoons. It is the turning of that weakness by an adversary to his own advantage — exploitation — that fills the cup of woe and exacerbates the misfortune. Creation of weakness is so much more difficult than locating and exploiting that which already exists, although specific weakness can also be created or induced over a period of time with a view to its subsequent exploitation. In Operation Gibraltar, infiltrators from Pakistan occupied Kashmir failed because they could not access the local population. Their tribal and Punjabi ethnicity did not allow them to communicate with the Kashmiri population in the Valley. Next time around, it is largely believed, Pakistan Inter Service Intelligence took away Kashmiri youths from the Valley sent them back after training as 'freedom-fighters'. They attracted punishment of the Indian security forces and spread disaffection amongst the affected local population. The ground was made ready for mass mobilization. Weakness was actually induced and the vulnerability was exploited. Strength cannot be advantageously sapped without reaching the critical individuals, institutions, and processes along a line of least or at least manageable resistance. Guarding of vulnerabilities, to be worthwhile, must successfully deny , at a lesser cost, a far greater advantage to the adversary that he would otherwise get. Exploiting of adversary's vulnerabilities is no less important that guarding one's own. One cannot be a substitute for the other. The pacifist view point that the security function ought pretty much to draw a line at guarding one's own vulnerabilities, tends to place own side at a disadvantage from which it may never recover. Without effective fear of becoming a victim in its own turn, there is no incentive for the adversary to refrain from undertaking low cost ventures to exploit some weakness or the other of which there is unlikely ever to be a dearth, particularly in fragile developing societies. Security in the third world societies is certainly unthinkable without development, but development merely in terms of growth of GDP, or even other human development indices, is unlikely to suffice as security. A strong state which fetters the individual, or a permissive state which allows exploitation by interest groups and strong men while succumbing to pressures, may so weaken the sense of collective endeavour, as to detract from the value of collective identity. An internal order which creates stakes in collective identity and endeavour, which supports inheritance and opportunity in an even handed manner, and keeps in focus long term goals while dealing with immediate problems is more likely to concern itself with matters of security in a realistic manner than that which is overly concerned with consumption oriented growth, globalization, and the so called universal values. Security can hardly be separated from the values that collective identities hold dear.

Security implies not only a desire, but also a capability to protect, nourish, and when possible, add on to the strength of identity and assets that give meaning and substance to life. This meaning and substance is sought often within the confines of a cultural context. It would appear that NATO, particularly in the context of the post Cold War World, is being nurtured as a repository of the European collective identity.

"In the post Cold-War world NATO is the security organization of the Western civilization[4]."

Apart from the geopolitics, that creates compulsion for the US to have a foot on the Eurasian landmass, the cultural concerns seem to matter a great deal. The concept of national security, does seem to have historical and cultural moorings. The desire to survive under all conditions and at all costs, to prosper as much as possible, and to aspire to greater achievement have all been considered very honourable goals alike by individuals and collective identities. National security seems to encompass pursuit of interests, and extends well beyond mere safety, that is, a reasonable freedom from hazards and aggression. Safety or plain survival does not hold an enduring satisfaction for nations any more than it does for individuals. How the US equate prosperity with security may be seen from the following :

"...It is a central lesson of this century that America must remain a European power. We have an interest in European security, because we wish to avoid the instability that drew five million Americans across the Atlantic to fight in two world wars. We have an interest in European democracy, because it was the triumph of freedom there that ended the Cold War. We have an interest in European prosperity, because our own prosperity depends on having partners that are open to our exports, investment and ideas[5]."

Most nations like to avoid conflicts if they can because of their inherent uncertainties and likelihood of at least some irreparable losses and avoidable costs. Very rarely can outcome of conflicts be predicted accurately on the basis of calculus of known power indices, and other information. Some losses are bound to be suffered, and although the long term prognostication of the overall impact of a successful outcome may be very encouraging, the population may not just be prepared to countenance losses. The element of risk in a conflict is substantial, and courting of unmanageable risks certainly seems to run counter to the concept of security.

Crises tend to occur as the struggle hots up; the more frequently so, if the forecasting of trends and their evaluation have been inadequate or faulty. Apart from exhausting stamina of the decision makers, and lowering confidence of the population, crises may cause a drift towards conflict. Crises may be only marginally less welcome than conflicts.

It would appear that the concept of national security encompasses protection and promotion of national interests while avoiding crises, conflicts, and risks that have the potential to threaten national well being. It also implies prevailing in crises and conflicts, when confronted, without suffering irreplaceable losses or sacrificing long term interests. National well being certainly has survival as the irreducible minimum, but pitches a little higher in terms of wherewithal and values.

A nation deems itself secure to the extent that it fulfils the following conditions:-

a. It is in a position not only to protect but also to promote national interests in a progressive manner without courting undue risks.

b. It is confident and capable of dealing with adverse influences and developments in a manner that, in due course, it will create a more favourable state of affairs if possible, and if not, at least restore status quo ante.

c. Least ways, it is capable of inflicting substantial and if possible, even unacceptable damage on those who threaten national security.

On a certain plane, security boils down to elimination or neutralization, of threats and risks at tolerable costs and penalties; if this turns out to be or remains an unattainable ideal, even effective management of threats and risks would be reckoned as security, as will be seen later. What does give rise to dispute is the enlargement of the concept of security to include promotion of interests. The separation between the two — mere protection, as against promotion of interests — is not as definite or clear as one would like to believe. It is rarely possible to make sizeable gains without treading on someone's toes. If a food deficient country, succeeds in becoming a food surplus country, it is likely to keep out imports, and cut into profits of food-exporters somewhere or the other; besides, it may want to enter export market and thereby threaten traditional trade links and the profits associated with it. Increase of petroleum production by any of the countries to earn extra profit tends to depress petroleum rates, and hurts others. Pursuit of 'legitimate' interests by one party, may be construed as a threat by the other party. Construction of war-ships by European powers and the United States was a subject of an agreement in the interregnum between two World Wars. Pakistani and Indian bombs are seen as an incipient threats by 'mature' nations. Which capability will appear on whose security horizon, and when, cannot be determined by reference only to the capability. Intentions also play a substantial part in the calculus. And apart from the perceptions proper of the threat, its management, which is a part of the security spectrum, also determines if, when, and how will the threat be acknowledged, and even more how will it be dealt with. The Chinese nuclear capability has not been viewed as an active or serious threat by India, but at least there is some concern expressed about it from time to time. But United States' B-52 bombers at Diego Garcia do not even seem to enter into many Indian calculations. Why worry about them, when so many nuclear powered sub-marines are also patrolling the oceans anyhow, may be the logic that informs such attitudes. Even the Soviets in the Stalin era tended to refer to the nuclear weapons as paper tigers. This is the counter-part of crying wolf, which is also a part of security management. It is well to remember that even when the Soviet Union ridiculed the atomic bomb, it was developing it own nuclear devices. Of course, burying of one's head in the sand cannot be passed off as security management.

Promotion of own interests also impacts on security in two palpable ways. On the one hand, it attracts attention of those who may see them as potential, if not direct, threats; on the other hand, accretion in own assets increases the burden of protection and compounds the security problem of others. The concern that was caused amongst Indian ocean states when a nuclear powered Soviet submarine — Chakra — was merely leased by India in 1980s was substantial, and that was understandable. Bombay High oil installations have brought in their wake, the need to guard them against surprise attacks. Whether it is accretion in assets or in operative power, the security sums have to be redone.

"[E]fforts by one state to increase its national security without attention to the reaction likely to result in other states can make two or more states less secure rather than more so[6]...".

If India were to become energy sufficient in years to come, such a development is more likely to cause alarm than satisfaction in the region. Of course, it needs to be stated right away that there is no such possibility in the near future.

The use of force to promote national interests outside of national borders elicits proforma condemnation. It is politically incorrect in our times to show preparedness to use force except against 'aggressors'. Simpkin distinguishes between the use of force to resist aggression against homeland — and calls it 'protectivism' — , and the use of force for furthering other interests. Protectivism is defined by him as -

"A policy in which resort to armed forces is rejected as an active instrument of policy but accepted as a means of protecting country's existing territory and territorial waters against armed force[7]."

We do not know if protectionism will also include the use of force to deal with an adversary who will take out, or otherwise render ineffective, own satellites ; and further, to qualify as protectivism, will the use of force have to be restricted to reciprocal or comparable counter-actions in space ? These questions have been raised merely to point out difficulties associated with drawing dividing lines between protection and promotion of legitimate interests. Simpkin himself, later in his work, says that Super-powers would not be expected to restrict themselves to protectivism[8]. Alliance philosophy and practice makes use of force to repel aggression against allies or to protect security interests of alliance partners, perfectly appropriate. Aggression against Kuwait had to be repelled; perhaps, aggression against Taiwan, if any, may have to be similarly dealt with. In short, the current practice and basic inferences as above indicate that security is as much a concern of the weak as it is of the strong. Force — with other means — may have to be used, and is most likely to be used by nations not only to protect, but also to promote interests. The case for continued need for armed forces with power-projection capability rests on the prevailing concept of security which accepts the use of force for promotion of national interests.

The concept of security in the popular mind, it seems, emerges and takes shape against the back drop of potential or ongoing conflict, and most of all when a major conflict seems imminent, or in the wake of serious lapses or failures. This possibly happens because the true nature of relationship between the ongoing and ceaseless struggle for survival and betterment on the one hand, and conflict on the other, is not seen for what it is. The latter is not viewed in the right perspective, namely, as a natural consequence and fall out of uncontrolled intensification of the former. Without willingness on the part of the people at large to bear the cost of security, and suffer punishment, if necessary, to protect and promote national interests, national security may get reduced merely to governmental activity, rather than be the centre piece of collective endeavour that it ought to be. An acid test, perhaps, for determining whether or not an interest is vital is to pose the questions about the cost that the nation will be prepared to bear and the punishment that it will withstand to protect it. Out of the two, it is the latter which is far and away the stronger determinant. Not only that national interests need to be determined, their hierarchy is also to be arrived at and accepted by the national policy makers and the nation alike, so that a national consensus emerges and nagging doubts are not allowed to weaken the resolve either to commit scarce resources to the maintenance of the armed forces, or, if need be, to take the punishment that invariably attracts the use of the armed forces. Operation Pawan in Sri Lanka suffered on this score. There was no consensus, leave alone at the national level, but even amongst those who were actually executing the policy. There was no awareness of the national interests which were being protected, and therefore, the casualties inflicted by the LTTE were hard to bear. Our then ambassador in Sri Lanka has stated his conclusion in vivid terms :

"Some of these [subordinate military] commanders themselves were not convinced about the logic of IPKF's presence and operations in Sri Lanka ", and beyond that, even the General Officer Commanding - in - Chief Southern Command Lt Gen Dipender had reportedly opposed the operations against the LTTE[9].

National security, as an on-going and continuing process, ought to aim at the following:

(a) Sensitising of the population in general, and opinion and decision makers in particular, to national security affairs with a view to eliciting their support, and participation.

(b) Creation and maintenance of capability and pursuit of policies - within and without - that -

(i)reduce, guard and protect national vulnerabilities,and-

(ii) keep open all options for correcting adverse situations that may arise, if possible, preemptively;

(iii) permit adoption of all effective measures — political, economic, and military — in national interests.

One hears of energy or food security, and now even of security of nutrition. One of the 'middles' from a national news-paper contained the following :

"Prime Minister I. K. Gujral wants to send the right signal across to foreign exporters. By allowing the import of a million tons of contaminated wheat from Australia, he has made it abundantly clear that India's food-grain requirements can even be met by imported cattle feed...After all, importing contaminated and diseased grain threatens not only the viability of the country's food production but also undermines the nutritional security of an otherwise actually malnourished nation[10]."

Shortage of electrical power can slow down transportation, tele-communication, industrial activity, trade and commerce, and even public distribution of rations on which several millions of the poorest depend. Perhaps, it can produce an adverse effect on irrigation and reduce agricultural out-put. Beyond that, and more immediately, it can hinder daily commutation, pumping of water and sewage disposal, medical treatment, and disrupt life in high rise buildings. The impact is likely to be felt severely in metropolitan cities.

Barry Buzan mentions the problems associated with the evolution of the concept of security in developing countries:

"National security properly refers to the relationship of the state to its environment, and becomes profoundly confused to the extent that the state is insecure within itself. In other words, the concept of national security can only be applied sensibly to the external side of the state's Hobbesian security functions[11]."

In developing countries, planning for development, whether it is state-centric, or in a liberalised mode, is quite rightly regarded as a holistic exercise which cannot succeed without political will, and a concerted and well directed effort by experts in various fields and the administration. Participation by politicians, generalists and experts at all stages of planning and implementation is necessary. On the other hand, security planning is often regarded as a tussle between those who ask for resources, and those who find it hard to spare them. Those who are concerned with promotion of interests ought to be concerned with their protection. Security as a concern and function cannot be separated from the main stream planning, development, or governance for that matter.

Internal Security (IS) was viewed peculiarly by Government of India in colonial times. It was during Kitchener's times that IS responsibilities of the British Indian Army meant no more than protection of communications, installations, and routes that the Army was required to use to carry out their primary function, namely that of fighting the enemies of the Empire. One of the four 'great' principles enunciated by Lord Kitchener on November 5, 1903 included the following :

"That the maintenance of internal security was a means to an end, namely to set free the field army to carry out its functions[12] [of defending the North-West Frontier against an aggressive enemy]."

Possibly because the heart and head of the Empire was located outside of India, the main IS concern was about channelising impulses and wherewithal of the Government to the Army. It was during the First World War and soon after that the inadequacy of the outlook was brought home. Those who were to guard the frontiers of the Empire, after they left their permanent stations and bases, needed logistic backing in materiel, personnel, and animals which could only come from bases in India which had to be guarded, along with the lines of communications. It was not as if security was not viewed by the British as anything other than nurturing and guarding of sources of strength, with the internal and external security being two facets of the indivisible whole. Problem for the British in India, perhaps, remained deeply embedded in their own imperial psyche. Nearly half a century after the rising of 1857, the British had generally come to believe that the uneducated Indian had total faith in the Imperial system, and but for the numerically insignificant agitators who were far removed from and out of touch with the rural India, the British-Indian rule of law, and the Administration which governed efficiently were the real sources of strength. For so long as the police and the Intelligence Bureau functioned efficiently, IS was taken care of. The Army supported the British-Indian Administration, when called upon to do so. It played no other part in the IS. Operationally, IS was taken to be no more than an extension of the police function. Law and order and IS were not viewed separately. Events following Jallianwala Bagh, and attempted uprisings in the units of the British Indian Army by the Indian revolutionaries like Pingle and Ras Bihari Bose brought home to the discerning the shortcoming of looking upon IS as an exclusive function of the Administration and the police. When a need was felt to employ the Army in the IS role in the Punjab, there was no policy, much less a doctrine. The then Lt Governor in Punjab took recourse to some outdated statute to deal with the situation.

Blinded as the British were by the vision of their Imperial destiny, it was not till the large scale defection of their prisoners of war to the Indian National Army, and subsequent mutinies by the Royal Indian Air Force, and the Royal Indian Navy, that the British-Indian Administration became aware that the sources of strength that needed to be nurtured and guarded had already been dissipated. They had failed to correctly locate their real sources of strength, and vulnerabilities. Having guarded the Empire against the external threat, they had failed on the IS front, and the armed forces were no longer useful in the IS role. The upshot was that Wansborough Jones report commissioned by the Interim Government in 1947 had recommended 'support of civil power' as one of the roles of the defence forces in India[13].

Threats to security which arise from within need to be responded to differently from those which arise abroad. The division could be premised on the following considerations: effective governance demands not only the enforcement of law of the land, but also elimination of threats which whittle down assets and sources of strengths. Threats which arise on own soil, principally from within, that is from own citizens, ought to be dealt with more by addressing the causes of disaffection or dissatisfaction rather than through the use of coercive means for the fear that a rise in 'force in use' will strike at stability, growth, and prosperity. With this approach to governance, threats need to be tackled or dealt with by due process of law, that is by designated guardians of law and order acting within confines of the law of the land. Bounds of IS could well be determined by what can be done within confines of law to deal with and eliminate threats on own soil.

There is always a temptation to stretch and expand the scope of the law of the land so that it includes the intended use of force by the government. The compulsion being that dealing with threats to IS is very much a 'domestic' matter for the nation state to deal with, and hopefully outside the international scrutiny or concerns. Initially, special purpose enactments in response to grave IS threats may be and are considered sufficient, MISA, TADA, NSA, for example. Insurgency — armed rebellion against established government — may be described initially as criminal activity — which most certainly it is — with a view to lopping off or under-playing the political content of the movement. At this stage, the agencies dealing with the problem must necessarily overcome the 'criminal activity' by using 'legitimate force'. Later, when legitimate force cannot deal with the problem, the special enactments are made, or invoked. At every stage, counter-insurgency operations seem to be conducted in a manner that the enabling legislation lags a little behind the actual requirements. Those actually dealing with the situation on the ground use force in the light of their own inclinations and practices in their service, because confines of the law of the land do not give them enough room in which to operate. Where force has already become an arbiter, not many are willing to be victims in unequal contests so that the law of the land is upheld. At the cutting edge, if the law cannot protect, and only inhibits, functionaries take recourse to being economical with truth — at least they do have a very good case. Pretence at the top — unwillingness to acknowledge the threat for what it is, and the circumstances for what they are — eventually create not only anarchy, but even chaos of which the worst victims are those who are caught in the cross-fire. The ultimate, in terms of stretching of the law of the land, being the declaration of the martial-law to quell grave disturbances. Even when it involves the use of substantive force, it is no more than an IS operation. Understandably, there is a natural reluctance to invoke martial law because it is politically incorrect for party in power to be seen to be ruling by force, and other political parties, and human right activists — and, on occasion, hostile foreign interests in their garb — are bound to style the governmental response as inappropriate and excessive. The nation state faces unique inhibitions in dealing with internal threats, and these are often debilitating.

The situation becomes even more disadvantageous when the threat is such that it cannot be dealt with in accordance with the law of the land, and force has to predominate, that is, sufficiency of force has to be the principal determinant of the response. Then matter may be about to slip out of the domain of IS. If threat to security is such that it cannot be dealt with except by force, employed for effect, in accordance with laws, customs, conventions, and principles that govern the use of force — and not, necessarily, law of the land —the matter clearly lies outside the domain of IS. In such circumstances, if the threat has to be dealt with principally on own soil, against own citizenry, it is civil war — the dread term of which most nation states are rightly afraid; even when a civil war is on, for all practical purposes, there is a desire to deal with it through euphemisms of one kind or the other. Perhaps, the purpose of denying the existence of civil war being the hope that the matter would get resolved, and rule of law established once again. In close proximity of the international border, and against a mix of own citizenry and hostile elements from across the border, it turns into a proxy- war. A proxy-war also creates situations , which may be politically inconvenient. An exception had been taken at one stage to one of the Chiefs of Staff of the Indian Army describing the situation in Kashmir as a proxy-war.

From this perspective, it is obvious that it is not so much the agencies which deal with countering of threats, or the origin of threat, that determine whether the matter lies within IS domain, or external security, but whether normal, 'governance' can adequatly eliminate the menace on own soil without stepping outside the rule of law. Since law of the land cannot be operative outside the nation-state boundaries, actions taken in the interest of IS cannot extend beyond the international border, although threats may emate extra-territorially.

External threats may. so inextricably be linked with threats which lie within that the idea of tackling them independently may be ill founded. A nation state, rightfully, may wish to deal with own citizens who may be 'misguided youths' — led astray, and therefore in need of special consideration — differently from intruders from other nations who may also be indulging in the self same acts of hostility as own citizens. Converting this very understandable desire into practical action may be an impractical proposition. Are individuals to be judged on the basis of their behaviour and actions, or in the light of their motives, or according to their identity, that is who they are. Questions such as these remain suppressed, ambiguously answered, or not answered at all. In point of fact, doubts on these vital issues spread confusion, and inhibit formulation of doctrine. Those empowered to use force on ground to deal with insurgents, need a clear doctrine to guide them. Armed forces custom says that your own sentry, if he has gone berserk will be dealt with like any other person indulging in similar acts. If he fires or threatens to fire, he will be overpowered by the most appropriate means. If your own aircraft, because of mistaken identity, starts firing on you, you treat it like any hostile aircraft. Is there a clearly enunciated doctrine, at the national level, to deal with insurgents? Perhaps, not.

It would appear that Government of India, taking over the reins from the British-Indian Administration, did not change the security paradigm. IS has been regarded as the exclusive domain of the Home Ministry :

"The problem of maintaining law and order and of preserving the morale of the nation in the face of a threat of external aggression is of great importance and this is the role of the Home Minister[14]."

There have been times when a Minister in the Home Ministry has held an independent charge of IS. It would appear that Security as a whole is not viewed or conceived in India as a comprehensive function well beyond the capacity of a single department or ministry; even the formulation or articulation of the basic and urgent security problems is well outside the ken of a single department or agency. As a consequence of opening up of the borders to foreign trade and travel, and unhindered activity in the electromagnetic spectrum, national assets and sources of strengths become more and more accessible to adversarial interests, unless of course, appropriate counter measures are already in place. Vulnerabilities may be exploited even before the host becomes aware of them. The divide between internal and external security with regard to the means used needs to be maintained, but it must still serve the over-riding purpose, and not fragment the unity of the national response. Proxy wars may also be fought by those who come in ostensibly as travellers, or drop down with parachutes, or destabilize the share, commodity, or currency markets from great distances, or through local agents. Decidedly in hot war, but also in during grave internal crises, satellite communications may be denied effectively at critical moments, shock waves sent by rising petroleum prices, or senior functionaries and experts in critical positions may be pressurised or tempted into inaction, or desertion when their services are required the most. To boot, they may also claim justification quoting supra-national and universal causes. There may be no immediate reason for such pessimism or alarm. India is not the only country which faces such hazards, some of which are admittedly exaggerated. But who can say that India is blessed and immune. Professional expertise, efficiency, good faith, foresight, executive ability, and a capacity for general comprehension and coordination are sine qua non in the domain of national security. National security is an area where the statement of the problem, even if a comprehensive definition proves elusive, would be a substantial contribution that academicians, generalist, specialists, professionals, and indeed all interested citizens, can make. It has necessarily to be tackled by the political leadership in the forefront, but not without contributions from all sections of the society. In a democratic polity, hope for mobilization of the national effort lies in formulating policies through open, forthright, and well-informed discussion. Government, on their own, and in secret conclaves, cannot determine national security policy. Notwithstanding the requirements of secrecy, this holds good as much in the matter of national security as in other weighty matters like development. National security can no more be addressed by a single ministry. The official view, it would appear, is otherwise :

"[H]ome ministry has the overall responsibility for national security management. .. [P]resent day crime patterns have serious across-the -border linkages — penetrating the public services and the polity — it can best be pursued by the home ministry through the national intelligence agencies and enforcement organisations, a number of which are under the finance ministry[15]."

Over a period of time, war ministries or departments became ministries or departments of defence — after all, how could democracies have war departments; basically, democracies defend themselves; occasionally they also create similar opportunities for others. Even so, ministry and department of defence concern themselves with those aspects of security which involve direct, and mostly overt, use of force. But they do not address the whole spectrum of national security concerns. It is not as if a single unified ministry for national security will address the problem. Every single department and ministry needs to create its own constructs of security that lie wholly or partially within their charter. The complete picture can only emerge through a unified, well coordinated, and cooperative effort. The command or top directed coordination is essential but it can never be enough. It has to be supplemented by coordination that is inspired by need, responsibility and desire to cooperate. As individuals become more autonomous, and 'empowered' — as much by virtue of the information, and skills that they possess, as by their ability to bring about results entirely by themselves by intervening directly and effectively through interlinked information and command and control channels — the scope for benefitting from their capability by giving them maximum freedom will increase. So will the need increase for the systems to protect themselves from the fancies, prejudices, and weaknesses of individuals. National security organization may have to emerge more on the lines of human brain which is without a single centre of supreme authority, and yet acts creatively, decisively, and in time to coordinate the effort of all body mechanisms. Cooperative effort is likely to emerge as the single most important determinant of successful national security policy and apparatus.

Understandably, this spirit of acting effectively on the basis of guidelines — instead of specific instructions in every situation, or not at all — will also have to percolate down to the executive agencies. Setting up of a national security council — or any other apparatus for the purpose — is certainly the beginning, but that is all it will remain, unless there is a change in perception and operations. Guidelines that can direct effort of so many individuals occupying so many rungs of the hierarchy have to be sufficiently general, well reasoned, and direct. That is the national security doctrine. Without a national security doctrine, national security council can be of little avail, unless of course, they themselves take on the task of evolving the national security doctrine.

Security, as a concept, serves a useful purpose for so long as it helps in evolving national 'intelligence' that senses the threats and opportunities in good time; defines the boundaries of the available strategic space; and integrates all the national resources for countering threats and exploiting opportunities.

NOTES

1. Joseph S. Nye, Jr, 'The Contribution of Strategic Studies', IISS, London, (p.23).

2.Henry Kissinger, 'Diplomacy', Simon and Schuster, London, 1994, (p.247).

3.Robert McNamara, 'The Essence of Security', Hodder & Stoughen, London,1968, (p.150).

4.Samuel P. Huntington, 'The Clash of Civilizations', (p.161).

5.US Secretary of State Madeleine Albright's statement before the Senate Foreign Relations Committee, on January 8, 1998, USIS, Mumbai.

6.Joseph S. Nye, Jr, 'The Contribution of Strategic Studies', IISS, London, (p.23).

7.Richard E. Simpkin, 'Race to the Swift, Thoughts on Twenty-First Century Warfare', Brassey's Defence Publishers, London, 1985.

8.ibid., (p. 292).

9.J. N. Dixit, 'Assignment Colombo', Konark Publishers, New Delhi, 1998, (p. p p. 212 - 341).

10.Devinder Sharma, 'Food for thought from Australia', Indian Express Pune, 19 July, 1997.

11.Barry Buzan,'People, States & Fear', Trans Asia Publishers, New Delhi,1983, (p.69).

12.Government of India, ' The Army in India, and its Evolution', Superintendent, Government Printing, India, Calcutta, 1924.

13.Chris Smith, 'India's Adhoc Arsenal', Oxford University Press, New York, 1994, (p. 49).

14.Venkateswaran, A.L., 'Defence Organization in India', Publications Division, Ministry of Information and Broadcasting, Government of India, New Delhi,1967,(p.88).

15.N. N. Vohra, former Home Secretary, quoted in the Times of India, Bombay, 6, October, 1996

7

Strategic Thought : Application of Power

Policy is informed by vision and dreams, idealism, and thoughts of a better world for everyone. It often mixes pragmatic considerations with grand ideas. It is justified and put across in a variety of ways, depending upon the cultural moorings and natural preferences of the people for whom it is meant and who it is intended to inspire: theories based on rigours of logic, or analysis of historical evidence, or faith, or 'scientific temper', or all of these are freely drawn upon in evolution of policy . Policy reflects totality of aspirations and interests without being inhibited by the actuals. Ends of policy ,on the other hand, are determined by hard facts, and reality as seen or perceived. Clausewitz reflected that the "policy administers the multitudes of interests in society as a whole[1]." Of course, those ends of policy which are to be held up as distant beacons are hardly distinguishable from policy it self and may well be allowed to remain on the ever receding time horizon, except for some propitiatory rites and gestures to realise them. But those policy-ends which it is intended to secure in a given time-frame - say, policy objectives - are differently treated, because this exercise calls for evolution of strategies and their implementation. It calls for ends and means dialectic, and a commitment to raise and apply resources to achieve the policy objectives.

> " The difference between high policy and total strategy lies primarily in the attitude of mind peculiar to each of them -— initiative, philosophical and creative in the case of policy, rational and constantly referring back to the political aim in the case of strategy[2] "

Inability to distinguish between the policy and policy objectives leads to needless confusion in minds of people. Such confusion tends to weaken the resolve while fanning expectations. Constitution of India contains the 'Directive Principles of State Policy', but Article 37 makes it clear that "The provisions contained in this Part shall not be enforceable by any court ...". In short, the principles of state policy are not policy-objectives. At least some of the problems associated with Article 44 dealing with uniform civil code, arise because grand policy objectives are mistaken in common perception for actual policy-objectives. Strategies are concerned with policy objectives, and not so much with policy, although the overall policy is their to guide and illuminate the path of strategists. But if there is a big gap between the stated policy and actual policy objectives, doublethink and doublespeak have to be resorted to, but not without confusing the common man and the talented alike :

> "We have not as yet set up all the doublethink ministries of the Orwellian regime, but we have made a significant start. The War Department has been changed to the Department of Defence, and the Navy and Air Force Departments have been brought within it. The Department of Justice has not been christened the Ministry of Love, nor as yet has it deserved any such designation in extreme Orwellian terms. There is not yet any unified Ministry of Truth, primarily because all the major departments of government have their own special propaganda agencies and have not been consolidated into one single organization[3]."

Policy objectives are none other than 'prizes' arranged in their order of priority and importance, that is to say that policy objectives state and define the hierarchy of prizes with respect to their relative importance and urgency. Obviously, prizes encompass all concerns - internal strength and cohesion, development, growth, favourable image, protection, and so on. The security perspective delimits the prizes on the one hand, and the means on the other hand. Striving for prizes is as natural for individuals as it is for collective identities, and associations. This pursuit of prizes, at some stage, sooner than later, invariably gives rise to rivalry amongst those who aspire to the same set of prizes or for greater share of them. If there is an agreement on the ends and means both, and in respect of the share of prizes with which the aspirants would feel satisfied, some kind of an adjustment among them may result; otherwise, a conflict may be in the offing.

The essence of adversarial relationship is the perception of mutual incompatibility, the greater the incompatibility the more intense the response — both pro-active and reactive. Adversarial feeling manifests as a desire to diminish and eliminate not only adversary's sources of strength and instruments of power, but also the adversary himself: destruction of his identity, order, culture, values, and assets. Only those assets which can be appropriated, exploited and used may be spared. It is not as if destruction and elimination spree is taken to ultimate conclusion every time. But such intent may often be apparent. Hitler's 'final solution' is the worst known example of this, although other examples are not rare. Adversarial relationship elicits such behaviour; conversely, infliction of extraordinary penalties, with or without intent creates adversarial relationships. The roots of attitudes which create adversarial relationships may go down deep in collective memories that draw upon past violations, violence, injustice, deprivation, obduracy, irresponsibility, or unconcern. Unwillingness to share prizes, or laying of claims on a disproportionately large share of a prize may give rise to adversarial relationships amongst contestants or competitors. In such situations, mutually agreed adjustments may cause the adversarial relationship to become less pronounced, or it may vanish altogether over a period of time. As long as adversarial relationship exists, a continuing search and effort to determine and exploit adversary's vulnerabilities is only to be expected. Soviets spied on the UK and the US through out World War II. They kept themselves well informed, and derived benefits from knowledge of differences between the two Allies about the emerging world order, apart from ferreting out the atomic secrets. Conversely, it can be argued, that undertaking of a search for vulnerabilities of a friend with a view to possible exploitation may turn him into a potential adversary.

Apart from the likelihood of dispute arising out of dissatisfaction with the share of prize, adversarial feelings or relationships may also give rise to trials of wills. Adversarial relationships may be actively pursued with a view to securing some prizes in entirety, or for maximising own share of prizes, or with a view to denying some prizes to the adversary, or with a view to subduing the adversary, or getting even, or avenging oneself. Whatever the cause of the adversarial relationalships, four faces on which adversaries work at all times seem to be the following:

(a) Locating and enlarging upon adversary's vulnerabilties in relation to own policy objectives; where necessary, creation of fresh vulnerabilties so that opportunities for deploying own power are created.

(b) Developement of own capability with a view to deploying it along the selected vulnerabilities of the adversary, pro-actively or in response, in pursuit of policy objectives.

(c) Reducing, concealing, and guarding own vulnerablities so that they may be easlily located or exploited by the adversaries.

(d) Development of own resistance and counter capability with a view to resisting and withstanding punishment.

In this context, vulnerability may be defined as the opening, access route, or corridor that may be used by the exploiter, by stealth or otherwise, to reach own vitals along lines of least resistance. Vitals are principal assets, resources, sources of strength and instruments of power, processes of making and communicating assessments and decisions, and 'pressure points'. Vitals could well include collective consciousness that sustains collective identities, and their structure which underpins nationhood, international associations and alliances, preferred internal and international order, government in power and its bases, non-governmental institutions that wield influence, economic infrastructure, natural resources, industry, trade, communications, armed forces, et al. Pressure points may be so termed, when even a little exertion on them produces disproportionate results, that is, loss of resistance of or compliance by decision makers, a pliant mood in the population, or a systemic dysfunction. Pressure points need not always be tangible objects, or places. They could well be faith in particular leadership, ideas, or notions that contribute to strength. Exploitation of vulnerabilities implies deploying own capability along lines or corridors of least resistance — after having located them successfully in the first instance — to obtain desired results, that is diminution of the adversary or his assets, strengths, and power — needless to add, at an acceptable cost. Protection of own vulnerability, on the other hand, implies concealing of not only openings and access routes, along which the adversary may be tempted to deploy his capability, but also of vitals in general, and of pressure points in particular; and beyond that, of so positioning own resources, that vulnerabilities can be plugged and sealed; if not all, then, at least those which are likely to give especial advantage to the adversary; if not preemptively, then at least, reactively, but before the ultimate damage is done. Exploitation of vulnerabilities implies securing of decisive advantage in reaching the desired goal. In terms of mechanics, it would be comparable to selecting the right points for application of force, and obtaining of the desired leverage so that the available power can be employed to lift the heavy load, or selection of the right slope for working ones way up. Application of power without considerations of vulnerabilities is unlikely to meet with success, and if it does, because of a substantial power differential in own favour, the venture is likely to prove much too costly or even disastrous. On the other hand, appropriate consideration of vulnerability factor, may even, on occasion, help to get over unfavourable power-differential. Essential difference between the attrition and manoeuvre techniques of warfare is that, in the former, the emphasis is on overwhelming or crushing by physical force as large a proportion of adversary's armed forces as possible ; whereas in the latter, or in manoeuvre warfare, the emphasis is on rendering dysfunctional the most critical components of adversary's armed forces through application of physical force at critical points, places, and times, and continuing the process, till the adversary loses his will to resist, even though a substantial proportion of his armed forces may still be in tact. Manoeuvre warfare is the technique of locating and exploiting all of adversary's vulnerabilities — systemic, psychological, and physical. Manoeuvre warfare, of course, uses force ruthlessly and efficiently to win battles, campaigns, and wars. Richard E. Simpkin has used the analogies of leverages from mechanics to make the point[4].

Exploitation of vulnerabilities of the adversary while guarding one's own, as a dictum, does provide the general direction for dealing with adversaries, but the actual power-dialectic takes into account the reality that there are a number of rivals and competitors in the field — not all of them adversaries — and they may subserve own purpose, more or less. All friends, no more than all adversaries, can be treated on par and gradations amongst friends and adversaries must be made.

Employment of power to win and secure prizes at an affordable cost and bearable punishment is the pivot of strategic policy and planning, that is, 'value maximization' is the goal in all endeavours.'Prizes' must be interpreted in the light of the overall situation and the context. While facing 'fearful odds', survival, or even death without dishonour, may also be reckoned as major achievements. It would appear that there are a few contributory factors which mainly subscribe to evolution of strategies in the context of competitive or adversarial relationships. The concern is with differentials: differences in capabilities, capacities, wills, and opportunities to prevail that actually exist, and even more significantly, their perception by the rivals, their protagonists, and antagonists. Assuming that, at a point of time, at least theoretically, an objective assessment of relative advantage that the rivals actually have is possible, subjective assessments, which are likely to be at some variance from the objective view, are bound to be made, the most critical of them being those by the adversaries themselves, not only of their own capability, but also that of their rival's. But in real life, most decisions have to be taken, in the light of assessment of own capability, and a speculation about what conclusions the adversary is likely to arrive at. Not only that variables are very large, but they are also prone to changes — sudden, and gradual both — and therefore, assessments need to be frequently updated. But, since there is no such thing as a comprehensive objective assessment, except as a mental construct, the picture gets more and more confusing, with updating and add-ons, particularly when the capability in respect of prospective allies has also to be taken into account. Mr. J. N. Dixit illustrates the kind of errors that creep in. He throws light on erroneous assessment about the LTTE motives and capability by Indian decision makers when they decided to sign the Sri Lanka Accord of 1987.

> " Representatives of RAW told Rajiv Gandhi that they had sufficient influence with the LTTE to prevent them from resiling from the Agreement once Prabhakaran gave his commitment...General K. Sundarji told Rajiv : this possibility [of the Indian armed forces getting involved in guerilla or anti-insurgency operations] should not be a matter of concern. The Indian armed forces can neutralise the LTTE in a fortnight or three to four weeks[5]."

All considerations of relative advantage/disadvantage are, even when the best of factual data is available, in the nature of considerable speculation and simplification both. Even so, these considerations contribute substantially to generation of strategic options and their evaluation, that is, evolution of strategies.

Adversarial feelings often give rise to a trend of thought, sometimes verging on strong conviction, that if the adversary is eliminated or reduced substantially, realization of own vision will be facilitated. It is presumed that the adversary is bound to harbour similar thoughts, and threats come into being, real and imaginary both. Threats are articulated, and force is used on occasions. From then onwards, there is an urge to defend, and beyond that, even a stronger urge to project power against the adversary.

Relative differences in compulsions, capabilities, and preferences of adversaries, that contribute significantly to the modes of projecting and resisting power do not seem to greatly change in their essence, though they are certainly influenced by technological advances. The following considerations appear to contribute significantly to evolution of strategies :

(1) What matters most is the ability to disarm the adversary, that is, to render the adversary's ability to resist ineffectual; ideally, with minimal damage, so that assets which can subsequently be exploited are not irretrievably lost. If that is not an attainable objective, the next best option is to possess a capability to overwhelm or exhaust the armed forces of the enemy. Situations in which adversary's forces can be subdued, overcome, or destroyed, with a degree of certainty, in a preemptive or, even better still, reactive mode gives the kind of whip hand that most contestants really desire. The main component of power is likely to be deployed to achieve this end, whenever possible. Malleson describes the battle of Laswari fought in 1803 between the Scindia's force and that commanded by General Lake. It was the excellent artillery of Scindia and its competent handling that held up Lake and his charge was repulsed. Ultimately, Lake became aware that without suppressing the guns, seventy of them, he could not carry the day. The main prop of the enemy's capacity to resist had to be knocked out by disarming the adversary. He decided to charge the guns.

> "Nothing stopped them; they [cavalry] carried the guns. Then Lake with his Infantry handy, dashed forward and secured greater number of them...Nor did they [the enemy] quit the field till they had been driven away from every position and every gun[6]."

Other means of dealing with the adversary are less direct and do not yield immediate or enduring results, and therefore, destroying or subduing the force remains an attractive proposition, a preferred option. Fuller quotes Marshal Foch from 'The Principles of War' :

> [The enemy] "will consider himself beaten when he is no longer able to fight; that is, his army will have been materially and morally destroyed. Therefore, modern war can only consider those arguments that lead to the destruction of that army : namely battle, overthrow by force[7]."

The situation has not greatly changed in the nuclear age. For so long as the US had the monopoly of nuclear devices and ability to deliver them with a degree of reasonable certainty, it opted for the strategy of 'massive retaliation', or assured destruction - hit anywhere and destroy. The relative advantage was totally with the US. Soon after the Soviets developed the countervailing nuclear weaponry, and put the first satellite in orbit, they gave a notice that they could hit any target anywhere and with a degree of certainty. Now the cities of the US and her allies needed protection, and the need for rendering the Soviet strike capability ineffective began to surface. "Counter-force strategy" may indeed have been a "no-cities strategy", and a contrived damage limitation exercise so that retaliatory or assured destruction forces did not have to be used[8]." If disarming also meant destruction of nuclear strike forces, so be it. Disarming of the adversary became a thrust area, as soon as it became a practical proposition, that is, with the advent of accurate ICBMs which could reach the launch sites, and tactical nuclear weapons which could deal with forces in the field. Even in the nuclear age, disarming remains a prime concern and consideration, whenever it is a practical proposition. The soldiers of the revolutionary warfare — guerillas — are so very difficult to defeat because they cannot be easily located, and therefore, they cannot be disarmed except, perhaps, at an unacceptable cost.

(2) A greater capacity to strike at adversary's vitals like important leaders, centres of decision making, communications, and trade, or other pressure points, has the potential to create a crisis for the adversary which may lead to panic, unwise decisions, mistakes in implementation of plans, and lack of coordination in application of effort, so that burden of his own incapacities will crush the adversary. It

does not suffice merely to strike from a distance, unless forces on ground, are available to take advantage of confusion and paralysis in adversary's decision making process, so that the transient loss of adversary's capacity and will is 'fixed' and fully exploited. 'Strike', in this context, is not intended to imply aerial or missile strike by itself. One of the main causes of success of the German blitzkrieg in the Second world War, when they made deep thrusts and incapacitated decision making in many of the headquarters of the Allies, was this ability to degrade the 'nervous system' so that adversary's mind and heart both were rendered ineffective. The decision making of the Allies was always overtaken by events, and the resultant confusion sapped the will to fight. Thereafter the troops, without leadership, were an easy prey. Relative advantage in ability to locate, penetrate, and paralyse or render less effective the central systems and critical subsystems that keep the adversary ticking, by itself may not produce all the results, but it can augment and magnify effects produced otherwise. A favourable differential is likely to lead, not only to quick but also decisive, results. A favourably placed adversary can achieve his policy objectives with minimum destruction, if that is what he desires. It was the ability of the Indian field forces to bypass the Pak field formations holding strong defence on the borders in what was then East Pakistan, and then pose a direct threat to the seat of government and military headquarters in Dacca in December 1971 that allowed India to obtain surrender of Pakistani forces with such remarkably limited destruction. Those who have no capacity to strike at the vitals have the choice of fighting slogging battles with attrition of forces on both sides, till decision can be reached in the field, or the conflict can no longer be pursued. Indian and Pak forces both seem to have resorted to limited attrition in the plains along the border between India and West Pakistan in 1965 and 1971, because of their inability or incapacity to strike at the vitals, or for want of strategic vision. If there is no capacity to strike at adversary's vitals, policy objectives may be only partially achieved in a given time frame, unless attrition itself happens to be a policy objective. India made it appear after 1965 that the thrust in the plains was a diversion, and the strategic objective was no more than attrition of Pak war-machine that had been built with the US aid.

> " With the exception of the HAJIPIR offensive, none of the remaining thrusts were pushed to a successful conclusion. This, to my mind, was due to a faulty strategic concept of the campaign which resulted in a number of ineffective jabs instead of a few selected thrusts in force. In consequence, there were fierce slogging matches spread over a vast area in which we destroyed each other's potential but reached no strategic decisions. Our strategy for war should have been confined to the concentration of effort on a few, well defined offensive actions on narrow frontages to achieve rapier like thrusts deep into enemy territory and aimed at objectives of military and political importance. The momentum of the offensives should then have been maintained by continual regrouping of forces to ensure the required superiority of effort along the chosen thrusts. In this lies the essence of higher direction of War[9]."

Pakistan, on the other hand, had decided upon deep thrusts to occupy Indian territory up to River Beas in Punjab. If Indian military leadership was found wanting in selecting strategic objectives, their counter parts across the border were unable to conduct operations to achieve their strategic goals. Neither did reach the adversary's vitals, or arrive at operationally significant objectives, with the exception of the Haji Pir pass in Pak occupied Kashmir, and therefore no possibilities for a 'better peace' were created. It is the ability to strike at vitals that creates the possibilities for quick results through application of force, or even more, allows effective articulation of threat without application of force. Those who have a favourable differential invariably take it into account while evolving strategies; those who are unfavourably placed, can hope to make up the gap, partially through surprise and 'operational skills', or wait till the differential becomes less favourable, if that is possible. Special and commando forces have the ability to reach and access the vitals in depth, and it is no wonder that they are being raised and maintained in larger proportions. With the increasing importance of command, control, communications and information systems, as well as the media, they have become the prime and vital assets. If these are disrupted or made dysfunctional at critical times through physical intervention by the special forces, the effect may be as great as that of blitzkrieg, if not greater.

(3) A favourable differential in abilities to deplete adversary's sources of strength and sustenance — resources — opens up the option of rendering the forces in the field ineffective, more or less, in peace and war. A petroleum producing country which depends upon its sale proceeds to sustain the economy, if effectively deprived of markets, can wither on the vine. Iraq under UN sanctions may be on the verge of collapse. At anv rate, Iraq is struggling for survival. But far more important, at a deeper level, the attributes of collective identity that create the nation, and the internal order that allows effective governance with minimal force, if attacked, can by-pass the whole of state apparatus, and the collective identity may disintegrate, as did the Soviet Union in 1989. From strategic strikes, to political support to separatist movements, to covert operations, to 'social and cultural engineering' in the target country the whole gamut of means and devices may be used to achieve results. With increased interdependence in matters of manufacture, denial of critical raw materials, or petroleum products, even for a short period of time, could produce results, although not as quickly. Most adversaries hardly ever refrain from covertly employing what capacity they have to erode the opponent's sources of strength. This capacity has great relevance in 'no war, no peace conditions', when the host governments themselves are keen to deny that a war is on. Under these conditions, when adversary's own media, and even the 'opposition' — in open societies — may do considerable damage out of indifference or unawareness, by falling into the trap set for them by the adversary. Those who are unfavourably placed in this regard, by virtue of inability, or having really given up such options in pursuit of their own

stated policies, have the option of making good the losses that result from continuing haemorrhaging, or 'appeasement' of the adversary till suitable capacities are developed.

(4) It was the very substantial differential in their capacities to replace and regenerate own forces that ultimately allowed the Allies to exhaust the Germans in both the World Wars. ultimately, Germany ran out of materiel and soldiers. It was the virtually inexhaustible supplies of materiel from the US, and equally astounding capacity of the Soviet Union to replace their dead and wounded that ultimately settled the score. This could be said without taking away from the great fighting prowess of the Allies. From stored materiel — reserves — conflicts of comparatively limited duration can be undertaken; alteratively, the intensity could be so reduced that contestants can replace and regenerate their resources. Low intensity conflict is a preferred option of an intrinsically lesser power. Kashmir proxy-war is kept by Pakistan at an intensity that it can afford to maintain, taking care that it remains below the provocation threshold. President Saddam Hussain was forced to conclude his conflict with Iran on terms which were not particularly attractive possibly because Iran has a greater capacity to prolong the conflict. Otherwise, the greater power has just to prolong the conflict at an intensity that it can easily support, and other things being equal, the lesser power will have lost. Even well thought out lightning strikes can go wrong, particularly under the pressure of having to conclude the operations in a predetermined time frame. More often than not, a restrictive time frame can tempt the lesser power to resort to audacity or gamble; alternatively, it may have to accept the status quo, or purely defensive attitudes. Pakistan, in 1965 and 1971 launched preemptive offensives in Chhamb area to preclude possibilities of Indian thrusts in the area.

(5) A favourable differential in ability to protect vitals is a proof against exploitation of success gained in preemptive or lightning strikes. This implies protection not only for national leadership, broadcasting and communication centres, and critical personnel and assets connected with vital decision making and its implementation, but also creation of a

calculated redundancy to compensate for some unavoidable losses and destruction. Adversaries are willing to try out confidence building measures and 'hot-lines' when there is a reasonable fear of being overcome in a matter of days, mainly because they are unable to protect their vitals. In such circumstances, avoidance of unintended or accidental conflict seems a reasonable and wise undertaking. Unfavourably or evenly placed adversaries are unlikely to strike at the adversaries vitals for the fear of provoking a retribution. It is worth recounting that India and Pakistan both avoided hitting each other's vitals or capitals in 1965 and 1971 conflicts in the Northern and Western portions of the Subcontinent, that is why vitals both in West Pakistan and India were generally spared. On the other hand, India, having gained air supremacy over what was then East Pakistan, hit the governor's palace, possibly because no retribution was feared. It is also believed that a few rockets delivered on the governor's palace by the IAF speeded up the process of capitulation by Pakistan in the eastern wing. Favourable differential in ability to protect own forces is a stabilizing influence, campaign against mines notwithstanding. When silo based missiles were no longer safe from block busters, second strike capability had to emerge before stability in terms of nuclear deterrence was restored. On the other hand, unchallenged ability to protect vitals may well lead to adventurist policies.

(6) Without the ability to renew sources of strength and sustenance, determination is likely to waver and fatigue is likely to set in much before the national resources are actually exhausted. Doubts about identity, prevailing order, policy objectives, leadership, chosen strategies, plans, and their implementation can sap the will of the nation. An unfavourable differential can cause a nation to give up a cause it holds dear, and accept a defeat even before it is inflicted by the adversary. The situation in India at the end of 1962, and in East Pakistan at the end of 1971 reflected such circumstances. The situation in the Soviet Union in 1989 was perhaps worse. The renewal of sources of strength is as much predicated upon the national leadership, as it is on the

institutions, innovation, industry, and technology, and in general, on the organizational ability. Powerful leadership is capable of achieving renewal by drawing upon material and non material resources of the nation which are not only within the reach of the state, but also those which are accessible mainly to private individuals. When facing an unfavourable differential in this regard, to move away from confrontation is a good option. There would be no disagreement about this.

(7) Willingness to face up to punishment that adversary may inflict or threaten with, is very nearly, the ultimate mark of commitment to an endeavour. A favourable differential in this capacity alone opens up possibilities which are not accessible to those who are not willing to face up to the punishment, accept the consequences of such an approach or decision, and persist in the endeavour in spite of the damage suffered. Willingness to face up to punishment has the capacity to take away the shine off 'deterrence'— strategy which relies upon 'inaction' or pure and simple threat. Mao exemplified this when he said, and perhaps meant, that China would survive nuclear strikes. This option is not open to many. Even the Soviets did not have it, or so it seems, because they chose to call the nuclear capability a paper tiger — of course, till they had it themselves — rather than proclaim on behalf the Soviet Union that they would face up to the punishment. Even minimal strikes on the mainland of the US was clearly unacceptable, and the assurance that the Soviets would be wiped out in the return strikes was not sufficient to steel the US during the Cuba missile stand-off. Deterrence was kept in place by unwillingness of the major contestants to face up to the minimal nuclear strikes. The balance seemed to have got vitiated only when Strategic Defence Initiative (SDI) was unveiled. Assured protection from missile or air strike was the precondition for the US to enter into a major conflict with an adversary who had comparable strike capability. What would it do when SDI gave it the desired shield, was a question that worried the Soviet Union and a new arms race was about to commence. Possibly, the increased cost burden imposed by the US on the

Soviet Union — which had no choice but to enter into a new race for the SDI, if it wanted deterrence in place —, as well as the awareness of the technological lead established by the US, contributed to the break up of the Soviet Union. The consequences of inability to take any punishment can be debilitating, even more than the damage that the punishment can cause. In conventional warfare, if the infantry is not willing to close in, or the mechanised columns are unlikely to achieve deep penetration till after the opposition is eliminated, or if the defence lines are unlikely to hold in face of intense bombardment or threat of chemical attack, the option of producing 'compellence' through ground action is no longer available. Recourse must be taken to stand-off strikes, and reliance must be placed on more and yet more destruction. If destruction does not still elicit compliance, policy objectives may have to be modified. In short, force projection, as well as defence capability is contingent on this factor to an extraordinary degree.

Individuals willing to suffer hardships and deprivation on a daily basis, risk their limbs, or throw away their lives, in encounters or captivity, confer on their leadership singular advantages in determining policy objectives and evolving strategic goals. Urban insurgency, terrorism, raids and strikes by special forces, irregular or guerilla warfare are some of the available, and decidedly cost effective, ways of pursuing goals. They may not be sufficient to achieve the ultimate goal, but they supplement the main instruments, and often achieve the limited purpose when the main instruments are not available or when it is not provident or prudent to use them. A kind of warfare is built mainly around this single factor: capacity and willingness of some individuals to stand up to and take punishment. Terrorism or insurgency are difficult to counter while remaining within bounds created by the letter and spirit of the rule of law, and for that reason, it is a great menace for the organized societies. But for that reason, they do not cease to be a kind of warfare — a cost-effective instrument — to be indulged in when advantageous, acknowledged when convenient, and denounced when necessary. The gap between urban insurgency and terrorism is not as significant as it is made out to be. Perhaps, terrorism does not always comprise acts of wanton destruction or criminality, perhaps not any more than strategic bombing of civilian targets does: both inflict death and injuries on civilian population, and indulge in destruction of civilian facilities of no special significance to military capability or the war effort. India supported Mukti Bahini; Pak supports 'freedom fighters' in Kashmir; the US did not just support the Afghan guerillas, they virtually maintained them, but it denounces PLA guerillas. This option is decidedly not open to those who do not want to, or cannot sufficiently motivate individuals to take punishment. The reasons for not resorting to insurgency or terrorism in pursuit of policy objectives could be many. Those mature host societies who cannot find willing hands for doing their dirty work — covert operations — may seek comfort from having reached a higher level of civilization and, at the same time, find others who are willing to do it for them, either for a cause or for money.

(8) Favourable differential in force projection and/or defence capabilities, mentioned at (1) to (7), is obviously desirable. But, first and foremost, creation and maintenance of such capabilities entail very heavy initial and recurring costs. Incurring of such expenditure may be at the cost of growth oriented investment. Expenditure on force projection capability or defence has to compete with development or social benefits, and welfare programmes. There are obvious spin-offs from which the industry and the society as a whole benefit: ideas and technologies passed on to other sectors by the defence R & D, disciplined and motivated man-power, with substantial residual working life that Services release into the main stream, and so on. Indirectly, and in a manner that may not be amenable to quantification, defence expenditure may confer indirect benefits. But, on the basis of available evidence in India, it can be assumed that in developing societies, expenditure on defence does not lead directly to development.

> "...Positive effects of defence expenditure on growth rate of out-puts are generally not confirmed. .... The second order negative influence of defence burden on the savings

- investment process is found. ...The link between defence burden and inflation is also established[10].. "

On the contrary, in some of the developing societies, heavy defence expenditure has produced deleterious effects: it has produced imbalances in the polity and, of course indirectly, conferred prestige on the armed forces which they seem to have exploited to usurp power. Although there may be no direct and visible links between heavy defence expenditure and derailing of the constitution, a suspicion may be justified that unrest occasioned by sectors starved of resources — which defence has appropriated — makes the task of governance doubly difficult and the resultant unrest gives a handle to those inclined to coup d'etats.

Non-availability of basic and raw materials, technologies, industrial capacity, and skills may also cause a country to opt for acquisition by import, particularly if the urgency is very great. Imports, apart from being an expensive proposition, may entail policy compromises and dependence on the one hand, and create problems of absorption ranging from formulation of doctrine to maintenance, on the other. The purpose of highlighting problems connected with substantial expenditure on defence is to emphasise that apart from depletion of resources, excessive expenditure on defence and acquisition by imports may ill serve the original purpose. Differential in abilities to incur costs and support a substantial defence apparatus on a continuing, long term, and competitive basis is one of the major contributory factors in selection of strategies. Imposition of cost burden as a punishment which the adversary cannot take can itself be a strategic option as noted in (7) above, apropos of SDI. If a nation is unable to react to moves by the competitor or adversary, by accepting the additional cost and other burdens, it may have to face up to a situation in which the unfavourable differential can only make things worse, or devise new strategic options. A shaken and impecunious Pakistan decided, in post 1971 period, to shift the emphasis from the conventional capability, always a costly proposition, to nuclear capability and proxy warfare, in which the returns on expenditure, in terms of deterrent and dissuasive capability are comparatively better. Pakistan committed itself to development of nuclear capability on the one hand, and resorted to supporting insurgency in Punjab, Kashmir, and in the Northeast, in a systematic, long term, and continuing basis.

Power dialectic — inter-action resulting from employment of power by aspirants to acquire, retain and or secure prizes — may be viewed in the context of aspirants either seeking a trial of wills, individually, or in groups, or of evading or avoiding such a trial of wills. A two dimensional model — admittedly, a somewhat contrived model — representing power-play amongst aspirants would be elliptical, with one of the foci signifying persuasion and cooperation, and the other, denoting contest and strife involving a trial of strength and wills. Trial of wills involves employment of power against rivals and adversaries with a view to imposing punishment and improving upon own state of assets and share of prizes. Trial of wills is predicated upon adversarial relationships the essence of which is a conviction that sharing of assets and prizes is a zero-sum game: adversary's loss must necessarily end up as own gain, and vice versa. Higher the intensity of adversarial feelings, the greater the desire to resort to trial of wills. If we also concede that subduing of adversaries in itself is viewed as a prime prize by many, and not only by a few sick individuals, trial of wills may well be the inevitable denouement of power-play. If, trial of wills is regarded as a natural culmination of power play, at least till the next round is begun, and therefore accepted as the thesis, then the antithesis is adjustment through persuasion and cooperation. The intensity of adversarial feelings is kept under check, and perhaps by passed, by finding commonality of interests. Movement away from strife may help in evolving new balances and equilibrium, as also in creating stability. Stability and freedom from strife may be utilized by many aspirants to prepare for the forthcoming trial of wills. If this were so, all the power-play that pivots around persuasion and cooperation could be interpreted merely as a preparation for a trial of wills. This is a cynical view, but perhaps justified, in the light of historical experience. Clausewitz seems to agree with this possibility :

> "It would be possible to talk about the conduct of peace or the conduct of the state's external affairs in 'peace time' and call it totaL 'strategy' provided we also recognize that in the absence of armed combat, the dialectic of wills is aimed at persuasion as much as at combat, or at a negotiated settlement or a compromise, rather than the use of force, evèn if the possibility that force can be used is always present in the background of relation between states[11]."

Without a trial of wills, reliance has necessarily to be placed on exploiting the prevailing power distribution; and order established on that basis. When power-differential is favourable, a stable equilibrium may be created by larger power(s) by deploying power in such a way that the disadvantaged get a feeling that they can somehow put up or live with transactions and exchanges that are actually 'offered' to them — unequal though they may be in real terms — and keep away from trials of will. This may be brought about by minimising 'power in use'— that is, power actually brought to bear to secure prizes — in relation to overall power that could possibly be employed in the event of need. It is the awareness of the unused power potential that drags the disadvantaged into acquiescence in transactions and exchanges which are unequal. An odd trial of wills may not be avoided, and may indeed be sought — to make an example — but not too often. Unused power potential can be brought to bear notionally to secure advantageous transactions on a continuing basis — exploitation . Its actual utility increasing in proportion to its non-use. Much less satisfaction would be forthcoming were the power to be actually employed to obtain favourable results in trials of wills. Greater the power-differential, greater is the benefit of non-use. Power-differential can also be increased by splitting or reducing the overall size of individual transactions or exchanges on which the same unused power potential can be effectively brought to bear.

Creation of great power differential and minimising power in use create conditions for establishing 'order' provided, of course, that a stable equilibrium is maintained, and frequent trials of wills are avoided. British power in India worked strenuously to create these conditions by 'demilitarizing' India before establishing pax-Britannica. Effective exploitation without a substantial power differential is unthinkable. Adjustments may well result in hegemonies, and further adjustments amongst them may yield a unipolar world. If trial of wills is fraught with risk and destruction, adjustment is fraught with exploitation which is ultimately seen as violation by the disadvantaged. Violence and violation are separated by stakes in the established order, and if they are not substantial, violence erupts, and adjustments make way for trial of wills.

Even those who do have a faith in efficacy and inevitability of trial of wills are well aware that it is invariably accompanied by a number of uncertainties, and at least some costs and losses; and consequently, the tally at the end may not reveal an advantageous outcome: the prizes secured after trial of wills may not fully compensate for the punishment taken. Equally, those who look upon adjustment as the most human and advantageous mode of bringing power to bear on disputes at hand, are fully aware that trial of wills cannot be totally avoided because force is autonomous, functions on a different plane, and may be unleashed at any time by those who possess it, wisely or unwisely, with or without valid reasons. The logic of strategy is indeed paradoxical, as eloquently and convincingly argued by Professor Luttwak : if a nation opts for strength by investing in development, and does not maintain a defence establishment, it may attract punishment; if it concentrates on defence establishment at the cost of development, it may collapse upon itself and subserve the adversary's purpose. In war,

- " the worst option may deliberately be chosen in the hope that the unfolding action will for that very reason be unexpected by the enemy, find him unready, and therefore diminish his ability to react[12]."

A nation which wishes to avoid trial of wills may appease only to find that the appetite of the opponent has been whetted. A nation which abjures treaties and alliances to retain its independence may in fact become so isolated that it cannot look after its own interests without outside help; on the other hand, it may be the fate of a member of an alliance to carry a large proportion of common burden without commensurate benefits. Perhaps, a right balance is struck by generating and employing power in a manner that neither contributes fully to the thesis of 'trial of wills' any more than it does to the antithesis of consensus and cooperation, or 'adjustment'. It would appear that most nations try to work out a synthesis which represents the most advantageous mix of the two, that is, they opt for a course of action or a choice of strategies which will bring the best possible returns, at minimum costs, reduced risks and punishments. In the power play, stability may be sought with a view to gathering greater strength and forging improved instruments of power. Stability may be secured through carefully controlled engagement with other systems or alliances, taking care to avoid isolation on the one hand, and absorption by others on the other hand. For this purpose itself, prizes may be exchanged just to avoid a trial of wills; even some opportunities may be allowed to pass by to avoid getting drawn into and inextricably absorbed by exploitive systems. When it is intended to secure prizes through trial of wills, the ultimate intent may be to absorb the opponent into an overarching system of own choice. that is, to annihilate. If alliances have to be entered into, to create a winning combination, some kind of absorption and counter-absorption is unavoidable. When an effort is made to isolate the opponent, it is to rob him of benefits of power that he derives by virtue of being a part of an alliance : the intent is to annihilate another alliance.

Power in action ,in pursuit of prizes, is brought to bear by aspirants in a number of ways — human ingenuity is indeed unlimited — but a model consisting of four broad 'bands' is proposed as a possible way of interpreting the power-dialectic. Application of power may be visualised as interaction along a few, well separated trunk routes or bands — analogous to 'frequency bands'—with distinct characteristics of their own[13]. Bands one and two lie in the 'adjustment ' half of the ellipse; Bands three and four in the 'strife and contest' half.

Band one, could be called 'concordance'. Power is employed in Band one by aspirants to secure prizes individually and collectively. Activity in this Band aims at seeking congruence of interests to the extent possible with other aspirants; if not, at least commonality of interests with respect to some prizes, so that the joint and combined effort may achieve that which is outside the capability of individual contestants. The larger in number and more important the prizes with respect to which congruence or commonality of interests is sought, the greater and more durable the understanding. This does not necessarily mean that the contestants have ceased to be contestants with respect to other prizes, or in entirety even with respect to those prizes which have brought them together to act in concert. The desire to protect and promote own interests is never really absent,in that separate identities are maintained. and nourished. Activities in the concordance band would include the garnering, accumulation, and generation of power that can be used in pursuit of prizes, and creation of grounds and opportunities for advantageous employment of that power. Internally, it would aim at removal of contradictions where possible and reconciliation of opposing pulls and pressures to arrive at working and workable arrangements. This may well mean a balancing act between short and long term prizes, between demands of the talented and the elite on the one hand and the countervailing needs of the common people on the other.

This would also mean redetermining the pale of collective identity to exclude those ideas, individuals, and entities which are likely to stand in the way of generation and harnessing of power. Pakistan pushed out members of minority community—Hindus—soon after it came into being. What happend in East Pakistan in March-Aril, 1971 was carry-over of this process. It is obvious that the full range of skills, assets, and activities are employed to create and modify circumstances in which power which can be employed in pursuit of prizes becomes available. Externally, it involves understandings and adjustments with other collective entities on contribution to the common causes and sharing of prizes. Unless there is effective communication and a minimum of understanding to start with, seeking commonality of interests would not be a practical proposition. A minimal receptiveness to mutual concerns is a virtual precondition for activity in this Band. It is diplomacy which holds the sway and there is always a temptation to subsume and underplay instruments which are vital for employment in activity in other bands. It would be quite appropriate to describe formation and strengthening of collective identities and associations as Band one activity. Considerable power-play is involved to bring about and sustain collective identities, and arriving at presiding identities. Similarly associations are not formed or sustained without power-play. Prizes are sought individually, and collectively, for which purpose strength is created, and accumulated to create instruments of power which will secure the desired prizes.

Activity in Band one, 'concordance', is aimed at obtaining best possible results should a trial of wills be considered necessary at a later stage, or forced upon the alliance partners. Agreements and deals about sharing instruments of power in collective and individual interests may lead to more enduring collective interests and eventually an emergent 'collective identity' in so far as the use of instruments of power are concerned. But this is not without the possibility of a negative fall out. Since the use of instruments of power, or the threats of their use invariably involves possibility of severe penalties, the agreement cannot become operative without a commitment to take some kind of punishment for the common cause, which may be disproportionate at times. Since the agreement is restricted to the use of instruments of power, national collective identities endure and thrive and assert themselves, at times to the detriment of the collective association or emergent identity.

All the talk of coupling and decoupling of alliance partners on the basis of who sees himself in the role of the whipping boy points out the fragility of the system. In every case, sources of strength are jealously guarded by the alliance partners. Alliances create a balance of power in international affairs, and not without giving rise to opposing or adversarial alliances. Alliances by themselves may not bring trial of wills any closer; perhaps, they stave it off to the extent that the stakes and wagers go up. But they give rise to arms racing with greater seriousness and commitment. Alliances may themselves get into concordance Band, while not allowing individual partners to do so across the divides. Alliances may develop into hegemonies and contribute to stability within alliances by undertaking activities in concordance Band. It is obvious that hegemonies within the alliances have a chance to take root when interdependence is strong, enduring, but unequal.

Power is employed in Band two 'appeasement', to bring about an exchange of prizes without an actual clash or trial of wills. Making over of the desired prizes to the other party, with almost nothing in return, in the hope of avoiding, evading, or delaying the threatened use of force or 'punitive' action is the usual pejorative sense in which appeasement is understood. But Band two, called 'appeasement' here, connotes the following : allowing, helping, or supporting other contestants to obtain or secure some of the prizes of their choice in exchange of good will, and or some prizes of own choice which are within their(the other contestants') gift, wholly or partially. There could be parity in exchange value - quid pro quo - at one end of Band two, and goodwill by itself at the other. Activities in the appeasement band could be inspired by a desire to avoid an immediate trial of wills, so as to be the better prepared for it in the future, or in the hope that altogether better circumstances would emerge, in the form of a more favourable balance of power that would render conflict unnecessary, in that the desired prizes could be secured by further exchanges; least ways, in the hope that the balance of power after the exchange of prizes would be less damaging, or more tolerable. The obvious benefit is that the element of uncertainty and risks is better managed. Such indeed was the case when detente was the outcome of Geneva Summit in 1955. After 1957, there was a change in attitude, and the US saw in the Soviet Union—

> "Not simply a threat to be encountered, but a partner whose collaboration was essential if nuclear war through accident was to be avoided[14]."

The traditional and pejorative connotation of appeasement in itself is a clear warning that activities in Band two are not devoid of risk, although the risk and uncertainty could be of a lower order in comparison with the trial of wills which would invariably result in some destruction. Band two activities naturally permit a greater exercise of control because the vehicle used is diplomacy. Depending upon the perspective, a short term disadvantage may be considered more acceptable in view of the anticipated long term gains. Aid by the developed nations and iniquitous concessions by the under-developed nations could also be construed as power dialectic in the appeasement band. Treaties, armistices, and truces agreed upon at the end of, or in the terminal stages of conflict, where the contestants are either exhausted or loath to continue application of power, for whatever reason, could also be included in Band two activity because no further trial of wills is visualised in the immediate future. Detente is an adjustment brought about by exchange of prizes - renunciation of overt hostility in mutually convenient areas. Band two activity is the prime field of diplomacy. Diplomats, like politicians are generalists, and may not be able to fully evaluate the value of prizes they agree to exchange and there may be no easy way of gauging the long term impact of trade and other protocols or agreements. Enthusiasm of politicians and diplomats may well ignore well-meaning and valuable advice from specialists. 'Peace in our time' may be too great a temptation.

Power is employed in Band three -'isolation'- to secure an advantage over rivals and competitors so that own claims on prizes, or share of prizes, are not adversely affected. Least ways, an effort is made so that ground is not lost. Even more so, activity in Band three is aimed at whittling down and debilitating adversaries and their alliances before and during trial of wills with a view to ensuring a favourable out-come. Power is applied in a reductionist mode to unravel bonds and strands that make up adversary's strength, and eventually, his ability to project power to secure prizes of his choice. The intention is to isolate elements of his strength to their basic components by reducing cohesiveness, sowing dissension, and weakening resolve. All means including minimal force, admittedly in an indirect mode and by proxy, are employed to achieve the purpose. Activity in Band three encompasses creation of incompatibility amongst partners of hostile alliances so that they are unable to act in concert to secure prizes through their collective effort, and consequently, some of the prizes of their choice are denied partially or entirely to them. Substantial success in Band three activity may convince the adversary that trial of wills is likely to prove disastrous, in which event it may be avoided or deferred by him. Unless the potential victims are accessible in the first place, and are some how made receptive to ideas and communications to which they are subjected, the success of activity in Band three is unlikely. A great deal of deviousness and overt and covert activity is sine qua non, and if there is lack of finesse, consistency, and co-ordination, the activity may not only be unproductive it can also back-fire. An upsurge in Band three activity was seen before and during the Gulf Conflict in 1991 and in the follow up by the US in 1998. Iraq was isolated from the Arab world with great care.

Apart from diplomacy, and activity by intelligence agencies, the sky wave and other media may be successfully employed with or without their awareness or active co-operation. All available fora,national, international, and regional, may be used to isolate, pressurise, and eventually neutralise the recalcitrant. Activity in Band three includes sanctions and blockades, in that force may be employed in a dissuasive mode.

Power may be employed in Band four, 'contest', to secure the desired prizes, or a larger share of prizes, through a direct trial of wills, using coercive instruments. It need not necessarily include the use of force, but without it, no real trial of wills is likely except in special circumstances. A nation state wholly dependent on international trade, and without instruments of force or allies, could be severely tested in a trial of wills that does not even include the use of force. Trade and tariff wars, rigging of elections, manipulation of Security Council, and the like could also fall in this category. Band four could include a conflict of whatever intensity, duration, or extent. The activities include the use of physical force or its threatened use to cause destruction, and/or imposition of privation, pain, and punishment. Activities in Band four aim at application of power to secure prizes against the will of other contestants, along with allies, or independently. Power may be employed to partly or wholly destroy some of adversary's assets in the hope that the adversary will comply by ceding prizes of own choosing. Although this is the ultimate form, other means such as embargo or sanctions may also be used to cause distress, deprivation, or extreme hardship to cause the adversary to yield. These means may also be backed up with the use of force or threat, and may often be indistinguishable from force in so far as the effects on the victim are concerned.

Trial of wills invariably involves damage and destruction which can only be minimised, and no matter how unevenly matched the contestants, the outcome is never fully guaranteed, although it can be predicted to an extent. The element of chance may set to nought some or all of the calculations made before the clash. The costs and risks can be partially controlled but never wholly since the adversary's actions and their effect may not be predictable in advance. Even an insignificant punishment, in comparative terms, may produce a devastating impact on the population, and further support from them may not be forthcoming. Political leadership may, in such circumstances, lose its power base. This hazard, in many situations, may seem more real to the political leadership than the likely gains to be reaped at the conclusion of the encounter. Activity in Band four is exhausting, and may have to be ended at a point in time which is not determined in advance. The tally at that time may show losses, in which case too the political leadership will be the losers. It is for this reason that activity in Band four is likely to produce results which are neither predictable nor controlled. Even so wars are not uncommon because force has a way of creating options for those who are unable to secure prizes of their choice through activities in other three Bands.

The use of force in Band four is more hazardous than its threatened use. If threats by themselves were to achieve their purpose few would use force. Threats become potent and effective instruments only when the will and ability to use force successfully is demonstrated time and again. Activities in Band four are more likely to achieve their purpose in an efficient manner when force and threat are blended in right proportion.

It would appear that the synthesis of 'trial of wills' and 'adjustment' is to be found in power operating concurrently, optimally and harmoniously in all the four Bands. Eschewing of any of the Bands in entirety and for long periods, or imbalance in application yields less than the best possible out come. Referring to the understanding between the super powers not to confront each other in the Middle East and Vietnam directly, Raymond Aron interprets the US - Soviet interaction as a deliberate movement away from 'conflict' to cooperation, no matter how limited.

> "From 1963 onwards ... the Soviet leaders resigned themselves... to explicit agreements with the United States... on arms control...in spite of Vietnam war, cooperation between Russia and America in these spheres, the common effort to avoid direct confrontation... still continues... Both parties have finally learnt from analysts ... that it is in the interest of both the super powers to close the atomic club and to keep their rivalry within narrow limits[15]."

Kissinger mentions advantages of the detente:

> "For so long as Nixon was domestically in a strong position, detente successfully linked the whole range of issues between East and West all around the world[16]."

Although it is advantageous,as a rule, to employ power concurrently in all the bands, it does not at all mean that one or more Bands cannot be shut down for a duration, or power must be equally distributed among all the Bands. The chords of total strategy are formed by controlling power-play in all the Bands.

It was a widely held belief for many years that power in action could not be brought to bear simultaneously in more than one Band. Diplomacy and force were expected to act sequentially and not concurrently. It was considered proper that only when diplomats seemed to have arrived at the end of their tether and could not proceed any further, should soldiers take the field and bring about a state of mind in which diplomats could resume their inter-course. At this stage, of course, soldiers were to leave the field to diplomats who were expected to arrive at an acceptable adjustment.

It is obvious that moral or ethical considerations have no great sanctity in power-play , particularly at the international level. If honesty is indeed the best policy, then it must prove efficacious, that is, it must yield the desired results, not only here and now, but also in the long run. Creation of illusions calculated to distort reality, and thereby so affect perception and judgement of other contestants, their supporters and allies, that they inadvertently sub- serve own purpose through their actions or inactions, is a time tested device that is often relied on, because it has a potential to magnify power in action through all the four Bands. This is not without cost, in that credibility and long term interests may suffer if enough care is not taken to exercise adequate restraint;equally,if contrivance becomes visible, the effect may be lost and credibility may also take a knock without any corresponding benefit.

Conceivably, power could be employed in a cooperative mode by all the aspirants in the international arena to secure prizes collectively so that they may be shared in an agreed manner, without giving rise to negative feelings ; generally to avoid conflict and to eliminate its causes. The possibility of alliances so wrought, prizes so secured, assets so created, growth so achieved, and the ensuing happiness cannot be disputed on the basis of logic. No such effort is being made in this Study. We are aware of and experience cooperative attitudes within the confines of collective identities and associations. But none are without the defining peripheries. Out side of defining peripheries, these very identities and associations enter into competitive, and confrontational relationships. Witness the attitude of the nuclear powers to those who do not conform to the demands of NPT. The cooperation is restricted to those who share special interests. Activities in Bands one to four could include but often excludes genuine cooperation and strategic cooperation takes its place. 'Strategic cooperation', is essentially a self-serving adjustment — for so long as necessary — although it could also include elements of genuine cooperation.

There is hardly any collective entity or nation which wholly seeks status quo; not any more than the one which is wholly committed to revision. Every nation seeks to retain and improve upon some of its assets, and at the same time wishes to bring about a revision so that new assets can be acquired. The difference lies between perceptions of where best chances lie: in working mostly within the confines of the existing international order, while improving upon it to suit one's own special interests, or in establishing a fresh or new order in which the acquisition and retention of assets is likely to be facilitated. In a very loose sense, and as a short hand, the term status quo nation or power has been used here to indicate those collective entities and nations which have higher stakes in continuation and gradual modification of prevailing order, as compared to those — revisionist powers or nations — who seek major and immediate changes because they fear that continuation of present order is progressively making things more difficult and intractable. They, revisionists, hope to achieve their ends by creation of turbulence which tends to upset and, if strong enough, eventually destroys the prevailing order. And, since order is based on maintenance of an equilibrium established by a preferred distribution of power, changes in order can only be brought about by attacking prevailing power distribution, and creating new centres of power which are considered more favourable. Turbulence is a means to an end. Turbulence, immediately, holds the prospect of reducing the share of prizes of those who benefit from the prevailing order. This is an age old and time tested method of engaging the powerful by the weak. It is not without cost. On the other hand, the maintenance and enforcement of prevailing order is the prime concern of those who find the power distribution to their liking. Preferences for activities in various bands is determined mainly by two set of factors: Stakes in stability, and possibility of benefitting from conflict and turbulence.

When there is a reasonable hope and possibility that, with the passage of time, and with the continuation of prevailing trends, differentials of strength and power amongst adversaries will even out, threats will attenuate, and security costs will not impose a burden of a kind that retards growth. There would be a natural inclination to restrict the activities mainly to Bands one to three, and restrict those in Band four to the minimum. This nice scheme of things is likely to succeed only if there is no conflict on a scale that is likely to give rise to chances of uncertain and unpredictable outcome. On the other hand, if there is an anxiety or fear, that unless conflict is resorted to, there is no possibility of bringing about new and favourable circumstances, recourse is likely to be taken to activity in Band four, even if it means facing up to and acceptance of risks and punishments even to an extent that they may jeopardise the future. If a feeling grows that opportunities are slipping away, and 'now or never' is the only practical option, turbulence in place of stability may be accepted as a price to be paid . This is not a small price, because turbulence, except in rare circumstances, takes the toll of the ruling elite and the leadership that opts for conflict, either in the wake of failure, or partial success. Even without the machinations of rivals, consequences and aftermath of conflicts — losses, problems of reconstruction, and changes in attitudes — are most likely to bring disenchantment of the population for those who took the 'brave' decisions.

It would appear that the basic propositions as above apply, if not equally and totally, then in a large measure, to the phenomena at national and international levels. Nations, political parties, interest groups, and lobbies generally operate in first three bands when conditions of stable equilibrium obtain. But occasionally they stray into Band four ie use all means including violence, if the prevailing order has become threadbare and stability is at stake, or if they desire to bring about a drastic change in the prevailing order. Notwithstanding other variables, there is one common policy objective of all seekers of political power at the national level, namely, to form the government. First of all, it is the continuation and perpetuation of their own government that political parties strive for internally, that is within the nation state. That does not necessarily mean that those forming the government are unconcerned with national interests, and would not share power with other contestants in times of grave threat. But it does mean that they will strive to promote and defend their governments, and the order that supports them, with as much steadfastness as they would show in warding off external threats and dangers. If and when there is an inconsistency between the demands of the nation and demands of the government in power, the matter may not always be resolved in favour of the nation state. Keeping the power base secure is a prime requirement and almost a compulsion, and activities in Bands one to four, and the strategies that they give rise to, will invariably be influenced by domestic considerations.This linkage between the internal and external policies is significant and is liable to be exploited by all contenders to their advantage. This situation is more likely in centrally controlled systems, or in developing countries not comfortable with the democratic systems, or where the checks and balances are not as effective as in mature democracies.

Strategies are formulated to help determine the prizes and prize sharing arragements; as also the means to be employed for the purpose, costs to be incurred, risks and chances to be taken, and punishment to be suffered and withstood, when it is unavoidable. Strategies in action call for generation and employment of power in various forms and ways to obtain and secure prizes, or to increase the available share of prizes, and/or to eliminate or diminish, or render ineffectual contenders and rivals who are likely to make their own claims for prizes or for larger share of prizes. By eliminating other contenders and rivals, the available share of prizes goes up, as a natural consequence. Of all the prizes, accumulation of power is perhaps the prime prize because power is most likely to be , at once, end and means both.

Some times there is reason enough to believe that even the seeker of prizes — the collective identity — may not always be an independent variable. But this is rare.

The desire to deal effectively with Israel — and by implication, its principal supporter, the USA — caused Egypt, Libya and Syria to federate in 1971 to emerge as Arab Republic of Egypt. But the experiment proved to be rather short lived. Mere convergence of interest in seeing or denying prizes may not lead to anything more than strategic alliances in most situations in which every alliance partner continues to utilize power at its disposal to seek prizes of its choice, perhaps with some adjustments in margins. Even congruence of interest may not always lead to merging of identities, because retention and perpetuation of identity itself may well be the principle prize sought in most cases. But as is evident, though, a passionate commitment to secure a single set of prizes does, sometimes, lead to redefinition and emergence of new identities. Splitting up of Pakistan and emergence of Bangladesh reinforce the view that a core collective identity, which for a time has joined with another in an alliance so close that their association takes on the attributes of a collective identity, does not totally move away from the original defining criteria. It in this context, perhaps, that proposition about the likelihood of wars in the future between civilizations may be viewed.

Submergence of those adversarial relationships that are primarily born of history and inheritance, and where no real clash of interests at present or in foreseeable future is visible, is not unthinkable. If the penalties of non-cooperation are sufficiently high and the likely benefits of submerging old animosities very substantial, congruence of interests among those of the same civilization is more likely than amongst those who belong to wholly different civilizations. New collective identities on the basis of civilizations may emerge, and indeed survive, without completely dissolving the original building blocks — the original collective identities which are so prized by the constituent individuals that they are the chosen entities for 'investment'. Cultures and civilizations do exert a unique pull, but they do not always or completely subsume the original presiding collective identity. That remains the core. Will Germans, Frenchmen, or the British for that matter accept to remain content with a lesser share of gains or profits so that the European civilization may prosper? That remains to be seen. It is not so surprising that the British and the French, who have been the best of allies in this century, have come together once again to further their collective interests, but what is surprising is that their former foe, Germany has actually taken a lead in cementing the European Union. It is all but obvious that affiliations on the basis of civilization will matter a great deal, but so will the building blocks, or the core collective identities. Even if a total redefinition of core identity is not a common occurrence, forming of strong associations, which often act as collective identities, is not so rare. European Union still remains an association, but it is on the verge of acquiring some of the symbols of a collective identity like the common currency.

NATO is already a collective identity, in which there appears to be a greater commitment to collective objectives than to objectives of individual nations. NATO is acting as a collective identity in securing new members. Commonality of interests in seeking or denying prizes can create new entities that exert collectively. It would appear that there are few independent variables in power play: appearance of vulnerabilities may be seen as an opportunity to seize prizes which had not been thought of: India, till very late in the campaign for liberation of East Pakistani territory for resettlement of Pakistani refugees, had not thought of capturing Dacca, not till vulnerability of East Pakistani capital became apparent after bypassing Pakistani troops holding strong positions on the border. Just as awareness of vulnerabilities gives rise to new objective — prizes—, so does the availability of newly secured instruments of power. It is now known that nuclear bombs were used against Hiroshima and Nagasaki even when surrender by the Japanese was under negotiations. If the rationale behind the dropping of a nuclear bomb was to pressurise the Japanese into surrender, then perhaps one would have sufficed. Why was the second bomb dropped. The newly emergent prize seems to have been the compulsion to demonstrate to the world the destructive power of the bomb with a view to claiming the supreme power status.

Expansion of NATO to include three of the former Warsaw Pact members is clearly intended to delimit the potential Russian power. The route taken was to play on the fear of the past Soviet allies of a possible communist backlash, or Russian expansion in some distant future. The sense of insecurity of the former Soviet allies proved to be the vulnerability of CIS. It seems to have been exploited to push the NATO security frontier eastward — closer to Russia— and to secure 'modernization' related sales of defence hardware and services to the new members in interest of interoperability. This gives rise to a strong possibility that NATO's interaction with CIS will remain adversarial in nature, whereas Russia as an addition to G 7, with some reservations, is no more than a member of an 'association' that looks to individual interests in preference to collective interests.

The Gulf War provides a good example of how 'power' was employed in all four 'bands' by the US to secure prizes at costs acceptable to G 7 countries. Russian concerns were relegated without any adverse impact on the effort of the allies led by the US.

Preparatory to the Gulf War in 1991, US were aware that their close relationship with Israel was a vulnerability that President of Iraq could exploit to crack open the Arab solidarity that was essential to the US policy of effectively isolating Iraq from other Gulf nations in general and Arab nations in particular. Common cause with Arabs was a source of strength for the Multi-national force, and its erosion could have hurt the Western powers in general and the US in particular, who did not, at that point of time, want to be seen as the ultimate arbiters in the region. Predictably, Iraq fired missiles on Israel in the hope of retaliation by Israel, so that Arabs opposed to Iraq could be painted pro-jew since they were fighting on the same side. This did not work because Americans had wisely foreseen this vulnerability and guarded it by persuading Israel not to retaliate.

It is evident that pressures created within Iraq, as a result of dropping of several hundred thousand tons of bombs by the Multi-national force, and continued UN sanctions against Iraq, have not been instrumental in removing President Saddam Hussein from power, although his removal was one of the stated objective of the US in the Gulf. It would seem that President Saddam Hussein's personal power bases, or access to them, were not correctly located; either that, or the power deployed by the US was not suitable for exploiting the vulnerabilities of Saddam Hussein. Massive application of power by itself may not yield results, and not economically in any case.

Similarly, the solidarity of the G 7 alliance — the hard core of the Multi-national force — was a major source of strength for the US. They wanted the industrialised nations to participate together so that the image of the Multi-national force, acting in the interest of the free world, would not take a beating. The vulnerability staring in the face was the possibility of some of the allies striking independent oil deals that a beleaguered Iraq might offer, on advantageous terms. This possibility had to be preempted. Trade sanctions could be by- passed, so their imposition on Iraq might not suffice. Besides, sanctions might leave the door open for independent deals. On the other hand,no body would want to deal with an aggressor who had used force to cross international border. It has been suggested that no specific idea of what would follow in the wake of an aggression on Kuwait by Iraq was given by US Ambassador Glaspie in a meeting on 25 July, 1990. Before that, in February, 1990, US Assistant Secretary of State for Near Eastern and South Asia Affairs, Mr.John Kelly, during his visit to Baghdad had praised Saddam Hussein for being a force for moderation. Did the US want

Iraq to act in a manner that would justifiably elicit from its G7 partners a severe and unified response. This is no proof of what was intended by the US. But reasonable surmise, on the basis of 'cui bono', would lead to a conclusion that by invasion of Kuwait, Saddam, unwittingly, contributed to holding the alliance partners together, and eventually cemented the alliance. The awareness of its domestic vulnerabilities by the US Administration, and the care it took to guard them, laid the foundation of US policies in the Gulf at strategic, operational, and tactical levels. Sensitivities in the US drawing rooms had to be respected. Horrors of Vietnam were not to be revisited. The US took care that the truly gory pictures of destruction in Iraq were kept out, and a ring-side view of surgical and virtually bloodless strikes by the Multi-national forces were shown. The punishment of the wicked by the righteous could only bring just satisfaction and a glow of achievement to the tax payer who made all this possible. Incidentally, a tax-burden on account of the conflict was to be avoided. With generous contribution from those whose freedom had been guaranteed by the Multi-national force and other sundry beneficiaries, there was a small surplus. No casualties would have been tolerated any more than a long drawn out conflict. Massive aerial strikes made this possible. Manoeuvre and direct force-on-force actions on ground could be delayed till resistance by the ground forces of Iraq was sapped.

Whether it is the province of national or military strategy, operational art, tactics, or even of weapon design, the concept of exploiting the adversary's vulnerability while protecting one's own is fundamental to success in all types of contests and conflicts, and across the entire spectrum of available means. The Cold War was a merely heightened state of these activities, but they have not ended with the Cold War. With substantial doubts about new configurations which are likely to emerge, potential adversaries — current friends and allies included — have increased. So, if anything, the 'post-cold-war' activity may have intensified. Russian invitation to double agents to come clean and cooperate may be an indication. Armed forces have to be equally capable of applying and/or resisting force, as the situation demands, in fulfilment of their role. While operating offensively, it is their principal business to inflict such punishment on the adversary as would exact from him, or cause him to yield, if not desired outcome, then, at least an acceptable adjustment — which may be called a 'better peace', or whatever else. While operating defensively, it is for them to withstand punishment while yielding not at all, or as little as would ensure survival, so that counter-force can eventually be employed against the adversary. No single action, either success or failure, is likely to lead to the desired or acceptable outcome, except in very rare circumstances.

Grand or national strategy begins by determining the policy objectives which can possibly be attained, by using all means — including the use of force — which are, either at the disposal of the country, or within its reach. It is a commonly held view that grand strategy must yield political goals and objectives, as also resources to be allotted for achieving them.

Allocation of resources implies, basically, the costs but not the punishment that an adversary is likely to impose in a conflict that may result from pursuit of policies. Grand strategy ought also to make an assessment of the punishment and trauma that can and may have to faced, withstood and overcome in achieving policy objectives and also think of means for creating the necessary strength and ability. Political objectives and means, having been broadly defined, the stage is set for allocating military resources for achieving one or more of the laid down political objectives. From the stand point of military strategy, the next stage is very crucial. What needs to be determined chiefly is the following:

Aims and objectives which are, wholly or mainly, amenable to the use of military means or force, including those which may so turn out to be at a later stage.

Objectives which may be amenable to the use of force to a certain extent and in achieving which the military is likely to play some part.

The nature and structure of military force that a country needs — its size, organization, equipment, recruitment, motivation, doctrine, and training — ought to be designed in response to the foreseen tasking in general terms, although all specific missions are unlikely to be predicted accurately. This kind of normative wisdom is not generally disputed, nor does it attract adverse criticism. This is an area in which the political leadership and the professionals should be interacting purposefully, and with utmost seriousness. But in reality, it is very difficult indeed to produce an agreement, particularly in a democratic polity, on the likely policy objectives to attain which military force is primarily to be used, and even more, on what kind of national commitment should be made to attain the related or corresponding capability. Defining specific missions, even for scenario building, or testing concepts, is something to which the political establishment is loath.

The second area of ambiguity, if not of discord, is about what is adequate for mission accomplishment. The political establishment always presumes that there is over-bidding by the military professionals, and instead of disputing the claims of the professionals, the easy way out is not to state the aims and objectives, not to get into a dialogue about specific missions or the wherewithal for their accomplishments, but merely to continue with the existing establishments with reduced expenditure and as few modifications as feasible, unless of course, the prevailing moods and atmospherics permit docking of defence budgets without a serious outcry from the opposition. This is not only true of developing nations, but also a common trait observed amongst yesteryear's empire builders. There were demands for economy and force reduction after every successful campaign conducted by the forces of the East India Company, and subsequently those of the British-Indian Government. The result often is that the military have to remain content with developing attitudes and skills that help in making the best of what is available. Missions, which are handed down in a crisis, produce their own compulsions, and cannot be avoided due to force of circumstances; at other times, opportunities may tempt. The logistic set up of the Indian defence forces did not have the intrinsic capacity to support peace-keeping operations in Sri-Lanka on the scale that they had been undertaken. The burgeoning defence budgets of the US in Reagan era were in response to a popular mood, and as we have seen earlier, also a part of the well orchestrated strategy. If private enterprise has a substantial stake in equipping the defence forces, it may act as lobby group for the defence establishment, and the political leadership may have to pay heed.

There is something to be said in respect of dominant influences that cradle two important aspects of the power dialectic: it is the political reasoning and logic which dominate at the policy and planning stages, but it is the 'grammar' — laws and principles which govern effective application power, for example, principles of war—that guides exeution of plans. Just as a meaningful statement can be made only when the grammar of the language is followed, force communicates most effectively when used in accordance with the accepted principles and tenets of war. A perfectly formed sentence will communicate the meaning, but unless the meaning makes sense in the context of the chosen logic, there is likely to be a mismatch. On the other hand, logic by itself cannot serve its purpose without accepting the grammar of the chosen medium. An all out war, if it is to be pursued, would call for , inter alia, creation of hate-objects and hatred on the one hand, and promises of a successful fight to the finish on the other. But for this, the motivation in combat, as also forbearance of civilians in face of aerial bombardments will be inadequate. Even if the wisdom of the political logic requires that the war is to be concluded after attaining predetermined objectives, well short of victory, the grammar of using the 'influence' component of power may dictate actions which it is hard to fit into the logic. The grammar of land warfare requires that a defensive battle can only be fought with 'depth'. The offensive force of the adversary must be broken up into packets, and then destroyed in detail after its momentum is lost. This calls for a battle to rage over a tract of land. If the defender is on own side of the international border, this involves some loss of ground, for a length of time in any case.

If the loss of ground in a particular area is unacceptable, some expedients could be used, like creating depth by occupying enemy territory if that is possible, or by launching a preemptive offensive which would sufficiently imbalance the adversary. Either the political logic which abhors preemption must be modified, or by a sleight of hand, by using other components of power, the adversary must be made to look an aggressor in another context, so that the preemptive strike looks like a retaliatory movement. The professional must be able to state the non negotiable grammar of his metier, and then the political logic must work it into its own purpose.

Power-play is a continuum with activities spread out in all the four 'bands' which make up the entire spectrum. During major wars and conflicts, power gets narrowly focused in a single 'band' to the detriment of all concerned. Fuller is at pains to point out that it was the obduracy of the Allies, in the last stages of both the world wars, that caused them to opt for unconditional surrender, foreclosing the possibility of negotiated end to wars against Germany ; they had opted out of the 'appeasement' band. Had they done so, negotiated settlement could have prevented utter and virtually irreparable exhaustion of Germany which ultimately led to the rise of Hitler at the end of the Great War, and vivisection of Germany, at the end of the Second World War. At the end of the Second World War, Morgenthau plan to extort the last ounce of German life-blood without giving anything in return, prevented Germans from giving up earlier. In contrast, Japanese conditional surrender was accepted, that is the institution of the Emperor was not eliminated. Peaceful disarming of the Japanese Army units without the direction from the Emperor may not have been possible.

Activities across the whole of the spectrum of power-play calls for ability to rein in hatreds and deal rationally with situations; it requires substantial and highly developed apparatus for correctly sensing the reality — acquisition of intelligence and its interpretation — and a system for utilizing and coordinating all the instruments of power at the disposal of the state. This ideal, of course, is difficult to achieve. It would appear that attributes of collective identity — character, nature, capacity, geographic location, and so on — dominate the urge to generate and employ power. Very often, rationalization rather than reason, passions and emotions rather than logic, capacities rather than objective need, opportunities rather than ethics, contribute toward how much and what kind of power is generated, and for what purpose, and against whom it is employed. It is the political logic that determines the strategies that are selected, and it is the compulsion inherent in the means that determine the way strategies are operationalized.

Considerations related to exploitation of vulnerabilities by the adversary determine the kind of warfare that a nation is likely to face. To foresee the situation that the nation will face, and to prepare for and prevail in the conflict is an act of supreme statesmanship. This would also involve, if need be, to opt for and design a new way of resisting power — as Mahatma Gandhi did —, or a new way of projecting power as Mao did.

If source of adversarial feelings and their intensity is not correctly perceived, and potential adversaries are not correctly identified, exploitation of own vulnerabilities cannot be prevented, nor can preparation be made to exploit adversary's vulnerability; nor can possibilities for alliances — strategic or otherwise — be created. Without friends or allies, not necessarily permanent ones, protection and promotion of own interests is not possible, and full potential of the nation cannot be realised.

NOTES

1.Raymond Aron, 'Clausewitz, Philosopher of War', Routeledge and Kegan Paul, London, 1976, (p.375).

2.General d 'Armee Andre Beaufre, 'Strategy of Action', Faber and Faber, London, 1966, (p.).

3.Harry Elmer Barnes, 'An Intellectual and Cultural History of the Western World', Volume Three, Dover Publications Inc., New York, 1965, (p.1331).

4.Simpkin, op. cit.

5.J. N. Dixit, ' Assignment Colombo', Konark Publishers Private Limited, Delhi, 1998, (p. 337).

6.Colonel G. B. Malleson, ' The Decisive Battles of India', Sagar Publications, New Delhi, 1969, [Originally published in 1883], (p. 289).

7.Major - General J.F.C. Fuller, 'The Conduct of War, 1789 - 1961', Eyre & Spottiswoode, London, 1961.,(p.126)

8.Robert T. Osgood, 'The Reappraisal of Limited War', Alastair Buchan (foreword), 'Problems of Modern Strategy', Praeger Publishers, New York, 1970.

9.Lt Gen Harbaksh Singh, 'War Despatches',Lancer International,New Delhi, 1991, (p. 193).

10.D. D.Khanna & P. N. Mehrotra, Defence Versus Development, Indus Publishing Company, New Delhi, 1993,(p.p. 162-163).

11.Raymond Aron, 'Clausewitz, Philosopher of War', Routeledge and Kegan Paul, London, 1976, (p.397).

12.Edward N. Luttwak,'Strategy', Harvard University Press, London, 1987, (p.8).

13.A broad division of stratagems into four 'upayas' or means is a part of Indian tradition and folklore. These are : conciliation, bribery, sowing of dissension, and punishment. Some authorities also add three more to the list, viz deceit, deception, and conjuring or creation of illusion. { V. S. Apte, ' The Student's Sanskrit English Dictionary', Motilal Banarsidass Publishers, Delhi, 1965, (p.116).} Kautilya commented on these and made a distinction between the use of these stratagems to achieve the desired results while dealing with kith and kin, and the rest. Some of his teachings are interesting. " He [the aspiring conqueror] should secure the members (of the king's circle [that is, kings ruling states in proximity]) who are immediately next to him and who are separated by one intervening state, by the exclusive use, the alternative use or the combined use (of the four means)."

" In the case of allies and enemies, success (should be sought) by a combination (of the means). "{ R. P. Kangle (translator and commentator), ' Kautiliya Arthasastra', Part II, Motilal Banarsidas s, Delhi, (p. 373).}

" For the means help [complement] each other." { ibid., (p.43).

14.Michael Howard, 'Classical Strategist', Alastair Buchan (foreword).'Problems of Modern Strategy, Praeger Publishers, New

15.Raymond Aron, 'Modern Strategic Thought ', Alastair Buchan (foreword), 'Problems of Modern Strategy', Praeger Publishers, New York, 1970, (p.40).

16.Henry Kissinger, 'Diplomacy', (p. 737).

8

Forces and Force Structure

Policy, if it is viewed and interpreted as the spirit of the nation state, or its intelligence, is virtually autonomous, particularly so if the policy is isolationist in nature, or inward looking. Wherewithal to pursue the policy may not enter into the calculation till policy objectives are defined and means are created to achieve those objectives. Means are the instruments of power that aspirants inherit or acquire. Major changes or shifts in accumulated power cannot but create or intensify adversarial relationships. Adversarial feelings, particularly those rooted in collective identities, quicken at the thought of fresh gains by competitors — which must necessarily be denied to them — or likely threats that those gains may give rise to. Therefore, creation of means is a much less autonomous process, in comparison with policy-making, in that, means can no more be created in isolation than they can be so employed. Economic, industrial, or technological development by itself may not cause concern, unless it directly assists in accumulation of strength or power potential, which can be realised when expedient, and converted into instruments of power like armed forces, or goods and services for export, or influence, in which case it can hardly escape the attention of adversaries and competitors. No wonder therefore, that, not only the actual creation of means, but even the potential to create the means is not a process that can be carried out in isolation. It invariably raises alarm amongst those most likely to be affected, and attracts counter-action. Anything and everything that takes into account likely interaction with adversaries and competitors cannot be separated from strategic thinking. Strategy is readily understood to mean the art of using all available means to achieve the policy objectives. With adversaries informed by the self same logic, operative strategy turns out to be a power dialectic. But far more seminal is the outcome of considerations that inform the creation and maintenance of the armed forces. Raising and maintaining of armed forces is also acknowledged to be within the domain of the art of war.

> " Clausewitz agrees to extend the art of war to include the levying, arming, equipping, and training of troops[1]."

If the nature of wars that a nation may be required to face cannot be foreseen, the resources committed to armed forces are likely to produce only indifferent results. But in contemporary times, the science and art part of this segment of strategy seems to get submerged with greater thought to the quantum of defence spending rather than the why and how of it. Interestingly, the high powered committee headed by Mr. Arun Singh that Government of India had appointed for reviewing all matters connected with the reorganization of the armed forces was called Committee for Defence Expenditure. The nature of war that a country is likely to face up to, or wage must indeed be the first of the considerations from which the force structure should be derived.

Wars are said to aim at extortion or annihilation of the adversary. Ludwig Renn[2] calls wars to seize property by the direct use of force, 'predatory wars', wars waged merely to obtain certain concessions, 'wars of extortion', and wars undertaken to destroy the prevailing form of rule, 'wars of annihilation'. The types of war posited in this book have been developed from the terminology used by Renn. 'Predatory ' campaigns or raids may not be distinguished from extortion, because seizure by main force invariably includes application of force in a manner that prizes are conceded more through fear than actual disability to hold on to them. Total destruction or displacement of population may have to be differentiated from depredation, or the outcome of predatory wars, by describing it as 'extermination or extirpation'.

The aim of extortion is to grab and hold on to prizes that can be retained for so long as necessary, and thereby to inflict pain on the victim with a purpose. The aim is to secure those prizes which cannot be seized by direct application of force, and which the victim is unlikely to concede except under pain which he cannot face up to or endure. Extortion may be effected initially through physical duress, and later through 'compellence', although a mix of both may be employed in varying proportions. Extortion is more effective at the tactical rather than at the strategic level. In the course of battles, that is at the tactical level, the decision lies more or less completely with those who are directly subjected to punishment which they can avoid or evade through compliance. At the higher levels, the decision makers are at one remove from those who are the direct victims of force, and so are the prizes which are sought, with the result, that extortion may not yield the desired prizes.

Besides, over a period of time, greater and greater pain might have to be applied to achieve the self same result, so much so, that extortion disappears as a practical proposition, and annihilation might have to be resorted to, if that is within the capability of the would be victor. Annihilation aims at bringing about such changes in the political, military, economic, and or social-structures of the adversary which are calculated to yield the desired prizes on a continuing and long term basis.

Extortion shows a greater concern with prizes to be secured on the one hand, and the impact that the securing of prizes is likely to produce on own polity and concerns on the other hand. The calculus of extortion excludes the impact that the ceding of prizes is likely to produce on the adversary's polity and concerns. That is kept out of the reckoning except to the extent that the pain should be adequate to secure the prizes, and that the adversary should find it more profitable to cede the prizes rather than prolong or extend the conflict.

If India were to bombard a base in Pakistan Occupied Kashmir (POK) that trains and shelters guerillas for insurgency in the Kashmir Valley, and makes it known that similar punishment would continue to be inflicted unless Pakistan ceases to harbour and train guerillas, it is quite likely that the directly affected and threatened base, and one or two in close proximity, may become dormant. But, on the basis of this experience, if it were to be assumed that Government of Pakistan would desist from inspiring and actively supporting the insurgency, the expectation may be belied. The pain of the affected bases may not get transmitted to the decision making centres in Pakistan. In fact something very similar happened in 1965. Three thrusts into Pakistan were launched by India, in response to infiltration into Jammu and Kashmir by Pakistani guerillas in August, 1965, and a subsequent attack on Chhamb and Jaurian by Pakistani armour in September, 1965. In the ensuing battles, both sides seized some border-territory by force, till a cease-fire agreement was reached after about three weeks of fighting. Since the prizes seized by either side were not enough to produce sufficient duress on the adversary, a status-quo-ante was accepted by both the sides in the course of talks at Tashkhent under the Soviet aegis. As a war of extortion, it was ineffective at the operational or strategic levels. India did not succeed in getting Pakistan to abjure claims on Kashmir. India never intended it to be a war of annihilation, in that it did not want to absorb Pakistani territory ; Pakistan, obviously wanted to absorb part of Jammu and Kashmir. Both failed in their objectives. Pakistan did not select the right kind of warfare, nor did it have a force structure that would allow it to annihilate even parts of Jammu and Kashmir. India reacted, and tried unsuccessfully to 'extort' the right concessions from Pakistan. India did not achieve its policy objectives, because it did not choose the right strategy. In contrast, the Chinese did successfully extort the concessions that they wanted from India during and after their campaign at the end of 1962 : they successfully persuaded India not to challenge either the absorption of Aksaichin, or their interpretation of the line of control in the Northeast part of India.

Annihilation is aimed at bringing about changes in polity of the adversary so that prizes that the adversary is unlikely or unable to concede are brought within reach. The obvious assumption being that the changes in the polity will indirectly secure the desired prizes on a continuing basis. Desire for extortion is derived from adversarial relationships that result from differences about what should be shared and how; desire for annihilation results from adversarial relationships that are rooted in irreconcilable differences of perceptions about major dimensions of collective identity. Renn holds that

> "Our theory that a dissimilarity between opponents leads to absolute war, whilst similarity leads to regulated warfare according to accepted rules seems to be confirmed by Fascist Germany's insistence on absolute or totalitarian warfare[3]."

This is an interesting observation: if there are major discontinuities across international borders, the nature of conflict may become more absolute, but continuities across the border do not eliminate possibilities of conflict; to that extent, they do not make things very much better: they go no farther than inveighing in favour of limited conflict. But continuities and discontinuities are also a matter of interpretation. 'Muslim' Pakistan regards a 'secular' India as totally dissimilar, and on that basis, wishes to lay claims on Muslim majority Kashmir. Pakistan wished to retain hold over its Eastern Wing on the basis of religion alone and discounted dissimilarities engendered by language and culture. Dissimilarities caused it to resort to genocide in what is now Bangladesh, notwithstanding similarity of religion. It is perhaps the dominant dimensions of collective identity that contribute to perceptions of similarity or dissimilarity, rather than totally objective criteria, although that also matters.

When adversarial relationships derive from both, perceived dissimilarity and prize related disputes, mere expediency may well determine when a war of extortion will turn into a war of annihilation. If we were to construct a pyramid of sources of power — and strength — with the government at the top, and the population of the nation state — collective identity — at the bottom, intervening strata could be labelled prevailing order, regime, and the ruling elite in an ascending order. The main instruments of power, would be directly accessible to the government, with each lower layer exercising some indirect control over them. In this representation of an orderly society, if the adversary were to seek prizes through extortion, he may be able to have his way only by bearing upon the government, and forcing it into parting with what they are loath to give. If it is perceived, that it is the government which resists and steels the will of the people, an effort could be made to physically eliminate the head of the government, or the ruling junta by precision strikes, or other means of assassination If this does not prove to be a practical proposition, recourse may be taken to indirect means like punishing the population by physical strikes, or through blockades and isolation in the hope that the beleaguered population may rise against the government and replace it with a new government which will be more amenable to yielding the desired prizes. Short of physical presence that allows removal and displacement of the persons constituting the government, and their replacement by those who are willing to govern, and capable of actually governing, the element of chance that the pressure exerted may be insufficient to achieve the desired purpose is very great. Besides, there could be a subsequent change of heart and reversal to status quo ante. Sufficiency of punishment cannot be determined in advance, for one thing, and returns that it produces must also diminish in accordance with the universal laws. It is the capability of the victim which has to be reduced to a level that he is unable to react, should he decide to change his mind. Annihilation is, ultimately, a process of absorption. It does involve a lot of destruction, dismantling, and melting down, and yet, absorption implies a desire for cooperation, admittedly iniquitous cooperation with a view to exploitation, that is, strategic cooperation. Annihilation is predicated upon a vision of an overarching order that the attacker prefers, an order in which the desired bilateral relationships would emerge. If the victim is such as to be considered unfit for initial annihilation and subsequent absorption, then he may be excluded from the system through the mechanism of extirpation or destruction[4]. Annihilation is successful only to the extent that the force in use can be minimised, by fashioning of new collective identities that adjust to the new order. Annihilation through force alone is a vastly destructive process which leaves the task of picking up the pieces to the victor — a task which cannot be completed without taking a lot of punishment. Assimilation is facilitated when the victim himself has been drained of his strength by loss of faith in his collective identity, order, regime, ruling elite, and government. Force from outside was hardly necessary to pull down the edifice of the Soviet Union. Extortion requires application of force to an extent that conceding of the prize by the victim appears a better proposition to him that continued suffering. If resistance to annihilation is the desired objective, in the concluding stages of an unfavourable trial of wills, the victim may desire to resist annihilation by conceding some of the immediate prizes sought by the victor with a view to protecting sources of strength Japan resisted annihilation by accepting to surrender at the end of the Second World War. In an unequal contest, or in a contest which has turned unequal, the loser may want to convert a war of annihilation into a war of extortion. The victor on the other hand, may want to convert what started as a war of extortion into a war of annihilation, if he finds that the victim has lost internal strength and will to resist annihilation : equally if the victor finds that annihilation involves punishment, because of unavoidable proximity with the victim who has retained a lot of residual strength, he may choose to remain content with prizes that he may extort from a distance. He would like to emerge with a favourable balance · gains must not be washed away by the impact of punishment. The United States, as a part of the Multi National Force(MNF) could and did inflict enormous punishment on Iraq from great distances, with few penalties by way of costs incurred, and casualties taken. They used their ground forces to close in and destroy the Iraqi armour. Two questions arise : why did they make no effort to absorb Iraq into a new regional order; and why, what had set out to be a war of annihilation, turned out to be a war of extortion. Withdrawal of Iraq from Kuwait was one of the prizes secured, apart from a few sundries like imposition of no flying zone and inspection teams, and so on. A simple explanation is, perhaps, that MNF was not willing to get into Iraq to create and enforce a new order, that is, they were not willing to take consequences of occupation. Although Iraq was subjected to the kind of punishment that the Germans and the Japanese were during the Second World War, for want of suitable forces of occupation, annihilation might not have seemed a practical proposition to the US and allies, at the time. Sanctions and the pressures that it produces, if allowed to work over a period of time, could lead to annihilation with minimum use of force.

Professional soldiers are known to demand bigger and better equipped armed forces, understandably so because they want to increase chances of success and reduce risk. Political masters are equally keen to either reduce the resources committed to the armed forces, or ask more of armed forces from the resources made available, depending upon their political philosophy and calculus of what will fetch the best political dividend. Armed forces are accused of wanting to play it safe, if not of empire building in personal and/or organizational interest while playing upon the popular patriotic motive. Armed forces are also accused of asking for more than what is essential by creating artificial scenarios of having to deal simultaneously with more than one adversary. Political masters are expected to resort to popular and soothing announcements containing assurances that no effort would be spared while allocating resources for the security of the country. They may do so while cutting down on the defence budget by resorting to a variety of stratagems like not offsetting the impact of inflation, or reappropriating a portion of the defence budget for drought relief[5]. The armed forces are pretty well aware that when faced with a clash of wills, they have to perform with what they actually have, or can lay hands on. Regrets for the past neglect, or promises to allot resources in the future is a route the politician can take. He may not have to face up to much worse than loss of office. In any case, because of the long time interval between denial of resources and its consequences, the political leadership may be in a position to get away by pointing out tnat the incumbents at the time of disaster are not really responsible. In the midst of this tug of war, in reality, man-power is pared or increased, equipment is designed and manufactured or purchased, operational directives are issued, and plans are made and training goes on. An aircraft carrier gets purchased, tank factories are established, and aircrafts are purchased. How are these decisions made, in the midst of all the imponderables. What logic in action informs those decisions.

It is believed, that starting with 1964, the armed forces have made five year plans, and on that basis, demanded resources for implementing those plans. The sanctity of plans prepared by the armed forces, without strategic and operational directive from Government is not hard to guess. Armed forces are unlikely to have a designed force structure, and they would be expected to do what they can with available resources.

The approach adopted against Pakistan in 1971 seemed to have been to stretch available resources -- armed forces — fully, without courting undue risk, and achieve whatever that was possible to cope up with refugee menace created by Pakistan. The policy objective was to seize enough real estate by force and settle Pakistani refugees on it. We had a situation in December, 1971 in which the forces that set out to carve out an area of East Pakistan in order to settle ten million refugees, forced all the Pakistani forces in the Eastern Wing to surrender and thereby facilitated the emergence of a new country. Regular Indian forces adept in manoeuvre were used along side the irregulars from the former East Pakistan who waged guerilla warfare. The forces employed in the East by India had certainly not been created or designed for the purpose. The mountain divisions had been raised to deter Chinese aggression in the wake of the Chinese attacks on the Indian territory in November 1962. Without doubting the political and military wisdom of changing the goals initially set to the armed forces, so that the success gained in the field could be exploited, the question could still be asked about what kind of forces should have existed had assistance in emergence of Bangladesh been one of the policy objectives. The success achieved masked the basic inadequacies. Contrast this with what Pakistan was doing ever since 1947. The difference in approaches adopted by Pakistan and India were markedly different. Pakistan being a revisionist state, its basic policy has always been based on annihilation of India as the ultimate objective. Its immediate objective in 1947 was to appropriate the Muslim majority areas of J & K and the state of Junagarh, and to maintain the State of Hyderabad in the Indian Union as a focus of infection that would eventually lead to communal violence and instability in which Pakistan would remain a dominant actor. It used raiders and tribals to achieve its objectives in Kashmir, diplomatic manoeuvre in Junagarh, and supported the Nizam of Hyderabad and his advisors with arms and ammunition to stiffen their will. Later, after the treaty with the United States in 1954, it acquired Patton tanks which could be used in the plains across the international border with India. In 1965, it used commandos and guerillas in J & K, and tanks in the plains to seize Kashmir. Very recently, a responsible journalist in Pakistan who later became a minister in the government of Mr. Nawaz Sharif, said as much: Rajiv Nanda of IDSA quoted Mr. Mushahid Hussain in a conversation,

> " Mr. Hussain told me that India in its present form can never be friend of any South Asian Country and therefore favoured, in the name of stability and security of South Asia, India's disintegration[6]."

The point being made here is that policy objectives of annihilation of India guided Pakistan in adopting a variety of means to attain the policy objectives. But the principle means used in 1965 — conventional forces — and the type of warfare — manoeuvre — did not serve the purpose well. Pakistan obviously learnt the lesson well after their experience in the East, and adopted guerilla warfare and subversion as the principle means of weakening India with a view to destabilization. The results obviously satisfy Pakistan.

The art and science of creating and maintaining a power structure, including the armed forces, is amenable to end and means analysis, like any other strategic proposition. Policy objectives and the time frame in which they are to be attained could be taken as the end, and the nature of warfare, actual techniques, and technology to be adopted, would be means in this frame of analysis. Here it is proposed to deal primarily with the armed forces — rather than with other components of the power structure. This is not intended to detract from the holistic approach which remains all important, but merely as a matter of convenience.

When force is employed to attain policy objectives, its very use produces an impact which needs to be taken into reckoning while deciding goals which are to be attained. The use of force must be governed in a manner that it does not vitiate the chances of attaining the policy objectives; equally, goals selected must be such that they are amenable to the use of force. Force is unique amongst instruments of power because of the finality it can produce. Violence is employed to produce desirable, and if that is not possible, at least, a 'better' peace. This 'heterogeneity' between means and ends has been pointed out by Clausewitz. It is the certainty of total and virtually uncontrolled destruction that has reduced the utility of nuclear devices as versatile means, and their utility, ever since, has been confined to a well defined area — deterrence.

Disarming is the age old method whereby the capability of the victim is reduced or eliminated. Disarming may be done, once again, by physically taking possession of arms, or by causing the victims to surrender them under grave physical duress. Disarming from a distance can only be achieved through an agreement provided it is seen to serve mutual purpose, or as a corollary to such a heavy dose of destruction, and if then. Disarming would involve taking on the responsibility of governance, or allowing the newly emergent governments to recreate instruments of power so that some kind of order can be maintained, otherwise iniquitous exchanges or exploitation cannot be carried out, unless of course, the intent is to take away the assets, and leave the victims to their own fate. If it is felt that, even after disarming and installation of new government, the victim is likely to revert to old and recalcitrant ways, it may be more provident to bring about changes in the 'regime', by devising a new constitution that guards against the known predilections. Understandably, this cannot be done from a distance, and not without occupation. This kind of exercise involves de-construction and re-construction, something that cannot be done without proximity and involvement. The results, of such exercise from the stand point of the aggressor, may be more lasting. If the social and economic structure in the victim's nation is such that it is unlikely to adopt the new regime, then there would be a need to create a new order, a task which cannot be attempted without direct and long involvement. If the prize sought is such that it involves major changes in the dominant dimensions of collective identity, like for example, merger with another nation, or fragmentation and partition, it calls for acceptance , if not acquiescence, at the level of common man. Starting top down, securing of prizes that involve major transformations and changes, respectively, of government, ruling elite, regime, order, and identity, call for greater and more direct involvement and direct presence of the potential beneficiary. They also call for more and more time consuming deconstruction and reconstruction with all the attendant uncertainties.

Without disarming, even if some of the desired prizes are conceded by the victim in a state of shock, extortion on a continuing basis is not likely to be successful. It is obvious that such changes can only be brought about after inflicting an unbearable punishment on the adversary which makes him amenable to any kind of settlement. To make the settlement credible and lasting, the adversary would necessarily have to be disarmed, partially or totally. Total disarmament can result into chaos or anarchy which cannot always be expected to serve the annihilator's purpose. Depending upon his requirements, he (annihilator) may maintain a level of anarchy, more or less controlled, if that is the desired object. The desired object may be to deny political space to the adversary, if and when, such space cannot be occupied or defended at reasonable costs. More likely, he will impose or allow evolution of power structures that he considers suitable for his own purpose. Annihilation cannot be achieved without major break and make — deconstruction and reconstruction — exercises. The breaking part is not achieved without destruction, in all probability, substantial destruction, unless subversion is also employed to reduce the level of physical violence.

Extortion is predicated upon a functioning system which is responsive, rational, and efficient to a degree that it is capable of fulfilling the commitment to concede the agreed prizes — territory, reparations, war prisoners for trial for crimes against humanity and so on. Extortion and annihilation both involve creation of consensus with adversary at some stage, which means negotiations. If threat of pain and punishment can achieve results, extortion can be effectively accomplished with minimal destruction occasioned by the need to demonstrate the victor's power.

Far and beyond extortion and annihilation, in the territory of death and destruction, lie extermination or extirpation. Annihilation, if successfully accomplished, ordinarily, should satisfy those requirements of the victor or the annihilator which cause him to undertake such ventures, provided of course that they are rational. But if the level of hatred born of perceived or real incompatibility is so great that the very existence of the adversary is seen as undesirable or polluting, then mere annihilation, as described above, and not in the literal sense, may not constitute the desired prize. Extermination or extirpation may be attempted when the offending segment of the population is seen to be polluting, as was done by Hitler, or when it is felt that there is a need to rid the land and seas of the people or species that overload the system, or vitiate the desired balance. Extermination has a finality about it, and no negotiations are involved or necessary, except perhaps to ensnare the unwary. None of this, of course, means that extermination cannot be preceded by either extortion or annihilation, or both. Hitler's concentration camps gave ample evidence of the sequential use of all the three.

Effective use of force, is never without elements of persuasion and dissuasion since physical force, by itself, is an inadequate instrument to achieve the purpose of obtaining meaningful compliance. Compliance involves an element of cooperation from the victim, no matter how unwilling or grudging. Force can do no more than destroy, constrain, or deprive. It is the fear induced by force, demonstrated force, that can be used to manipulate the victim's psyche to achieve the desired results. Physical force, when it prevails over that of the adversary, may be used or employed to physically dispossess the adversary of what he has got, or to dispel or displace him, or to constrain and place him in bondage, or to deprive and exhaust him. In this, the pain of injury, deprival, bondage, and or isolation is inseparable from dispossession of assets of the victim. All of these can be accomplished without cooperation of the victim. There may be no negotiation with the victim whereby he, under duress, or in fear, is made to cede or yield, or perform. In contrast, coercion must necessarily involve negotiation or bargaining, with the victim offering something in return for withholding of further punishment, or some other concession, or even offer of some prize by the subject using force. Coercion is bargaining to achieve an iniquitous exchange in which force, or more often, a combination of force and its threat are employed in the hope of achieving the desired results.

Though effects that force can produce, destruction, death, injury, and so on, have been strung together, there is a need to distinguish between the nature of force that destroys and kills on the one hand , and one that injures, constrains, or deprives, on the other hand. Death and destruction can be inflicted on the victim from very great distances and there is no upper ceiling on how much force can be used. Although death has a finality, with respect to an individual, the use of additional force may not be viewed by the attacker as superfluous. Additional application of force could well be aimed at many more deaths, or for increasing the probability of the death of the intended victims. In so far as destruction is concerned, pulverization has no finality. It can go on indefinitely. In contrast, the amount of force that can be used to cause injury, constraint, deprival, exhaustion, and so on, cannot be unlimited. Its limiting values are not infinite. Force that is not to be used to inflict punishment of death and unlimited destruction must be employed 'economically', otherwise, it may be counter productive, apart from being wasteful. 'Constraining' force cannot be employed indiscriminately and from great distance. It calls for proximity of the subject to the object of the force. Destructive force, will necessarily yield a crop of some injury and constraint, just as constraining forces will cause some deaths and destruction. A battalion charging with fixed bayonets, while approaching the enemy's dug - outs, which have already been pounded with artillery and aircraft, is unlikely to be sparing with rocket propelled and other grenades and assault charges, before running them over, and asking the defender to surrender. Only at that stage, they may want to ask the vanquished defenders to come out of the shelters and dug - outs, and then, march them to prisoners of war camp. This is a very different proposition from bombarding the defender with aircraft for thirty days from stand off distances, and hoping that absolutely nothing would be left on ground. There is likely to be no 'negotiation' — such as that carried out between the platoon commander who shouts that those who come out of the dug - outs without weapons will be spared, and those who reply by filing out with their arms raised — between attacker using 'destructive force' and the victim, except perhaps at the highest level. Constraining force on land reduces destruction, and achieves results mainly through coercion at many more levels including the lowest, provided proximity with the subject can be established.

Understandably, constraining forces take punishment, and not necessarily in inverse proportion to the differential of technology available to the opposing sides. Even the most sophisticated constraining forces will have to take punishment, which is the cost of closing in, if they have to succeed in their mission.

'Negotiation' is basic to coercion. Negotiation can be carried out using only the threat if there is a mutual understanding amongst adversaries or competitors about one another's capabilities. If not, some demonstration of force to bring the realization home could take place, followed by negotiation. Dissuasion — or deterrence — merely indicates what the adversary is not to do, of course, on the pain of punishment, but positive persuasion — compellence — requires the adversary to positively perform. Theoretically, or in mathematical terms, dissuasion may be reflected as persuasion not to perform. But that would distort reality. Dissuasion would cover a very small segment of activities that the adversary is not required to carry out — like, for example, targeting his missiles at own cities, or attacking own nuclear installations — but 'compellence' could well mean dismantling the nuclear facilities. Deterrence is achievable through destructive forces and coercion, but compellence is not. It calls for constraining forces. But for constraining forces, it is not possible for the subject to physically move in the proximity of the object of force and obtain his compliance.

Coercive or violent diplomacy relies on posing credible threats of the ability of the subject to inflict unacceptable punishment on the adversary, with strikes against his hard and soft targets. even after having taken a substantial punishment in the first instance. In our times, it has been circumscribed to the extent that, on the one hand the host is unable to protect his own assets, and on the other hand, he is incapable of disarming the adversary before he inflicts an unacceptable damage. Deterrence, that is thus achieved, is governed mainly by what is considered an unacceptable punishment by the potential victim, and the assured capacity of the attacker to inflict that punishment, or a little more of it for good effect. The compulsion for the arms race was derived, at one stage, from the desire to be one up, if possible, so that deterrence may be converted into compellence. With the realization that under conditions of parity, higher and higher levels of strike capability limited the chances of creating compellence, attention switched to risk management — risk of instability, escalation, and accidents. Limitation and reduction talks aim at retaining deterrence without unnecessary risks.

Though deterrence is meant to frighten the adversary into inaction, it's only effective, in the most critical areas involving nuclear exchange. Fear of instability and escalation inhibits the actual use of the deterrent means till adversary's actions seem to deserve the threatened punishment in full measure. Deterrent capability may be of doubtful utility value, but it cannot be forgone because the lack of it may tempt the adversary to attempt extermination. Deterrent capability without avowed renunciation of first strike, spells 'inaction' with an offensive content. If no first strike policy is announced, the edge of its offensive content is blunted. A capacity to strike from long distances with weapons of mass destruction has particular relevance to wars of extermination.

Wars of extortion aim at correcting power imbalances between adversaries. The aim is to achieve this by exchange of prizes under duress. There is no serious attempt to interfere with the internal power distribution of the victim. Therefore, it is possible to reduce the contact area and the duration over which force is applied. Essentially, they are prize related wars, and therefore, they are likely to end as soon as the commonly understood conditions are fulfilled, or when all the adversaries perceive that the prizes are out of reach, and the 'match ' needs to be ended, at least for the time being. Not being driven by the concerns of collective or national identities, they may not give rise to intense hatreds which tend to prolong the conflict. Wars of annihilation, by their very nature, call for fight to finish or mutual exhaustion, with every possibility that the hostilities will be resumed no sooner than power to make war is renewed.

Capability for extortion calls for a limited ability to create compellence : inflicting enough punishment, from distance and by closing in, so that the desired prizes, or prizes within easy reach, can be seized by force and retained for a sufficiently long time, so that the adversary agrees to continued retention of adverse possession obtained by force, or concedes the desired prizes. Wars of extortion do not touch the core interests — that is, they do not make claims on prizes that are unlikely to be conceded by the adversary without a prolonged and/or intense trial of wills. They are waged to get at prizes which the host or the defender finds it difficult to secure or retain, apart from their value being more to the contender than to the possessor. In short, they are considered good picks or killings. There is no desire to press the claim beyond a point, or to rock the edifice. Disarming is not the intent in wars of extortion, so they do not call for forces that would surround and capture the adversary's forces. The offensive content is small, but the defensive content is proportionately larger. The change in status quo that is aimed at by the attacker is comparatively small. The defender may also be willing to concede the change in return for a matching change desired by him. No large-scale mobilization of resources is required. It is a limited war in every sense.

Regular forces required for wars of annihilation — that includes power projection — must be able to strike deep — into vitals, and at pressure points. They must be able to evade, by pass or jump over the adversary's peripheral defence to disarm the reserves, and to starve the defenders of their sustenance. They must bring about break down in prevailing order and disrupt governance. They must have the capacity to impose isolation on the country as a whole so that they can interdict the inflow of vital materiel and help. They must be able to present their 'reasonable' demands to the affected population, and create the prospects of rapid restoration of order and peace no sooner than the demands are met. War of annihilation implies creation of asymmetry in the mobilization of resources, speed of mobilization, and most of all, in the mobility of forces in the field, and their ability to close in. The emphasis of forces designed for wars of annihilation is, in decreasing order, on mobility, strike power, and survival. Wars of annihilation, if they have to be carried out mainly by regular forces have to be preemptive and swift. Otherwise they are likely to deteriorate into slogging matches that do not serve the security interest of the country.

Irregular forces, as defenders can also win a war of annihilation by exhausting the adversary over a long period of time, never once winning a battle conclusively, many times disengaging in disadvantageous situation, but winning through survival. Led by charismatic leadership, and a sprinkling of some regular units, and trained man-power, the guerillas and partisans can wear out a foreign force. As a force of resistance, they are par excellence, because they can raise the resistance to the level of people's or national war. If war of annihilation against another country without a dominating regular component is unthinkable, resistance to war of annihilation except with the help of local militia is unlikely to succeed. Emphasis is on survival, mobility, and strike power.

War of annihilation without a well defined purpose and a predetermined idea of where to end it, and on what conditions, invariably leads to disaster. Parts of Japan in the Second World War need not have been reduced to a rubble.

Forces raised for prevailing in war of extortion cannot deal effectively with an adversary bent upon wars of annihilation. Purely defensive forces are condemned to fight every few years on their own territory, and in a disadvantageous position, because the initiative does not lie with them. The thinking that informs such forces is to stop the fight on a winning note whatever that means, and then to exchange prizes.

Both the World Wars in this century were wars of annihilation. Discounting the 'Hitler' phenomenon, it could even be said that the Second World War took up where the First had left off. Wars of annihilation are driven by concerns of collective identity, rather than by concerns of prizes. Denial of prizes to the adversary, or his elimination in the current and offending form, is more likely to create the drive for wars of annihilation. By their very nature, wars of liberation, revolutionary wars, and civil wars are wars of annihilation. Revolutionary warfare aims at annihilation of social, economic, and political order, some of the major dimensions of the national identity, and nearly all of the concepts and institutions on which the system is based. Revolutionary wars reserve death for the adversaries — the 'classes', 'enemies of the people', 'parasites and the exploiters' and so on. Revolutionary wars are more about redefining individual identities, creating new collective identities, and a new order. A lot has to go into the melting pot which may include some of the national boundaries. The changes desired are so far reaching that the violence used has necessarily to be abiding and pervasive. Therefore, revolutionary wars may have a recognizable beginning, but they may not have an easily recognizable end. Continuation of violence till attainment of vaguely defined objectives itself may turn out to be the end that is sought, and ends and means may become inextricably mixed.

Civil wars also aim at thwarting attempts to cast off established national identities on the one hand, and to recreate new collective identities on the other hand. Civil wars could have facets of revolution or reaction on the one hand, and colonization or liberation on the other hand, but the aspect of annihilation is never absent. Often impelled by extreme hatred, civil wars tend to bring out the worst in mankind. Wars of liberation can and do have foreign components. Insurgencies may have small beginnings and, if these are not eliminated in time, they can mushroom into civil wars, or wars of libration with foreign components and involvement. But being in the nature of wars of annihilation, the participants and adversaries tend to prolong and extend violence with a view to achieving their goals : insurgents make efforts to involve increasing proportion of the population in violence either of their own making, or by exposing them to the 'government' troops; 'governments' tend to snuff out insurgents and supporters by using massive force whenever they can. This common and recurring practice is depicted as lack of sensitivity and/or concern for human rights, in their allegations against each other, by the opposing sides, and construed as barbarity by the commentators who take both the sides to task. But it is best to remember, that in warfare of annihilation, the above is only to be expected. Prolonged, pervasive, and intrusive violence is necessary for the melt-down. The violence need not be severe but it must be real and threatening to a large proportion of the victim's population. The agents of violence can dole out punishment, and disarm or frighten into submission only when they are in close proximity. Unspoken negotiation between the victim and the attacker must be a practical proposition. Surrender or mere inaction must bring rewards by immediate remission in pain and fear.

The nature of warfare is also governed by the desire and ability of the leadership to mobilize all possible sources of strength, to convert them into instruments of power, and to utilize them to attain policy objectives. All strength and power, ultimately, can be sourced to the population. As an individual, a citizen may begin by producing more than what he consumes. He may store a part of the surplus in a manner that is directly accessible to him — his private property —, he may pay taxes, and invest. The government may lay hands on taxes to raise and maintain forces; it may also make use of other public assets for the same purpose, and beyond that, it may also take public loans for the same purpose. But the forces so raised would be limited. Soldiers bearing arms could not exceed the number that can be paid for, and their quality would be governed by the market forces. Warfare conducted by such forces would indeed be limited on two counts : One, except for those bearing arms, the contribution of others would be strictly limited, and generally confined to what they have willingly given. Therefore, a substantial proportion of the totality of all available means would either be withheld, or remain unmobilized. Two, the probability of the common man having to suffer direct punishment as a result of war would be appreciably smaller in comparison with those bearing arms. The upshot would be that the involvement of the total population would be of a low order, in proportion to their contribution and commitment. Comparatively small forces of professional soldiers, sailors, or airmen, would fight limited wars. Their professional skills, competence, and technology at their disposal would, in the course of a few wars or campaigns lead to massive extortion or annihilation of their own side or that of their adversary. Totality of war, starts off by widening the base of population from which man power is drawn, through national service, or conscription. It mobilizes resources not only at the direct disposal of the government, but also at the disposal of what is now called the private sector, and the common man. Last of all, by exposing most of the population to the hazards and dangers of war, the scale is near total.

Napoleon is credited with having made the war total. Faced with the prospect of leading an impecunious France against coalitions of powerful nations, he raised a national army, and not only that, he developed tactics and staff procedures to suit his national army. Napoleon was a master strategist in this sense too, although what is better known and acknowledged is his mastery of the operational art and military strategy. It was his ability to mobilize national resources and enthuse the nation that created the possibilities for his victories. Totality of war is not a function merely of the war aims, or the precise instruments of war, but also of the proportion of resources employed. Both the World Wars which came in the wake of the last phases of the industrial revolution in the Northern hemisphere, allowed nations to focus all their industrial resources, including the raw materials from the colonies they controlled, to achieve production of warlike stores and materials on a scale hitherto unthought of. Larger and larger forces with greater and greater access to munitions brought to the conclusion the philosophy of Napoleon : national mobilization to raise forces capable of annihilation of the adversary Napoleon relied on his generals and his own generalship to secure strategic victories, and achieve annihilation by over-running the enemy territory to secure subjugation. He aimed at annihilation through intrusive and invasive application of massive force.

If Napoleon made war total in one sense, it was Douhet who made it in another. He propagated the doctrine of hitting the sources of strength — what are called value targets in our times. Douhet fervently believed that punishment from air alone was enough to achieve the policy objectives of the attacker : extortion or annihilation. In fact he believed that application of force from a distance was enough provided it was sufficient.

What did happen, however, that by threatening every thing and any thing, no matter how deep in adversary's territory, or how unconnected with military operations, he got the whole of the adversary nation involved in the war and made the latent sources of resistance and strength that the nation possessed accessible to the war leaders. It was proved in the Second World War that the so called strategic bombing against value targets did not achieve the desired results: neither did Great Britain get cowed down during the Battle of Britain, nor did Germany buckle under massive and savage aerial attacks against the industrial and population centres. It is doubtful if the use of weapons of mass destruction against value targets could have gained its pride of place in the saga of total warfare but for the ideas propagated by Douhet. It is worth recalling that the nuclear bomb was developed and used during a period that the doctrine born of Douhet's ideas held sway, and application of massively destructive weapons from long distances seemed to be a practical and complete method of winning the war. It would appear that disarming from a distance seemed a very practical proposition at the time. Douhet held that -

> " In order to assure an adequate national defence, it is necessary — and sufficient — to be in a position in case of war to achieve the command of air[7] "

And then went on to predict that -

> "War will always be inhuman... the purpose of war is to harm the enemy as much as possible ... and all means to this end will be employed[8]."

He predicted and approved the use of 'poison gas' in defence of his country and riled against those who would abide by the 'formal agreements'. He condemned them as nothing but 'patricides'. What would Douhet had said about the use of nuclear weapons delivered by air is not hard to guess.

It is reasonable to conclude that coercive or 'violent' diplomacy cannot be fruitfully practised without highly destructive forces that have the capacity to reach out to the adversary's sources of strength and power with a degree of certainty. Similarly wars of extermination or extirpation rely on assured and near total destruction. Wars of annihilation, in addition to the forces that are capable of inflicting punishment and attrition, also call for forces capable of imposing constraint in direct proportion to the extent of annihilation that is desired. Wars of extortion can be prosecuted with forces that can inflict just the right amount of punishment, and no more, because excess or uncontrolled punishment is likely to prove counter productive.

The above taxonomy of war, on the basis of policy objectives on the one hand, and that of force on the basis of effects that it is expected to produce on the other hand, establishes some very obvious correlations between the two. These have been illustrated in the form of a 'map' on the next page.

It links nature of forces and the policy objectives that they can be expected to help in attaining. Instruments for

CORRELATION : POLICY OBJECTIVES AND NATURE OF FORCES

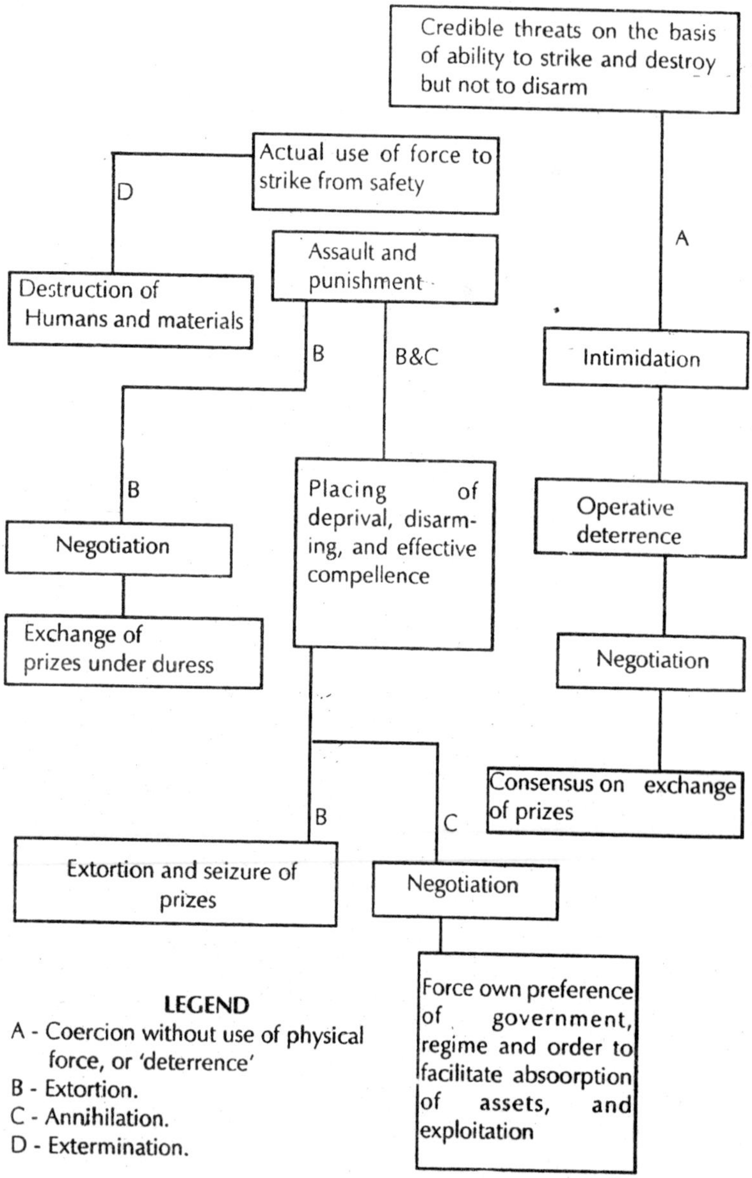

application of, or resistance to, physical force draw upon three elements, viz strike power, mobility, and protection. Strike power is the ability to inflict punishment on the adversary. Mobility is the ability to move towards or away from the victim or attacker, or in relation to him, directly or by a circuitous route, quickly or slowly. Protection implies ability to protect oneself from the punishment that the attacker may want to inflict either by direct strikes, or through deprivation or denial, without appreciable degradation of own mobility or strike power. Strike power could be evaluated in terms of distance at which it can be brought to bear, the nature and extent of punishment it inflicts, the duration for which punishment can be imposed, and the residual after effects that the punishment gives rise to. Mobility could be evaluated with reference to the medium on or through which the movement takes place — across the country, on rails or prepared surfaces, on or under water, in the air, or in space for that matter — , the speed of movement, and the duration for which it can be maintained. Protection could be judged in terms of the ability to evade punishment, as also of the severity and the duration of punishment that can be withstood.

Mobility is a very crucial factor in that it can, very substantially, compensate for deficiencies in strike power. Three different facets of mobility need to be viewed. (1) Ability to create and exploit adversary's vulnerability 'by - passing ' obstacles and/or difficult terrain or by 'jumping over' them to arrive close to points of decision. Capture of crossings across Albert Canal in Belgium by the German paratroopers in the Second World War made a lightning advance possible.It is the ability to travel through air without noise and at low altitude, using hang gliders, that allows the Palestinian terrorists to invade Israeli space. Low altitude air space is a new vulnerability created by hang gliders, or dirigible parachutes. (2) Ability to reach behind the enemy lines in the first place, and then to maintain momentum of attack on successive targets and victims not capable of putting up stiff resistance is the essence of Blitzkrieg. Blitzkrieg is a technique that enables the attacker to make the adversary's decision making process ineffectual, if not irrelevant, by retaining initiative through sheer pace of movement and action, or 'tempo'. (3) Ability to create shock through momentum of attack so that victims are overcome in detail and constrained before they have time to react.

Ability to move in air, and below or on water offer unprecedented possibilities for creating new vulnerabilities and exploiting them. Even a limited strike power at a vital point can produce the desired results. Mobility thus creates leverage, and constitutes the most fundamental force multiplier.

Ability to remain submerged and move under water gives protection to submarines. Similar protection is also availed by missiles mounted on railway flats or moving trailers. Troops airlifted by helicopters or airdropped behind enemy lines have their power multiplied by virtue of being able to reach the adversary's pressure points.

Primary source of force is, undoubtedly, strike power, but without mobility it cannot be brought to bear on the victim where and when it hurts him most, and without protection, the chances of own losses and costs getting out of hand cannot be ruled out. Even more, without protection and mobility, the chances of utilizing available strike power may be jeopardised. Mobility and protection complement the strike power on the one hand, and enhance its effect on the other hand. In its own right, strike power can confer some protection on own side, if indirectly and only for a length of time, by perplexing the victim and robbing him of some of his decision making apparatus and faculties. Protection may allow the attacker to close in and overcome some of the deficiencies in strike power.

Turning the problem around, mobility can be used to compensate for protection : the probability of a force or a missile on a moving platform being hit is low in comparison with those in static locations. Strike power can be employed to keep a pursuing attacker at bay till slow moving elements can get away. Protection and endurance may lead to wastage of adversary's strike power, and thereby tilt the differential in own favour at critical time.

Each of the primary elements — and sub-elements — can be employed effectively to complement each other as well as to compensate for unavoidable deficiencies.

The basic engines or instruments of force could be divided into three broad categories : armed men, manned or unmanned fighting platforms, and projectiles — smart or otherwise. Armed men have the intrinsic ability to employ the whole range of force: they can destroy, kill, injure, constrain, deprive, and deny. Their constraining capacity is outside the capability of fighting platforms and projectiles. Fighting platforms cannot renew their capacity except for short durations. They need a great deal of time in workshops and with maintenance echelons. Their recycling is more difficult than recycling of armed men. Projectiles can dole out any kind of punishment but not yet with sufficient discrimination. Their effect is transient, except when they use NBC warheads. Only armed men seem to have a capacity to benefit from difficult terrain and living conditions, directly in proportion to their training in hardship morale, and competence. Their mobility though is extremely limited, and they cannot compete with fighting platforms except in built up areas, in close and mountainous terrain, or in extreme bad weather when the platforms are rendered inoperative. But with technological advances, fighting platforms, manned and unmanned, will be able to get over many of their limitations in so far as their mobility is concerned.

Projectile themselves cannot be thwarted except in hi-technology — and extremely high cost — regime of Strategic Defence Initiative (SDI), or Anti Ballistic Missile Defence (ABMD). Projectile launchers or fighting platforms guard their vulnerabilities through movement, concealment, and deception. Armed men, by themselves, are extremely vulnerable and their mobility does not afford them much protection. In fact, they are most vulnerable when moving, that is in the open. They need to seek protection either in defence works, or in protected fighting platforms. Armed men may sometimes avoid severe punishment by being in the close proximity of the adversary.

In the light of the foregoing, it is feasible to argue that the national armed forces should comprise five functional components, characteristics and mode of operation of which are set out in succeeding pages.

(1) Destruction oriented with capability forces for striking at adversary's value targets, launchers, and bases, as a deterrent.

Characteristics

They have the capacity to inflict intolerable pain and punishment on the adversary without necessarily conferring any direct benefit on the attacker. To be fully effective, they have to have nuclear warheads or warheads which can inflict comparable damage. They serve the purpose of deterrence—keeping the adversary from undertaking unfriendly acts with hostility content above a well understood 'threshold' —but may not serve the purpose of getting the adversary to act in a particular manner. They are almost totally dependent on the relative superiority of technology, and for nations who can remain ahead in the technological race, they always confer advantages. Their effectiveness is prone to quick and rapid shifts in response to additions of 'technology value', or degradation because of counter action by the adversary. The pace of change is likely to be often unpredicatable, depending upon the technology that is developed or accessed by the adversary. Being technological marvels, they remain in the domain of closely guarded secrets, and in the hands of scientists and technologists. They are highly amenable to centralized control and there is always a temptation for the political masters to plan for their use in isolation, on the basis of concepts and ideas harboured by their makers, rather than in conjunction with other forces. Their incorporation in the organic structure of the armed forces is one of the biggest problem areas because these forces derive utility from 'inaction', rather than actual use. Therefore, their incorporation in the strategic, operational, training, and logistic doctrine is problematic. Very expensive in the long run, and because they do not allow the use of force in a graduated manner, or 'in retail', they always need to be supplemented by conventional forces. But as tools of deterrence they remain unsurpassed. If delivered by missiles, they really do not need to find adversary's vulnerabilities. Short of effective missile defence — unlikely to be total — very little can be done to stop them from inflicting punishment that they are designed to deliver except their own shortcomings , that is unforced errors, or technical snags. If they are aircraft or submarine delivered, vulnerability on ground, at sea, and in flight has to be guarded with great care, and effectiveness is suspect till the moment of actual delivery of the weapon load. Added to that are the very real problems of effective target location, evaluation and acquisition on the one hand, and the gravity of decision making process on the other hand. If targets are static, the problems may be more manageable. These forces depend either upon mobility and deception to guard their own vulnerabilities, or they need to be protected in underground structures which further complicates the technological problems. Credibility of the forces is the most critical factor in 'operations', in that it is the threat which is expected to do most work. Built into the strategic doctrine, there has to be a method of 'demonstrating' the capability — decision making and all — in a convincing manner.

Mode of operations

Periodic capability demonstration exercises are sine qua non. The essence is the holding out and articulation of the threat. If and when called upon to be prepared for preemptive or reactive strikes, instant readiness has to be maintained with provisions for recall at every stage. Reactive strike launch procedures may call for computer control in the last stages, when human interface cannot keep up with the demands of speed. Capacity to deliver weapons on a given target from a variety of launchers, and from multiple locations enhances credibility. Launchers used may be in concealed locations, or mobile, on land, in the air, or on below the surface of water. Surfeit of destructive power is held in reserve, well concealed and protected, to deny to the adversary the possibility of preemptive elimination of own strike capability.

(2) Destruction oriented surface forces for inflicting punishment that is adequate to permit extortion and/or annihilation, when necessary.

Characteristics

These are the forces that are meant to inflict substantial and heavy punishment on the adversary's forces in the field so that his ability to wage war is degraded to the extent, that he sues for peace. The intent is to physically cripple the adversary's forces and dictate terms which include an agreement to disarm or substantially reduce his forces, or inflict sufficiently heavy punishment from which he would not be able to recover for a length of time. This presupposes a favourable differential in capability derived from a combination of quality and quantity of equipment, and a willingness to withstand punishment. Advantages in technology could be offset, to a limited extent, by good training and handling of forces. The trial of wills in this mode is likely to turn into a slogging match, and greater endurance and staying power would be the dominant factors. Intrinsic organizational and industrial strength, self reliance, and stability would be more telling than marginal technological advantages. These forces would be very sensitive to terrain and local conditions, and outcome of an individual engagement would be hard to predict, with generalship and chance playing major roles. Adversary's similar forces are best dealt with in concentration areas, and on the line of march, because they can then be destroyed in bulk and before they develop fully their capacity to counter and resist force. Equally, ability to hide concentration and movement before striking preemptively gives major advantage. If a choice has to be made, between the two, it is the tactical mobility which is more important than the strategic mobility for destruction oriented surface forces. Exercise of political control over military operations has necessarily to be at one remove, with grant of autonomy to the military in the operational matters. There is a presupposition of ability to obtain reliable intelligence on the opposing forces and its field logistics, adequate capacity for renewal of own forces for as long as necessary, and a capacity to protect own vitals and sources of strength for the duration of the conflict.

Mode of operations

Battlefield is so chosen and prepared that the adversary feels compelled to give battle with as large a proportion of main components of his forces as possible. Sudden and heavy disarming strikes against adversary's forces are made, if possible in his concentration areas. The aim is to bleed the enemy, through attrition, till his forces are effectively disarmed, or the adversary accepts terms that result in his being disarmed. This may involve 'fixing' of the adversary's force so that it cannot avoid or evade punishment.

(3)Manoeuvre oriented forces to enable conduct of swift campaigns in aid of annihilation.

Characteristics

Manoeuvre implies a shift in emphasis from direct punishment of force in the field to exploitation of adversary's vulnerabilities to exert on his pressure points by entering his vitals and disrupting his administration and governance. Such a force relies as much on its ability to move and maintain itself in the adversary's areas as it relies on its ability to deal with hard and soft targets. Its forte is movement and speed of movement. If it acts in unison with the destruction oriented surface forces, it can hasten capitulation of adversary. This force needs state of the art technology that must have a clear edge over that of the adversary. It must have a capacity to win a sequence of many small engagements so that it can successfully avoid major battles. These forces to be effective, need reliable intelligence covering the whole range of adversary's forces and government, capacity to mount raids and effect recovery after inflicting punishment, ability to create holding forces that derive maximum benefit from terrain and local conditions to survive in face of heavy punishment, and ability to make deep penetrations. The grammar that underlies the effective use of force is most dominant ; and military commanders need a great deal of autonomy and freedom to act.

Mode of operations

These forces act in cooperation with destruction oriented forces, or on their own, creating their own 'pivots' and holding elements. They induct manoeuvre components behind the enemy's lines and in depth areas so that they have access to the adversary's vitals. They maintain ceaseless movement of manoeuvre components and exert pressure on vitals to dislocate adversary's mind and communications. They impose sufficient punishment — savage but not mindless — to distract the adversary, principally as a means of own protection. The denouement is to attack sources of strength and sustenance of the armed forces and the decision making apparatus through and from which the armed forces take direction.

(4)Resistance oriented forces to counter annihilation and extortion

Characteristics of force

Resistance cannot be offered without total and complete mobilization of the population — including personal and private means at the disposal of private individuals — on the one hand, and well organized regular and irregular forces on the other. Regular and irregular forces have to act together and they need unflinching support of the population to turn resistance into peoples' war. Indigenous, competent and inspiring leadership at the national and regional levels, and its integration with the military leadership is sine qua non. If not, the forces of resistance would not be any more than defending units and formations of regular forces in trenches. The model for the forces of resistance has to reflect the spirit of " We shall fight on beaches ..... " , more so now that the weapons of mass destruction are available for use. The regular forces have to be able to survive to fight, but the rest must at least survive and eventually resist. India before Independence has had experience of a totally unified and centralized authority. But it was alien, and the regular forces were trained to remain totally isolated from the civilian population. The regulars were not expected to fight aliens on Indian soil. They were to fight the raiders and tribals outside the Indian borders. There were thoughts and fears about the Russian invasion from time to time, but resistance was to be offered in Afghanistan where a carefully crafted disorder was maintained. The buffer state was there to ensure that governance in Afghanistan was so rudimentary that disorder on call was available. Disorder in Afghanistan plus the Imperial regulars were to constitute the resistance. After Independence, resistance to foreign aggressors on own soil has not received much attention. A combination of para-military forces, home guards and militia has to take the brunt, leaving the regulars—manoeuvre forces, and commandos both—to isolate and punish the aggressor. The model of a thin line of trenches and obstacles creating a screen behind which the life would go on normally is not a realistic expectation in years to come. This model suffers from the twin disadvantage: it absorbs most of the regulars into purely defensive role and gives virtual immunity to the adversary from counter strokes ; it still does not provide enough protection in depth areas. Former Defence Secretary P. V. R. Rao advocated these thoughts in his `Defence Without Drift. Resistance oriented forces thrive on total integration of political and military strength, and political awareness of matters military is of essence. Resistance forces must necessarily rely a great deal on timely and accurate dissemination of intelligence, further they need a capacity to renew themselves from locally available resources. At the same time they cannot do without a capacity to reach out to and recoup from distant resources in depth areas. Detailed and exact knowledge of ground and climatic conditions of area of interest is their forte. They need technology suitable for inflicting damage at short ranges at many points in a coordinated manner, or in response to local opportunity, and for impeding mobility of the adversary on and off roads. Proximity to the adversary cannot be avoided by resistance oriented forces; in fact,that is a source of their strength.

Mode of operations

Resistance implies attrition, dissipation of adversary's momentum, fragmentation of his forces into bits with increasingly reduced coherence and effectiveness, interpenetration of opposing forces and a stalemate which is more disadvantageous to the adversary. Substantial punishment is the cost of offering resistance, and at least in the initial phases, the losses in terms of casualties taken and ground surrendered may be greater than the penalties imposed on the adversary in most encounters. The age old wisdom of gaining time , or imposing delay on the adversary, is based on the often observed outcome of long conflicts : they tend to favour the defender, that is if he can remain in reckoning till then. Sheer passage of time brings about unanticipated changes and chances which are more likely to favour the defender on his own ground, rather than the attacker who is operating at the end of extended lines of communications. Progressive infliction of greater and greater punishment on the adversary as and when opportunity occurs is what finally turns the balance in favour of the defender. This is achieved through denial of logistic resources to the adversary and disruption of his lines of communications by careful selection of ground and circumstances for chosen battles and active engagement for so long as advantageous. Creation of disorder in areas under adversary's occupation leads to further dissipation of his strength in rear areas and for maintaining the minimal order that is essential for the business of living from day to day, even in the combat zone and rear areas. Wearying down of the adversary over a prolonged period is the heart of the matter, and not so much the fighting of decisive battles. Regaining of freedom from constraints imposed by the adversary aims at the ultimate restoration of old order. Resistance does not imply victories in the initial stages.

(5)Constraint oriented forces which, when required, help in occupying and holding captured territory till decisive results are obtained.

Characteristics

These forces, originally, are a component of the resistance oriented forces. They are forces specially trained into a cadre based militia so that they can follow the manoeuvre oriented forces into the opponent's territory and fill the vacuum that invariably results from the displacement caused by the refugee movement. But for them, either the regulars will be sucked in , or a vacuum will be created.

Mode of operations

These forces maintain presence in direct and close contact with object or victim of power. They display a favourable power differential and create the impression of its immutability. They keep close watch over behaviour and mood of the victim with a view to inflicting pain and distributing rewards so that adverse developments are nipped in the bud. Their principle function is to maintain order with a view to minimising the force 'in use', as against force on display.

Notwithstanding the generalities mentioned above, the actual force structure must take into account the ground realities. It is not good enough to say that Force A constitutes the deterrence. The questions to be answered are, who will it prevent from doing what, in which circumstances. Similarly destruction oriented force must have a capacity to successfully engage and punish targets of given characteristics and attributes while operating on a given piece of terrain. Actual relative differences in capacity to strike and/or take punishment, and precise conditions of operations are all important. Annihilation is not a feasible proposition without there being at least a proportion of population in the adversary's country that seeks a change and may view even absorption with a degree of favour. Power projection for the purpose of annihilation without creating such a base in the first instance is unlikely to succeed.

A nation of India's size cannot do without a balanced mix of all the components of forces mentioned earlier in this Chapter. All of these do not have to be raised in a hurry, but the long term goals must not be lost sight of. Technologies and production capacities may be so developed that they converge to create the desired capacity at an appropriate time. This would only happen when there is a national consensus about what national security implies : what kind of benefits it would confer, and what kind of commitment and costs it would entail. For distant goals to be achieved, it is not good enough that leadership can make a reasonable assessment about demands of security over next five years, but the time-horizon must be stretched to something like 25 to 30 years. Only then would the room that is likely to become available for evolution of strategic options — ends and means both — would actually be utilized.

NOTES

1. Raymond Aron, 'Clausewitz, Philosopher of War', Routledge and Kegan Paul, London, 1976, (p.99)

2. Ludwig Renn, 'Warfare, The Relationship of War With Society', Faber and Faber, London, Mcmxxxix. (p.18).

3. Renn, op. cit., (p.87).

4. Legal — Indian Removal act of 1830 — and military measures adopted to move Indians — Cherokee and Seminole tribes — west of the Mississippi resulted in forcible movement of some 100,000 Indians. Comte de Tocqueville's comments indicates a desire to isolate Indians, possibly because they could not be absorbed :

" They [Indians] were isolated in their own country, and their race constituted a little colony of troublesome strangers in the midst of a numerous and dominant people."

Encyclopedia Britannica, Volume 11, 1964, (p.209).

5. According to Smith $ 2.5 billion were taken directly from the defence budget for drought-relief during 1987. Chris Smith, 'India's Adhoc Arsenal, Direction or Drift in Defence Policy?', SIPRI, Oxford University Press, New York, 1994, (p.88).

6. Rajiv Nanda, 'Analyst wary of Sharif's peace-intent', Times of India, Bombay, February 6, 1996.

7. Giulio Douhet, 'The Command of the Air', Faber and Faber Ltd, Mcmxliii, (p.3).

8. ibid., (p 147).

9

Geopolitics of the Sub-continent

A geopolitical entity is essentially a derivative of geography but not of geographical factors alone. Added to the geography is the human element : encrustations of human migrations, habitation, and institutions which have become a part of the history, and the living beings which populate the land, their civilization and culture(s), and politics. It is predicated upon the possibility of a certain minimal internal strength born of cohesion and coherence, an idea of a periphery with respect to which insiders and outsiders are determined, and the likelihood of generation and projection of power by people occupying a land-mass. While a geopolitical entity may only remain a strong possibility, awaiting the realization of potential, the existence of the possibility itself may be founded on certain geographical and historical factors, which tend to have a degree of permanence or persistence. A populated land mass is the most basic source of strength and power. When individuals decide to cooperate, on the basis of common perceptions of interdependence and a belief that collective effort will secure prizes for individuals for which individual effort by itself is inadequate, collective associations comprising individuals and groups of individuals emerge. Collective associations last for so long as they fulfil the promise. If they last long enough, and develop an enduring collective consciousness — on the basis of shared interests, preferences, and values — some groups get placed beyond the pale on account of some perceived difference with the presiding collective identity, or incompatibility, just as some choose to separate themselves because they feel to be at a disadvantage, or discriminated against, or persecuted. Collective identities which develop political strength and power demarcate their territory and create institutions and apparatus for guarding it, apart from using those instruments to acquire additional assets including territory, and for settling scores with adversaries. Collective identities with instruments of power — mainly nation states in our times — try to enlarge their territory, if that is possible, by whatever means. International borders stabilize if they are in conformity with 'discontinuities' in major dimensions of collective identities like language, race, civilization, religion, and most importantly, perceptions of what constitutes 'natural' limits of land mass and its 'ownership'. One set of parameters determine the periphery of the collective identity in terms of constituent people. Another set of parameters determine the extent of land that can be occupied by, and if need arises defended — against other claims and claimants — by the people constituting that collective identity. If and when an extended geographical area is occupied by a people who have the potential to constitute a collective identity, and when they assert it in political terms, a geopolitical mass emerges. Geopolitics is rooted in this basic and common phenomenon. The larger the number of people who contribute to accumulation of political power, the greater the likelihood of emergence of collective power. It is well known that the per capita income in China is appreciably lower than in the USA, even so there is a prediction that, China at current rate of progress will overtake the US gross domestic produce early in the 21st century.

> "It is difficult to see any set of circumstances where-measured in a sensible way — China will not be well on its way to becoming the world's largest economy by 2020[1]."

> "Assuming a starting population of 1.15 billion people and modest economic growth rates allowing for decay of the double-digit figures of the last decade , the population of China will reach 1.75 billion, and its gross domestic product (GDP) will overhaul that of the United States in the year 2023[2]."

Even India, in spite of the abject poverty of many of its citizens, may perform a similar feat in times to come.

> "Step forward, India. Before the political pundits fall off their bar stools in shock, let me click on my mouse and bring up my India 'spread sheet': by 2051 India's aggregate GDP will also have exceeded that of the United States. Of course, if one assumes a rapprochement with its erstwhile inhabitants in Pakistan and rapidly developing Bangladesh (now about 135 million people each), then the economic power of the Indian sub-continental block will overhaul the United States much sooner[3]. "

These predictions are based on an important assumption that Chinese and Indians will retain their ability to accumulate and combine power of most individuals in political terms, that is, they will continue as nation states. Similarly, although the Soviet Union has disintegrated, Russia is expected to continue as a nations state. A geopolitical entity may live on for centuries without its potential ever being realized. A coherent political regime in control of a geopolitical entity is most likely to realize its potential, that is, convert it into a geopolitical mass — something that exerts influence by its mere existence because of its strength. A geopolitical entity endures almost indefinitely, vulnerable only to major demographic upheavals -- and not mere changes — which cannot be predicted through logic of linear progression. Political regimes are more prone to change and fragmentation. They can also be more or less competent, vigourous, innovative, or ambitious. Therefore, for how long, how often, or when the potential of a geopolitical entity will be realized is difficult to predict.

There was a time in Europe when fervour of Christian faith could realize geopolitical potential.

> "There was even for a while — in crusades — a single foreign policy and a common military task force, something which Europe cannot begin to agree upon now[4]. "

It took several centuries and two cataclysmic wars thereafter, for a major part of Europe to emerge as European Union (EU). EU looks like the beginning of geopolitical realization of Europe.

It is tempting to refer to Buzan's concept of 'security complex'.

> "A security complex is defined as a group of states whose primary security concerns link together sufficiently closely that their national securities cannot realistically be considered apart from one another. Security complexes tend to be durable, but they are neither permanent nor internally rigid[5]."

What is implied here by geopolitical entity is not without strong over-tones of 'security complex'.

Napoleon's observation about China's potential was a clear acknowledgement that it constituted a geopolitical entity. Assessment of geopolitical potential implies informed guess-work about the likely strength or power projection capability that a geopolitical entity is likely to manifest in a given set of circumstances.

If international borders are such that they disregard 'continuities' in population and geography, geopolitical mass can be viewed as 'divided'. Divided parts of the same geopolitical entity are likely to show a desire for unification, at some point of time. East and West Germany did unite, and this could have been foreseen, although the exact circumstances of their unification could not have been forecast by rational analysis. Any long term planning on the basis of divided Germanies was bound to come unstuck at some point of time. Same could be said of the divided Korea, although the present animosity and trading of charges between the two make it difficult to repose faith in such a proposition. What constitutes a natural geopolitical entity cannot possibly be determined by purely geographical factors, any more than it can be done with reference to either demographic factors — civilization, culture, languages, religion — or history. All of these matter. The United States of America and Canada certainly constitute a geopolitical entity that has turned into a geopolitical land mass. A large number of substantive 'continuities' straddle the international border between the two countries. In these circumstances, had there been an emergence of animosity or adversarial feelings between the two, it could have led, perhaps, to a major conflict and subsequent 'unification'. It did not come about because they evolved into a collective association and agreed to share instruments of power. Their sovereignties are so well adjusted that they make one whole. On the eve of the Great War, there had been some resentment in Canada on account of American statement that Canadian union with the US was only a matter of time. Creation of a Permanent Joint Board on Defence during World War II and subsequent agreements on defence of North America created conditions in which sovereignties of both countries could reach comfortable adjustments [6]. The international border between the two, in effect, is not very different from those that separate the states from each other in the US. But anything south of the United States forms a different geopolitical entity. Yes, the demography is different. It is not merely the Rio Grande, or the Gulf of Mexico that create a separate geopolitical entity.

If there is a lack of cooperation, and ill will, across the international borders that cut across — what would otherwise be —a geopolitical entity, the result is a crop of conflicts both major and minor. Demographic continuities create insidious threats : threats that arise from shared feelings and reactions. Disturbances tend to travel through the medium of undifferentiated continuities in population. Genocide launched by President Yahya Khan in the then east wing of Pakistan resulted in refugee movement. Bengali speaking people, particularly the Hindus, were aware that they could find succour in India. Had there been a hostile population in the territory surrounding the east wing of Pakistan, the refugees would have had to make a far more difficult choice — death at the hands of the Pakistani soldiery and police, or a worse fate at the hands of those waiting to pounce on them across the international border. Way back in 1919, when there were grave disturbances in India, the Shah of Afghanistan feared that the disturbances would travel into his territory.

> " On 3 March 1919, Amir Amanulla wrote to the Viceroy of india, announcing his accession as Amir of free and independent Afghanistan...Amir Amanulla wrote to the Viceroy on India criticising British handling of the internal security situation in India in general , and at Amritsar in particular, and said that he was moving troops close to the border to ensure that virus of discontent did not seep into his country[7] ."

It is another matter that he unilaterally decided to invade India to nip the trouble in the bud. Apart from the fear of refugees, there is the danger of contagion : of the fear of the spread of disruptive ideas, anarchy and revolution. Notice the reaction of the European royalty to the rise of Napoleon, or later, that of the then European governments to the overthrow of the Tsars by the communists. Continuities in population also create opportunities for subversion on the one hand, and treating minorities like hostages, on the other hand. Years before the partition of India in 1947, even before the British had even thought of Pakistan, there was a section of the Muslim opinion, then working on the concept of Pakistan, who held that if Pakistan was totally devoid of Hindus, they would be left without any leverage to exert pressure on the government of India in the event of ill treatment of Muslim minorities in India.

> "Pakistan without its large non-Muslim minorities in the Punjab and Bengal was hardly well placed to demand safe guard for Muslim minorities in India[8]. "

That was some thinking ahead. Even so, it helps to focus attention on the problems and opportunities that continuities divided by international borders are likely to throw up. If there is a lack of near total understanding and adjustment — a la United States and Canada, or countries in the European Union — continuities may prove to be vulnerabilities which lead to erosion of strength. The fear that strength may be eroded is far more frightening than the likelihood of a direct attack or invasion because without the minimum strength — the mother substance from which power and its instruments are forged — even the possibility of countering an intrusion does not arise. Repression of Tamils in Sri Lanka caused the resentment to travel across the straits to Tamilnadu in India, and the Government of Tamilnadu or Government of India, for that matters could have remained mute spectators only to their disadvantage.

> "Sri Lanka's geographical location so near India, and the deep socio-cultural link between Sri Lankan Tamils and Indian Tamils ... compelled India to perceive critical developments in Sri Lanka not purely as an internal affair of a neighbour but as an issue which could affect India's own unity and territorial integrity if India did not respect the sentiments of its own Tamil citizens[9]."

Geographical barriers like mountain ranges and deserts create discontinuities when they do not easily yield sustenance for human habitation. If the hazards of travel across the ranges are such that life on either side appears to offer better chances and opportunities, geographical barriers tend to become divides that separate civilizational, cultural, and linguistic entities. Geopolitical barriers may not prevent invasions, as every student of Indian history well knows, but they tend to contain and demarcate. The sub-continent is as much the creation of mountain ranges as it is of the Indian Ocean. There is a debate about whether seas should be treated as a barrier or an unlimited opportunity to set out on voyages. Unlike the land which permits travel and movement along a few well defined passage-ways, seas do not restrict travel. If travel on the surface of the earth generally restricts choice to a few routes, travel on — or under the — surface of seas opens up many opportunities. But since seas do not allow habitation, shore lines create either abrupt discontinuities on the one hand, or, at the same time, allow continuities without major changes, to be transplanted across long distances. England is separated from main land Europe by the Channel, but more particularly, by the language(s). The United States and Canada basically represent transplantation of European Civilization, across thousands of miles, without major changes. Whereas land barriers create possibilities of fault-lines or lines along which discontinuities occur mainly because of compartmentalised populations on either side, seas in our own times, act as bridges or barriers depending upon, whether the separated populations represent continuities or not. North Atlantic community would not have materialized but for the close links that bind Canada and United states with Europe in general but the United Kingdom in particular. Similarly, continuities across oceans are exemplified by Australia and New Zealand. Land barriers are more prone to create discontinuities. Tibet across the Himalayas, and Afghanistan across the Hindukush do not appear to be the natural extensions of the sub-continent, but they constitute grey areas. Incidentally, the creator of [the word] Pakistan, Chaudhri Rahmat Ali, had added 'A' for Afghanistan or North West Frontier Province, possibly because he believed that Afghanistan is a part of the sub-continent.[10].

Discontinuities in demography and those due to geographical barriers or seas certainly make for stable borders. Conflicts between states separated by 'discontinuities' are also to be expected, and border claims cannot also be ruled out, but the sense of security that is born of conviction that the affected states cannot be totally annihilated or 'absorbed' in entirety prevents panic reactions in the would be victims, just as it bridles would be victors from more ambitious plans. Most of the fears of the Pakistan government spring from the notion that the cultural continuities across the international border may tempt India to annihilate Pakistan, particularly if India turns out to be more prosperous, and people in Pakistan develop doubts about separate nation-hood that has not contributed materially to the realization of their dreams. Equally, Pakistan can and does exploit cultural linkages to its own advantage.

> "Conceivably, with sufficient support and encouragement, Muslims and Sikhs could provide a Trojan horse on behalf of the Pakistani Government which could break up the Indian Union and thereby reduce the security problem for Pakistan[11]."

Although Chanakya, three centuries before Christ, had thought of the sub-continent being brought under one rule, in reality, except for short periods in history, this has not been so. History of India has been full of warring kings; those who fought against the invaders, those who made common cause with them, but most of all, those who fought against each other. No wonder India was only seen as a term describing a geographical area and nothing more, by the British. The sub-continent had never been a nation state. It simply could not have been, because, by the time the notion and idea of the nation state took root, India was already a colony. Later Indian intelligentsia lost no time in thinking of the sub-continent as a nation state. Though the undercurrent of the cultural unity of the sub-continent, on the one hand, was a matter of direct experience, the reality of numerous divisions within, on the other hand, could not be wished away. New divides of race and class had been added to religions, languages, and castes. The imperial order, and new technologies of production and communications seemed to converge when it came to destruction of old bonds forged over centuries of inter-dependence. The nation state as the ultimate repository of all loyalties, something which clearly held the promise of submerging most divides, seemed extremely attractive to those who embraced Indian nationalism as a panacea for all ills afflicting fortunes of the sub-continent. Just as they strove for the objective of home rule — which ipso facto meant a nation state covering the whole of the sub-continent — they faced the cutting edge of the divide and rule policy of the British. The British mastery over the sub-continent had been gained, inter alia, by exploiting social, religious, and political divides. Expression in political terms of a presiding collective identity, with sights on the whole of the sub-continent, was anathema to the British rulers. Neutralization of such ideas was fundamental to the continuation of the British rule in India.

The British India consisted of presidencies, provinces, and administrations, where the British ruled directly, and of a hierarchy of 'native' states over whom they ruled as a paramount power. This intricate but essentially unitary administration of British India may only in part have been due to the historical process by which the whole of the sub-continent was acquired by the British. British were always apprehensive of the possibility of Russia seeking access to the seas through the sub-continent. Mobilization of the resources of the sub-continent was absolutely essential for countering the Russian threat. India was also to be the base for ventures into the Far East. Resources of India and Indians had to be centrally controlled and managed. It was precisely because the British were not unaware either of the continuities that spanned the whole of the sub-continent, or of the divides that crisscrossed it, that they persisted with the system that created islands or discontinuities of their choice in the sub-continent. Though the sub-continent had been pulled together into an administrative unity by the British as a matter of necessity, particularly after their experience in the wake of events in 1857, they wanted fire-breaks for arresting the spread of nationalist sentiments. The British wanted a unified administration for the sub-continent, but did not look upon the possibility of the emergence of the sub-continental — Indian —identity with any degree of favour. Geographical and demographic continuities in the sub-continent created such possibilities was something to which the British were indeed not blind. At the same time the British were more than aware that divides in the subcontinent made it a practical proposition to rule over it with minimal resources.

Indian sub-continent as a geopolitical entity posed a peculiar problem to the British. In the imperial context, the sub-continent was to be used as a base for campaigns outside the sub-continent. During the Second World War, India was successfully employed as a base to fight the Japanese in Burma and South East Asia. Resources of the sub-continent were to be exploited and used — manpower and raw materials — for power projection. This called for cohesion, coherence, and synergy within the sub-continent, if serious effort was intended. This could not occur without giving rise to self identification and self esteem. And yet, the sub-continent was to be kept unaware of its own potential strength. This was a tall order. That the British succeeded at all, and they did succeed to a large extent, is no small wonder. It may be attributed to the ingenuity and vigour of the British on the one hand, and the apathy, greed, and shortsightedness of the Indians on the other. The view of the sub-continent as a geopolitical entity was partly taken in India office, and partly by the Government of India. The India office viewed the sub-continent as an entity that contributed towards the protection and promotion of imperial interests in the East. It was India office that determined the role that India played in fulfilment of the imperial design. That is where the plans took shape, perhaps in consultation with the Viceroy and the Commander-in Chief in India. The rest of the Government of India played very little part in this exercise. Indians had no access to imperial vision, not even in the closing years of the British rule. The Government of India implemented the imperial plans, even as it practised the divide and rule policies, mostly with finesse. The British administration in India, Government of India, which brought off this miracle, was unified, efficient, and responsive to the imperial purpose and needs.

Efficient governance of the whole of the sub-continent from Calcutta, Simla, or New Delhi was shown to have been a practical proposition by the British. The point was not lost on the politically conscious Indians. No matter how much they disliked or hated the British, many from the intelligentsia admired the efficiency and despatch of British governance in India, and looked upon a single unitary government for the sub-continent with considerable approval. It was considered to be a unifying force. Indian nationalism continued to remain inward looking, and mostly concerned itself with unity within, and home-rule, or political independence. All these objectives seemed to be beyond the distant horizon in any case. This was the nationalist view of the majority.

A large number of disadvantaged Indians — and there were so many of them — were led to believe that they owed their misfortunes either to their 'minority' status, or that they were victims of powerful interest groups. In either case, they had much to gain from loyalty to the British. With British support, minorities could stand up to the oppressive majorities, just as the deprived sections of the majority could get even with the upper cast or educated 'Hindoos'. Loyalty in exchange for support seemed eminently justified, because only then could they hold their own against their exploitive and rapacious compatriots. Most nationalists showed awareness of the divide and rule policies of the British, and amply resented them. They did emphasize the need for all the Indians to unite, in their fight against the British, but that was mainly to shake off the colonial masters. Nationalists wanted a unified India under a unified administration. The separatists wanted protection and guaranteed privilege disproportionate to their numbers and/or merit. Indian nationalists wanted a united effort against the British, as a hostile response to the divide and rule policy; the separatist wanted divisions to subserve their interests — as a natural consequence and by product of the British policies in India. But beyond that, the geopolitical potential of the sub-continent, and its implications remained hidden from separatists and nationalists alike. Except the rarest of the rare, none had given thought to the likely consequences of drawing international borders across a geopolitical entity. The British solution to the management of contradictions inherent in the imperial purpose — unification for power projection, and division for cost effective rule — could have but one denouement in the closing years of the British empire : fragmentation of the sub-continent, rendering it incapable of strength and power, and susceptible to internal conflict. It is highly unlikely that the British establishment, in the dying days of the empire, had the energy or vision to have actually thought this through. It was a natural culmination of policies that had developed their own momentum and inexorably, almost 'intelligently', sought to fulfil the purpose of their progenitors. It is not without irony that Governments of India and Pakistan turned to the British and the Americans to seek advice on how to cope up with the consequences of divided sub-continent.

It is readily understood by most Indians at present that it was the divide and rule policy of the British that gave a fillip to the concepts of separate electorates, and eventually to the two nation theory and partition of the sub-continent. Opposition to the British and their sympathizers manifested as a demand for a unified nation corresponding to India under British rule. As has been noted earlier that it was the British rule that brought to colonial India the idea of nation state which seemed especially tailored to suit conditions in the sub-continent, in that it had the intrinsic ability to cope up with enormous diversity in the sub-continent by invoking national loyalties. Britain as a nation state demonstrated repeatedly the concept of the total sovereignty and autonomy of the nation state. Models that are predicated upon positive cooperation among and between nation states that occupy a single geopolitical entity were not available in Europe where the concept of nation state took root, until recently. Post partition states in the sub-continent had been part of the imperial hegemony and had the experience of being on the bottom rung. They had no problems in adjusting to the new hegemonies established by the First World or the second World. They seemed to have slipped into the pattern by becoming parts of the Third World with more or less alacrity or reluctance. What was available was the balance of power achieved in the sub-continent by India and Pakistan being on the two opposite sides of the Cold War divide. This model not only ruled out evolution of relationships amongst sovereign nation states, but also created a mind-set, that became oblivious of the sub-continent as a geopolitical entity.

A geopolitical entity, when not under a unified political regime, tends to dissipate its strength and potential for generation and projection of power on account of adversarial relationships which unavoidably develop among constituent political units. An equilibrium derived from balance of power, for so long as it lasts, may prevent violent eruptions unless it also supports and holds in place a regional order that not only permits but even encourages cooperation. But experience in the sub-continent since at least the tenth century indicated that by far and large, lack of a unified political regime did lead to violence and dissipation, so much so that in Indian consciousness geopolitical entity — something that actually exists irrespective of the nature and number of the political units occupying the land mass — does not seem to have figured.

Most Indians can think of a united and unitary sub-continent, with a unified administration — something on the lines of what existed under the British rule — as the ideal. This is not at all surprising because it was nationalism, which had it roots firmly embedded in fight against the British rule, that brought to Indians hopes of ending feuds in the sub-continent. Ever since, sub-nationalism is equated with a dissipated sub-continent in minds of a large majority of Indians ; in many minds, sub-nationalism is scarcely differentiated from treason. It is only now that there are some signs of awareness that fragmentation of the sub-continent into warring factions might have been due, at least partly, to the inability of the leaders in the sub-continent to work out or devise a political structure that could 'contain' the sub-continent, and build it into a geopolitical entity.

> "Why was India divided? The simple answer is that the Hindus, as represented by the Congress, and Muslims, as represented by the League, could not agree upon a constitutional framework for a united India.
>
> "The land, which had been one unit for more than a thousand years with the two communities living and working together and contributing richly to its composite culture, was divided ; it was the most tragic blow, struck at its very heart. It happened because, as Dr. Ramohan Ruia, pointed out, 'a tired and an ageing leadership, hungry for power', surrendered to the subtle intrigues of Mountbatten[12]."
>
> " The choice with which Jinnah was presented with in the end by the Congress and the British was either an undivided India without any guarantee of the Muslim share of power at the all-India centre or a sovereign Pakistan carved out of Muslim-majority districts of the Punjab and Bengal. Had Jinnah been more sure of his following in the Muslim provinces he might conceivably have decided to work the mission's plan for an all-India federal structure[13]. "

These two views, appearing on the opposite sides of the divide, are an indication that a realistic view of the sub-continent as a geopolitical entity may yet emerge.

Creation of Pakistan was seen as a victory of the British and the sub-nationalism — two nation theory — that they supported. This was the perception not only of the common man, but also of national leadership in India. As against this, the leadership in Pakistan was equally jubilant that Muslims in India had secured a nation state for themselves not because of Hindu goodwill, but in face of heavy odds. Indians in the sub-continent rued the partition because a 'nation-state' had been divided, and creators of Pakistan were elated because they had effectively eliminated the possibility of, what was in their perception, domination by the majority. Pakistanis had succeeded in isolating themselves from the rest of the sub-continent ; or they, at least, thought so. If Indians, in their minds, hankered after a united India — that is splicing together of threads broken by the partition into a single nation state — most Pakistanis thought of establishing new continuities with the Islamic world. Indians tried to come to terms with their newly acquired political identity in secular and socialistic terms, while Pakistanis tried to establish their Islamic identity in contradistinction with India. If Indian nationalism, as a carry over of pre-partition days, did not quite overlook the sub-continent, Pakistani nationalism lost no time in seeking support from outside the sub-continent so that the newly formed Pakistan had the best chance to prevail against India. Both seem to have given a short shrift to the geopolitical entity that is the sub-continent.

All the three major conflicts that India faced after independence in 1947, and several minor ones since then, seem to have a lot to do with perceptions — or misperceptions —about demographic and geographical continuities that actually exist in the sub-continent, because of which it is a geopolitical entity, something which cannot be wished away.

Religious continuities between Muslim majority areas of Jammu and Kashmir in general, and Kashmir Valley in particular, with the adjoining territory of Pakistan created the possibility of the merger of the state with Pakistan in Pakistani mind. They concluded that it was a natural corollary to the partition of the country notwithstanding the legally valid instrument of accession signed by the Maharaja of Jammu and Kashmir in favour of India. What was a very good argument against India proved to be embarrassing to Pakistan when the self same continuities were invoked by the supporters of the Pakhtoon movement which sought to integrate Pakhtoon speaking areas into an independent political unit, and laid claims on Pak territory. Pakistan then had to take recourse to the arguments advanced by the British in support of the 'Durand Line' which essentially supports the view that the sub-continent does not extend beyond that line, irrespective of the spill over of tribes on both the sides of the border.

> "Lord Curzon came out as Viceroy in 1899...One of his first official acts was to take up the question, which the Frontier campaigns of 1897-98 had revived, of separating the North-West Frontier districts and the adjoining tribal areas up to the Durand line(fixed in Kabul in 1894 between Sir Mortimer Durand, Foreign Secretary, and the Amir Abdur Rahman, to delimit the British and Afghan spheres of influence) from the control of the Punjab Government[22]."

The understanding was clear enough; the sub-continent did not extend much beyond the Durand Line, and that there was a need to prevent Afghan turmoil from seeping into it.

Baluch sub-nationalism is also dealt with by Pakistan by using arguments which emphasize that continuities within Pakistan are stronger than those which extend outwards. It is undoubtedly easier for Pakistan to retain Baluchistan than for Iran or Afghanistan to absorb it. One or more continuities, or one or more dimensions of those continuities — since all continuities have multiple dimensions — dominate the collective consciousness on the basis of which the urges and movements for unification gather momentum. Continuities created by geography, civilization, culture, language, religion, and history do not either materialize or vanish into the thin air in a jiffy. But prevailing moods and the leadership — which feed upon each other — decide the dominant theme. Splintering of Bangladesh from Pakistan was, or should have been, a strong reminder to people in India and Pakistan that linguistic and sub-cultural affinities can turn out to be as strong as religious affinities, if not stronger. Before the partition of the sub-continent became a reality, there was just a beginning of a movement for a united Bengal. Geopolitics is based on an assessment of continuities — and discontinuities — which are likely to express themselves in the contemporary political structures and idiom.

Emergence of the sub-continent as a geopolitical mass is likely to be of great concern to China for two reasons: firstly, China has always regarded itself as a geopolitical mass with a unified political system — the middle kingdom — which has a civilising mission, and therefore it must have a capacity to project superior power in comparison with its competitors ; and secondly, the close proximity and common border it has with the sub-continent makes it obligatory for China to take note and initiate action to neutralize the power potential of the neighbour with whom some kind of rivalry, at some point of time, would be unavoidable. Chinese resented Indian efforts to secure the leadership of the newly liberated colonies and the Afro-Asian bloc. Not only did they bring down India a peg or two in 1962 border conflict, but since then, took active steps to befriend, support, and arm Pakistan even when Pakistan was firmly in the US camp. Chinese support of Pakistan did not await developments in the 70s, but started as early as 1965. Their friendship with Pakistan undoubtedly had an anti-India angle, but perhaps it was not restricted only to that. Decidedly after the liberation of Bangladesh, they seemed to have pulled all the stops in helping Pakistan. They have supported Pak nuclear and missile programmes so that it remains confident of its deterrence capability vis a vis India. General Raghavan quotes CIA Director J. Woolsey from his testimony to the Senate Government Affairs Committee :

> "China has consistently regarded a nuclear armed Pakistan as a crucial ally and a counterweight to India[15]. "

> "This strategy of encircling India is not being orchestrated by Washington, but Beijing. The Americans do not give a damn because they have decided to ally with Germany in Europe and China in Asia.China is militarily powerful, has big market and rivalries with Japan and Russia, the same countries the US perceives as problems in the future. China sees India as a nuisance which needs restraining through Pakistan. The latter has little autonomy and will do what its sponsors require...India should deal with the dog owner and not the dog[16]."

Clearly, the Chinese policy is intended to encourage Pakistani truculence and hard attitude against India. Pakistan's nuclear capability is an insurance that China has taken out against the realization of the sub-continental geopolitical potential which can indeed create problems for China. Should the sub-continent develop such a potential it will be sought out by the United States, Russia, Japan, and several East Asian countries as a countervailing mass against the Chinese. Even the United States, when it saw an opening into India in the wake of the Chinese aggression, went all out to help India and even restrained Pakistan from taking advantage of India's difficulties. The possibility of the whole of the sub-continent acting in unison is attractive to the United States, provided it does not act at cross purpose to its own policies. Was the sub-continent, as a geopolitical entity, in the reckoning of the United States, when it aided India in 1963, is a difficult question to answer. Perhaps, the aid signified no more than the desire to add one more nation to the ring that was to contain communism. It would appear that the sub-continent as a geopolitical entity has started to appeal to the policy makers in the United States in the second half of 1990s. United States have not always encouraged Pakistan not to fight with India ; perhaps, they have indulged Pakistan, in recognition of the services rendered, and given it a long rope, particularly when it became the front-line state. Now in the post Cold-War world, geopolitical interests of the United States and India may converge. It may actually look upon the emergence of the sub-continent as a geopolitical mass with a degree of favour.

Geopolitical calculus could have and should have made India aware that try as it might — even by going to the extent of championing the cause of Peoples Republic of China for the membership of the United Nations, and accepting its suzerainty over Tibet without demurring — it cannot avoid rivalry with China. Rivalry is unavoidable precisely because India and China are two huge geopolitical entities with a common border. As and when they develop power projection capability they must ineluctably bring within their reach and range huge tracts of each other's territories. When they choose to extend trade or influence, their areas of interest must overlap. Similarity in the size of population must make them both prime producers of labour intensive goods. They may both look for more land to accommodate their burgeoning populations. Land may not be a very attractive prize to developed countries because their productivity and prosperity is not directly linked to per capita availability of land. But in so far as China and India are concerned, that cannot be the case. Their actual requirements of lands will be empirically established only when their growing populations stabilize and they attain a reasonable self sufficiency in food and water. Till that happens a zero-sum solution to the problem may appeal to one side or the other. China is today admittedly in the league of great powers, but that need not make India necessarily believe that China will deem it infra dig to compete with India. If India does not find it inappropriate to compete with much smaller Pakistan, it is highly unlikely that China will ignore India, even in its depleted state. China does take Indian potential seriously, if not the present prowess. It abundantly exploits Indo-Pak rivalry as a part of the answer to the geopolitical problem, and has taken steps to sharpen it. India, on its part, at one point of time, tried out appeasement as a strategy, but perhaps not coherently or cogently enough. India received no prize in exchange for acceding to Chinese claims on Tibet, nor did it secure any tangible benefit for championing Chinese cause at the international fora. When the crisis came, perhaps it was the opportunity of balancing the geopolitical mass of India against China that kindled the interest of the United States to start with, and subsequently that of the Soviet Union. In the post Cold War era, the United States and Russia both are not unmindful of the importance of India as countervailing mass to China.

The difference in capability and power of Pakistan and India will grow with time, other things remaining the same, in favour of India. In another fifteen years Pakistan will be left further behind by India. Status quo favours India. The opposite is true in respect of India-China in-equation. In years to come, China is likely to further improve upon differences which are already in its favour. The comparison of power quotients creates a frame of analysis in which India-Pakistan and China-India relationships can be brought on the same plane and measured on the same scale. If India outranks Pakistan, China outranks India. What is noted less often is that China outranks Pakistan with even greater margin, and this in itself may be sufficient for Pakistan to ensure that their relationships remain free of rivalry or hostility. In no circumstances can Pakistan afford to annoy China. It is another matter than Chinese support to Pakistan, in holding its own against India, gives added incentive to Pakistan to court the Chinese. It is quite likely that at least some of the oil and gas out of the Central Asian Republics may flow through Afghanistan and Pakistan. China could get access to these through good offices of Pakistan. Pakistan also has a unique access into the Islamic world, many divides of which it straddles.

The sub-continent as a geopolitical entity, does not admit of a traditional balance of power : all of the other nations together, including Pakistan, cannot overcome India. It could well be a planetary structure with the central mass being provided by India, with co-existence as the avowed goal. Howsoever it might please India, such an arrangement leaves others dissatisfied and distrustful. A structured hegemony in the sub-continent, with India as the hegemon, is what Pakistan resents the most. Pakistan is willing to see itself as an extension of the Middle-East, with a view to drawing upon the pan-Islamic sentiment and support, so that it could deal with India on equal terms. Pakistan befriended the US and

China for the same purpose. During Cold-War, this approach worked up to a point. But now a search must begin to create a new political architecture for the sub-continent in which all its nations are truly equal for certain stated purposes, and in common interest. This is difficult to bring about particularly because almost fifty years have been spent by India and Pakistan in confrontation.

It is obvious that in the emerging multi-polar world, the US, Russia, China, Japan, and Europe are going to be the major players. They need to create or maintain a balance of power which takes into account the numerous variables, and a few certainties : militarily, the US will remain the most powerful nation, but economically, China may well forge ahead. Russia may bound back; it still has nuclear weapons, and a great reservoir of resources, and a matching population. Japan may want to create a power balance which takes into account the US tilt towards China. Europe will compete with the US, while making the US bear most of its security costs. And yet, in spite of numerous complexities, comparatively simple policy options have to be worked out. For want of such options, national security doctrine cannot emerge.

> "America's permanent interests, he [Kissinger] felt, was in preventing hegemony in Asia of any power and the US would react to attempts by any country to dominate Asia, including China. The United States needs China to maintain a balance of power among Asian countries, including India, according to former US Secretary of State Henry Kissinger[17]."

> "The Americans and the Japanese are here because India offers the geopolitical and commercial possibilities.

> "In the years to come America's relations with china and Russia, will determine its relations with India. It is an unspoken fact that in the next fifteen years — the time span which the Pentagon is using for projections — the United States see China as its main adversary in Asia, Russia in Europe[18].'

Even if one were to disregard over-simplification, it cannot be denied that numerous options are being considered by those aspiring to be or wanting to remain great powers. In all of these, the sub-continent would have a place provided it develops its full geopolitical potential. As and when Pakistan feels convinced that the value of its geopolitical assets — location in relation to the Islamic world, China, and Russia, oil rich Central Asian Republics (CARs), access into the whole of the Muslim world, irrespective of divides in it, and so on — will only go up when it desists from confronting India, a change in attitudes will come about. India, equally, will benefit if a large chunk of its power projection potential is not set back by Pakistan. Being the largest member of the sub-continent, it may benefit the most by re-establishing the economic zone in the sub-continent. Perhaps, there is a need to bring about this realization. It is only after the end of the Cold War, that the US have perhaps considered the possibility of India as a player in working out balances in Asia. Views expressed by one of the former Chiefs of the Pakistan Army give some idea of perceptions of the elites of Pakistan in this regard. It is obvious that major changes in attitudes are visible all around, and India must now make good use of this opportunity.

> "It is customary that whenever United States desires to implement any strategic decision in the South Asian region, a number of think tank scholars are commissioned to provide a trailer to the strategic move.
>
> "In 1992, United States scholar Selig Harrison was the speaker at a colloquium on 'United States and South-Asia after the Cold War: Implications and Reflections', organized by Foundation for Research on International Environment, National Development and Security.) His statements are quoted to reveal as to what is in the offing in the 'held Kashmir' :
>
> "India as the bigger state, having sustainable linkages with the United States, ought to have the primary responsibility with respect to the subcontinent. This should neither be

> ignored nor forgotten in any calculations or combinations. The status quo has therefore to be in her favour... Pakistan being the lesser member with loosening ties with United States, should adjust herself in the larger context. In her secondary role, as subservient to the regional frame, she must shorten her activities and curtail her aspirations[19]...".

This discussion about the geopolitics of the sub-continent would be incomplete without reference to its location on the rim of the Indian Ocean. Sea lanes carrying oil from the Gulf will always have the greatest significance for most countries of the world. So much depends on uninterrupted supply of energy. This is an area of total convergence of interest for the United States and the sub-continent.

The US presence in the Indian Ocean is significant. Its two operational commands — the Central and the Pacific — hold a sway over the Indian Ocean now that the Soviet Union has opted out, at least for the time being. The sub-continent has an inherent capacity to be a major player in the region. India and Pakistan can actively cooperate with the United States and her allies in maintaining uninterrupted flow of oil, that is in policing the Indian Ocean. As the sub-continent turns into a prosperous economic-zone, the needs of secure trade would also call for the same approach.

India cannot, ever, remain out of Chinese reckoning and attention because of its sheer size, and location ; rivalry between the two is unavoidable, although this rivalry need not always manifest as confrontation. It is obvious that China has taken steps to encircle India and deepen the divide in the sub-continent. This is clearly aimed at preempting the possibility of India's emergence as a great power, and improving upon its own chances of a substantive victory, should a conflict take place. Indo-Pakistani rivalry is an outcome of colonial past. There is a scope for creating a political identity of the sub-continent and adjusting all the nations including Pakistan within that structure so that the geopolitical potential of the sub-continent is realized to everyone's advantage. India is hobbled by Pakistani rivalry, and Pakistan is haemorrhaging because of her spending on the armed forces. SAARC should ultimately assist in this direction. The sub-continent is a civilizational and cultural unity, and it ought to conduct its affairs accordingly, to register a meaningful say in the world order.

Pakistan split open in 1971, because it showed insensitivity to civilizational and cultural continuities in the sub-continent. Relationships and bonds between the two wings of Pakistan were predicated upon a sub-continental identity. Had these continuities not existed in pre-partition days, there would indeed have been no possibility of a country with two geographically unconnected wings. If Pakistan shows incomprehension of this reality, it may split again, under the burden of its expenditure on armed forces. In the face of the implacable hostility of Pakistan, India may have to offer unilateral 'no-war' guarantees to Sindh and Baluchistan, so that the jingoistic ruling elite of Pakistan are isolated. Realization may then come that an architecture of identities in the sub-continent will gradually, but inexorably, emerge. It would be on the basis of equitably protecting and promoting interests of all the collective identities of the sub-continent. Pakistan may yet draw the right lessons from the secession of its eastern wing, and seek accommodation within such architecture, on terms it would find advantageous. Should it not adjust to emerging reality, its regions might.

Survival of over-populated and under-nourished countries of the sub-continent, with any kind of self respect or honour, in the emerging world order will be that much more difficult unless they take note of the unifying factors in the sub-continent and cooperate.

NOTES

1.Hamish MacRae,' The World in 2020 ', Harper Collins, London, 1994, (p.p.253-255).

2.Francis Pike, 'Mandate from heaven : China will wear the crown', Asian Age, Bombay, 22 July,1997. By arrangement with Spectator.

3.ibid.

4.MacRae, op. cit., (p.225).

5.Barry Buzan,'People, States & Fear', TransAsia Publishers, New Delhi,1983, (p.106).

6.Encyclopedia Britannica, Volume 4, 1964, (p.p. 744-745).

7.Edgar O'Ballance. Afghan Wars 1839-1992. Brassey's, London,1992.(pp.54-55).

86.Ayesha Jalal.The State of Martial Rule', Cambridge University Press, 1990, (p.23).

9.J.N. Dixit, 'Assignment Colombo', Konark Publishers pvt ltd., 1998, (p. 17).

10.Jalal, op.cit., (p. 13).

11.Chris Smith, India's Adhoc Arsenal, Direction or Drift in Defence Policy? SIPRI,Oxford University Press, New York, 1994, Pakistan, (p.29).

12.Rafiq Zakaria,'The price of partition', Indian Express, Pune, 14 August, 1997.

13.Jalal, op. cit., (p. 22).

14.Michael O' Dwyer, 'India As I Knew It - 1885-1925', Mittal Publications, 1988 [originally published around 1930], (p.106).

15.Raghavan, R. V. Lt Gen, 'India's Need for Strategic Balance',Delhi Policy Group, Delhi.

16.Gautam Sen, writing on China in Indian Express, Pune, 2 November, 1996.

17.Henry Kissinger, 'US needs China for balance of power', Indian Express, Pune, 4 November, 1997, quoting an article by Kissinger in Newsweek.

18.Rajan Gupta,'Look West through the East',Indian Express, Pune, 22 August,1997.

19.Gen (Retd) Mirza Aslam Beg,'Trilateral zone', Asian Age, Bombay, 14 October,1997. By arrangement with the Dawn. Beg is a former Chief of the Pak Army.

10

New World Order and Emerging Conflict

The architects of the new world order (NWO) have uniformly concentrated on nation states developing international institutions, conventions, agreements, and treaties that would allow better and improved inter-course among nations with enhanced security for all law abiding nations, and punishment for the guilty. There is a desire to create a common corpus of universal values which nation states will subscribe to and uphold in the interest of common security, progress and prosperity, with the onus of doing so resting more firmly on those who have the competence, authority, and power to do so. Referring to President Wilson in 1918, Presidents Roosevelt and Truman towards the end of World War II, and later, to speeches of Presidents Bush and Clinton, Kissinger comments that -

> " for the third time in this century, America thus proclaimed its intention to build a new world order by applying its domestic values to the world at large[1]."

There are others who are of the view that the economic factors — productivity, profits, investment opportunities, prosperity, distribution of wealth, consumer satisfaction, and so on — will make nation states, less and less relevant. Other groups and interests will contribute to the emergence of the NWO.

> "What is happening is the shift from a global system based on nations to a three tier system based on states...Soon to be included in the newest, third tier of the system, are

regional 'technopoles'...areas like Orange County, California; Osaka, Japan;the Lyon region of France [They] will acquire the predominant status..... The real decision-making power of the future wil be transnational companies in alliance with city-regional governments[2]...."

Similar views are also expressed by Ohmae:

> " The old world has fallen apart. The modern nation state — the artifact of the 18th and 19th centuries — has begun to crumble. Nation states have lost their role as meaningful units of participation in the global economy of today's borderless world. They have become remarkably inefficient engines of wealth distribution[3]."

Amongst the main objections to the continuation of the nation states as the principal players and determinants of the world order is that many of them do not constitute production and market oriented units by themselves, and much worse, they come in way of formation of economically viable regional blocks from which all concerned have a chance to benefit.

> "In a borderless world, there are the natural economic zones. These region states may or may not fall within the borders of a particular nation. It really does not matter... Nation states do, of course, have a vital interest in propagating and enforcing the values of inclusiveness that hold their societies together. But it is the economic engine of region states that ties this abstract concept to very tangible pocket books[4]. "

Thus there are two dominant views of and about the emerging world order : the first school would have us believe that the world order will be derived from relations among nation states, as it has always been ; the second school rejects this world view, and asserts that the main or principal inter-actors would be the economic giants, mostly multi-national corporations (MNCs), who will make boundaries between nation states less and less relevant, and serve the purpose of the consumer better than ever before. The first view-point focuses on nation state identities and security ; the second, on improved living conditions and pursuit of happiness. Nation states are a reality and these international persons seem to determine not only issues of war and peace, but also those of international trade and commerce. But we are also no less aware, that international investments and trade, are in the hands of private parties and individuals — and no so much in the domain of the governments, now that the centrally controlled states of the socialist bloc have taken a beating. MNCs are on the scene, they build plants in a number of countries, and seem to deal with governments on very nearly equal terms. Does the rise of economic zones and MNCs herald the decline of the nation state is a question that needs to be answered. And beyond that, the impact that such development would have on nation states that populate the world, deserves attention.

Perhaps there is no zero-sum model in which the rise of economic players and dominance of the economic order must necessarily subsume the political system of which nation states are the main building blocks. Nation states are identity oriented, with firmly defined peripheries; they seek perpetuation of their collective beings and values that they hold dear, for which purpose they invest as individuals and collectively. That does not mean that nation states abjure prosperity. Creation of empires and exploitation of colonies are ample testimony to the desire to proposer that nations have. In fact, pursuit of national interests is a prime concern of all nations : some wish to exploit; others wish to avoid being victims of exploitation. The architecture of collective identities which fulfils the purpose, minimally of survival, and ideally of perpetuation on acceptable terms, cannot outstrip the space created by presiding loyalty. Individuals who form or contribute to collective identities, and collective identities themselves, make adjustments and accept the primacy of collective endeavour for so long as they trust that the presiding loyalty will cause the constituents to subsume individual and collective pursuits and preferences whenever survival and/or perpetuation are at stake. The political space that owes its existence to the presiding loyalty cannot endure for long in a situation in which the desire to share equitably is totally absent; and particularly so, when a fair proportion of individuals and constituents have to make do with insufferably small portions of prizes secured with collective effort. The largest such architecture of collective identities which is capable of enduring and surviving is nation state. The size of architecture of collective associations, whether formed by individuals, or collective identities, or associations, which has prosperity of constituents as its moving spirit, is not limited by any considerations of loyalty. Expediency, pragmatism, and chances of good gains, at least when the going is good, is all that matters. Constituents of collective associations are there to make gains for themselves.

Questions are being raised at present about the relevance of the nation state to the international systems on the one hand; and to the individual, and to the most basic collective identities that individuals make up, family upwards, on the other hand. Various incompatibilities and contradictions are pointed out between the security of the individual and the security of the nation state. They are real enough : a repressive state may pose a greater threat to the individual — from whom it draws sustenance — than an external threat. An impression is often formed that, if the state boundaries are eliminated, the individual would have a better chance of survival and betterment both.

Much of the confusion may get eliminated if MNCs are recognized as collective associations. They are there in business for so long as it is profitable. Nothing binds them to the people or lands from which they earn their profits except considerations of productivity and gains. MNCs by themselves have no desire to perpetuate themselves; they are there to perpetuate profits and other gains of their chief executives, directors, share holders, and employees. The organization can be wound up when necessary. New companies can be formed, new factories can be raised, and new markets can be found. Yesterdays employees and customers can be dumped, no sooner than they cease to contributes to quick and substantial returns on investments. There are no stakes in the fortunes or well-being of former employees, and even less in continuation of ventures which no longer pay. Concern is with profitability, and not with perpetuation of a collective identity. There may be no sense of loss associated with such a closure. They are an instrument. MNCs are not predicated upon enduring collective consciousness, and therefore, they do not constitute a collective identity. They cannot and will not compete with the nation state as an enduring alternative. Yes, the controllers and real owners of the MNCs have an identity, it resides in one or more nations, and they will invest for the future in the people and institutions of their kind, located very obviously, in the first world.

It is idle to pretend that there is a movement away from the nation state or that economic space and players will replace political space and political leadership. Collective identities themselves form larger collective identities — for security — , and collective associations for prosperity. The North Atlantic Treaty Organization (NATO) may be interpreted as a collective identity within the 'solidarity', or space created by loyalty to the cause of collective defence. NATO relies on a substantial and disproportionate burden being carried by the USA in financial terms in the interest of the Alliance. But the USA, as a constituent member of the G-7 club, which is an association, is not willing to concede advantage to other constituents. Within the nations, individuals and corporations merge and collaborate. This ability to form collective identities and associations is major feature of NWO. What is happening, perhaps, is that the political leadership is making greater room for economic activity because 'e' component of power can be employed in our times far more advantageously that 'c' component : relationships can be as short lived as desired; there is no need to occupy high moral or ethical ground, as would be the case if an armed aggression were to be concluded on an advantageous note; there is no commitment to the disadvantaged.

World Order is to be construed primarily as an agreement or understanding amongst nations about norms and bounds governing power projection — by nations — in pursuit of their interests. It conforms to the resultant of potential and operative powers, or in other words, it reflects the power distribution amongst nations who have the capability to script the world order, and what can be done to support it. World order is meant to facilitate power-projection : it is sculpting of terrain and shaping of space to guide, regulate, and control application of power so that the advantage enjoyed is in proportion to the 'power-index' of the nations. World order incorporates biases and preferences of the script-writers.

> "The idea of using air strikes originated in the White House well before the present occupant was born. It was in May, 1942, at a dinner given by President Franklin D. Roosevelt in honour of Vyacheslav Molotov, foreign minister of the Soviet Union. Roosevelt told his guest that " United States, Russia, England, and possibly China should police the world and enforce disarmament by inspection after the War ". He went on to point out that as small nations were incapable of defending themselves against powerful aggressors, " they might just as well remain unarmed after the war." If any of them were to try to violate the prohibition against the armament, " the police in power could then threaten to quarantine the offending state, and if that did not work, to bomb some part of it." Two days later, Molotov was able to tell the President that Stalin fully approved of the proposal. That was how the United Nation's security system was born. Roosevelt's Four Policemen, later joined by France as the fifth, put themselves in charge of international peace and security, empowered themselves to order economic sanctions, or "take such action by air sea or land forces as deemed necessary to maintain or restore international peace and security[5]."

Creation of a world order has been an oft stated dream of the USA. After a highly successful and beneficial intervention in the First World War, the USA started showing a marked inclination to create a secure world in which the US values held the sway, and obviously, the guiding hand was that of the US. For a brief while, at the end of the Second World War, the USA seemed to have almost arrived there: with the exception of the USA, the victors and vanquished alike were at the end of the tether, the US had the monopoly of the atomic bomb, and a gargantuan industry almost untouched by the ravages of the war. But the Cold War intervened, and the dream seemed to recede, only to revive when the USA emerged victorious at the head of the multi national force. President Bush spoke of NWO, now that the USA had really emerged as the only super-power. The essence of NWO in the US eyes, is the US leadership of the world. The isolationist US is definitely out. It is the super power that wishes to engage the whole world, as a right and as a duty. The picture has been sketched vividly, with details added by President's advisors. Some of the essential US foreign policy objectives, as enunciated by the US Secretary of State in her statement to the US Senate's Foreign Relations Committee on January 8, 1997 are as follows:-

> "...we must be the authors of the history of our age....our armed forces must remain the best-led, best-trained, best-equipped and most respected in the world...force, and the credible possibility of its use, are essential to defend out vital interests and to keep America safe.. .. framework for American leadership must include measures to control the threats posed by weapons of mass destruction and terror; to maintain America as the hub of an expanding global economy; ..At-the centre of that framework, however, are our key alliances and relationships....It is a central lesson of this century that America must remain a European power. We have an interest in European democracy, because it was the triumph of freedom there that ended the Cold War. We have an interest in European prosperity, because our own prosperity depends on having partners that are open to our exports, investment and ideas. NATO is a linchpin of stability NATO cannot and should not preserve the old iron curtain..What NATO must and will do is keep open the door to membership to every European nation that can shoulder alliance responsibilities and contribute to its goals.. while building partnership with all of Europe's democracies....We must and will remain a pacific power..to maintain the strength of our core alliances while successfully managing our multi-

faceted relationship with China.[We] have many interests in common [with China], and have worked together on issues including the Korean peninsula, crime, the global environment and nuclear testing..there should be no doubt, however, about the importance of this relationship, and about the need to pursue a strategy aimed at Chinese integration, and not isolation..chemical weapons ban will soon be in effect.....Arms control and nonproliferation are closely linked to our policies toward rogue states. We have a major interest in preventing weapons of mass destructing from being obtained by regimes with a proven disrespect for the rule of law....The primary obligation of the United States is to its own citizens. We are not a charity or fire department. We will defend firmly our own vital interests...the United States has been steadfast in supporting the peacemakers over the bomb throwers in historically troubled areas of the globe. Our goal has been to build an environment in which threats to our security and that of our allies are diminished, and likelihood of American forces being sent into combat are reduced..Competition for the world's markets is fierce..In the years ahead, we must continue shaping a global economic system that works for America..We will thrive in any true competition..... We will work with others to defeat the forces of international crime and to put those who traffic in drugs permanently out of business.. We will pursue hard line against international terror, insisting on the principle that sponsoring, sheltering or subsidizing terrorists cannot be rationalized; it is wrong; and those guilty should not be appeased, but isolated and punished....We will maintain our strong backing for the international war crimes tribunal ..American Constitution remains the most revolutionary and inspiring source of change in the world."

The above statement while sketching the thrust-lines of the US foreign policy gives the world clearly to understand that the prosperity and ascendancy of the US are the core ideas, and it is for the promotion of these ideas that NWO ought to evolve. Of course, partners in prosperity have equal stakes. It is easy to read 'G-7' plus for partners in prosperity.

NWO has to deal with a very large number of nations, which though theoretically equal and sovereign, in reality are very different from each other. In the days of the Cold-War they used to be divided into three worlds on the basis of camps they belonged, or did not belong to. Now they are divided into industrialized, newly industrialized, and least industrialized countries, or on the basis of development. World Development report classifies them on the basis of the size of their economies. The differences are stark when expressed in these terms. They are equally stark when the strength and maturity is compared, although scales for measuring these abstract qualities are difficult to construct. Barry Buzan notes that

> "The universalisation of the state system has extended the moderately mature norms of the older, stronger part of the system to cover the new members, many of these new members are so weak as states that they cannot adequately fulfil their role in such a relatively advanced system[6]. "

The fib of equality amongst nations has to be kept up where and when convenient. And this gives rise to some problems. Not that they have not been tackled. The General Assembly of the United Nations is not the seat of authority that it would have been, were the equality of nations a reality. There would have been no advocacy of non-proliferation while defending the necessity of the strategic weapons for the US and other nuclear weapons states. It is better to acknowledge and take into account the inequality among nations. Debating points do not alter the reality.

A highly stratified structure with the industrialised nations at the top does seem inevitable at least during the first quarter of the twenty-first century. In all probability, the 'G-7 plus' — Group of seven industrialised nations, viz USA, Canada, Japan, UK, Germany, France, and Italy, plus Russia seeking entry into the Group as a full-fledged member — will occupy the heights because not only are they the world's strongest nations, but their sources of strength are in fact, and they collectively command a majority of instruments of power, inter alia, nuclear weapons with global reach. They have already formed an 'association' for collective prosperity, that is, individual nations from G-7 will contribute to the collective entity for so long as there is a guarantee of at least proportionate share of prizes, with a further possibility of making better than proportionate gains. Strong national identities of G-7 plus nations are not being subsumed in the process. G-7 plus association may prove in the long run to have been one of the instruments for gathering of national strength and eventual assertion of national or regional identities. G-7 plus represents a limited coincidence of interests which indicates that there are prizes which they seek collectively, and for this purpose, it is an exclusive club. Members have certainly not abjured competition amongst themselves, but even so, they find cooperation provident in certain areas. It is not so much the supra-national interests that bring them together but, perhaps, the similarity in their sources of strengths, power, and vulnerabilities, as also the prizes that they seek. Theoretically, this kind of situation could create possibilities for conflict or cooperation in equal measure: desire to acquire precious metals for the capital formulation, raw materials for the establised factories, and markets for the finished goods gave rise to colonial wars spread over three continents, and ultimately the Great War itself. World War II was perhaps the unfinished business left over from the Great War, that was merely hastened by an inherently faulty treaty. The relative stability of the Cold War era endured in spite of a large similarity in prizes that the First and the Second World sought, because they not only possessed the main instruments of coercive power in comparable measure but also shared many of their vulnerabilities. Admittedly, the sources of strength were somewhat dissimilar, and consequently, the influence and the economic power that the First World could bring to bear ultimately prevailed in exploiting the vulnerabilities of the Second. It is only in the post Cold War era that there has been an effort to reconcile the similarity in ends and means into an understanding verging on cooperation. The main concerns of the industrialised nations are not very different:

the boom and bust cycles are to be avoided in favour of steady growth in the industrialised countries, new opportunities for productive investment of capital are to be found wherever opportunities can be created; inflation is to be held in check even if it creates some unemployment; productivity is to be the main instrument for earning profits even if it reduces steady jobs; cheapest labour and raw materials must be used in production no matter where they are located so that production costs do not eat into profits ; new and higher technology must be developed at a pace that allows transferring of the dated versions along with rights for licenced production, but for which exploitation of invested capital at an accelerated pace would not be possible. A status quo in standard of living — level of consumption, education and health care, life styles and leisure related activity — must at least be maintained, if not improved upon. Their life styles are rooted in open society, primacy of individual's freedom to choose, high rates of consumption, insistence on short term contractual arrangements in preference to lasting or long term commitments so that changes can be rung in without risks or loss, abiding faith in winner-take-all principle, ability to adjust to the demands of complex organizational structures, and unerring efficiency that contributes to making individuals so highly competitive that they cannot remain satisfied except when riding a rising prosperity curve. These lifestyles and philosophy have contributed to their development and prosperity, but they also render them particularly vulnerable to terrorism and drugs, on the one hand, and susceptible to quick disenchantment, in times of stress, with leadership, conventional wisdom and values, on the other. Slowing down of growth, or drop in improvement in standard of living are likely to be construed, in the industrialised nations, as major security threats that need to be tackle on a war footing. An unbridled competition amongst the industrialised nations will almost certainly have an adverse impact on all, and may be viewed by respective populations with disfavour. A unipolar, stratified world makes the avoidance of this risk a real possibility. A condominium arrangement at the top may well keep the risks at manageable levels provided there is an agreement on sharing and wielding of power, and creation of an international order that supports 'security' of G-7 plus, that is, facilitates pursuit of interests by members of this group, if need be by obviating or resolving internal contradictions. An emerging or potential power centre that is amenable to the rules and writs of G-7 may be gradually incorporated — that is how Russia seems to be creeping into the charmed circle — , or carefully watched, if it appears to be a maverick like China so that it does not threaten NWO. The Strategic Deterrence of the United States, and its willingness to foot a large bill for the security of Western Europe have allowed Western Europe to invest productively and grow in spite of the Soviet menace. The self same factors allow the United States to dominate the G-7 on the basis of Russian fear on the one hand, and to lead them collectively to cooperate with Russia on her own terms, on the other. The so called multipolar world, perhaps, is no more than a condominium arrangement, principally aimed at political status quo for G-7, with the United States at the top. One of the principle concerns is to obviate reemergence of bipolarity. G-7 plus account for a vast majority of strategic nuclear weapons with the exception of those in possession of China, and constitute the real mass of political and economic power. They are the determinants of the NWO. If Russia eventually joins the prosperous North, it may also occupy a place of honour at the table of G-7 headed by the United States. The geopolitical wisdom of keeping the two giant Asian landmasses separate will have been vindicated. Threat to this design may come principally from China. China has the potential to create another 'polarity', if it can make common cause with Russia, and/or India. Such an eventuality could threaten the unipolar world with the possibility not only of creating a countervailing power centre, but also of accessing the markets of the 'deprived South'. So soon after the breakup of the Soviet Union which had championed the cause of many of the non industrialised nations, this does seem far fetched, but such a possibility holds a far greater threat to the Unipolar scheme than possible differences within the G-7 like, for example, European Union asserting itself by subsuming trans-Atlantic linkages. It must be seen that but for the fear of the Russian nuclear weapons at present, and the conventional military power that Russia may eventually acquire, the need for US participation in the NATO gets diluted. A quiescent Russia on the fringe of the NATO, allows the USA an opportunity to continue with the effective leadership of the NATO.

The United Nations are not considered a wholly suitable forum by G-7 plus either to fashion, or to enforce the NWO except on those rare occasions when it is found expedient to do so. The United Nations are ponderous, slow, and 'democratically' inefficient. It is difficult to get on with a political agenda in the United Nations that addresses the concerns of the G-7 plus. In short, United Nations are no great help in creating the NWO which wishes to address the global concerns on the basis of other than absolute equality amongst sovereign nations. China, if it makes common cause with Russia, could on occasions hobble the Security Council even without using the veto powers. Not only that China does not possess at present either the economic power or the technology comparable with other members of G-7 plus, but it also gives rise to some doubts about its future as a single political entity at present. It is conjectured that China will overhaul the GDP of the USA by the year 2020 , and some parts of China will be as prosperous as Europe, while others may remain substantially underdeveloped. Conjectures are also made that China may not be able to remain a strong unitary structure because of the forces generated by the differential growth, in which case, those regions of China that develop faster than others could deal with the industrialised nations on the basis of their autonomy. Chunks of prosperous China could yield many of the advantages of rapid growth to the industrialised nations, without the hazards inseparable from a unified China in possession of strategic nuclear weapons. The utility of a unified China to USA, as a countervailing power against the former Soviet Union is never to be discounted. Russia occasionally, may show signs of making common cause with China possibly to extract some concessions from the United States or NATO, but other wise,

Russia has more to gain from G-7 at present, and in the future. This arrangement — G-7 plus at the apex — may create political space to virtually include the whole world, in a manner that the United Nations have not been able to do. The United Nations may well subserve the purpose of the G-7 plus, as it draws on their generosity for educational, welfare, and relief programmes. The United Nations, described often as talk-shop may on occasion give vent to the 'democratic aspirations' of the under-developed nations. The membership of the group — G-7 plus — may change, depending upon whether they continue to qualify or not, but the structure may hold intact for the next quarter of the century. G-7 plus will evolve and enforce the NWO through a variety of instruments and means : international treaties and conventions, like CTBT or CWC, resolutions of the United Nations General Assembly and the Security Council, pronouncements of the International Courts of Justice, verdicts of bodies like the WTO, and most of all through the conditioning power of the media.

If the main sources of prosperity for G-7 plus in the future are seen to be international trade on advantageous terms, high returns on investments and advances, lowering of costs of production and avoidance of environmental hazards associated with production, and access to hitherto closed or developing markets, then, the NWO will support the cause, and G-7 plus will enforce it.

Some salient indications of sculpted terrain and shaped space are there to be seen: there is a concern with instruments of force in the hands of immature states, and the method recommended is demilitarization. Under developed or least developed parts of the world are to be denied access to weapons of mass destruction, and methods of developing or delivering them. Nuclear weapons are to be retained only by those who are 'responsible'. Treaties like NPT, CTBT, and regimes like MTCR aim at fulfilling this purpose. At the other end of the spectrum, there is to be a ban on land mines, except perhaps those which can be disarmed at will and from a distance, or have self destruct mechanisms. Demilitarization is aimed at increasing the gap between the makers and script-writers of NWO, and the rest, so that international policing does not become a hazardous business. This has been the moving spirit behind the United Nations concept of security all along. United Nations, have reflected concerns and interests of the great powers. British, when they established their empire in India, proceeded along similar lines. They had promptly set out to disarm India.

> " What happened under the British rule was the elimination of the huge numbers of militia- like groups of soldiers subject to non-state control[7]."

Globalization implies submerging of national borders — some borders, to some extent. National borders in the developed world remain sacrosanct.

> "It is one of the paradoxes of the contemporary world system that the potential for international integration has never been so great, yet at the same time the forces ordering and channelling integration have never been so strong... regulatory mechanisms at border controls have never been so sophisticated or so fully enforced...Perhaps the major reason why immigration policies have become more forceful in recent years has been the rise of nationalism as an influence in contemporary society[8] "

Integration is measured in terms of trade and foreign direct investment. The prescriptive conclusion being that integration gives a fillip to development and growth. In reality, it pushes up sales of MNCs, and fetches good profits on foreign direct investment.

> "In fact, sales of foreign affiliates of MNCs in 1992 were $ 5.3 trillion — compared to the $ 4.6 trillion worth of goods and services that were traded world wide that year[9]."

Integration is a way of facilitating the access of capital and goods of the industrialized countries to the developing world. Integration means creating conditions in which 'co-operation' is possible.

> "Of course, integration in this context simply means doing one's utmost to ensure the largest possible market for the consumer and capital goods of the North[10]"

NWO is elitist, and the new elites are the experts in various fields, and not only technocrats. Elected representatives have necessarily to accept the advice of the experts; similarly, those who have accumulated or inherited wealth have no choice but to allow their industries and concerns to be run by the experts. Chief executive officers of MNCs are the new elites. Efficiency, productivity, and risk management are the new values that NWO supports. NWO is extremely complex and it has to depend on talent. Inflow of talent into the developed world remains unhampered. Understandably, this is on the basis of inducements, and not force.

The new elites across the globe form their own associations and organizations, and seek security through their links with the developed world.

> "The real decision-making powers of the future ... will be transnational companies in alliance with city-regional governments[11]."

What is underplayed is the source of power of the MNCs and their security. The hard core of MNCs has to have security for which it goes to its roots. The hard core relies on its parent nation states for security ; whereas, those who man foreign affiliates of MNCs, try to create an atmosphere which is conducive for their security in the host country.

> "The giant corporations who straddle the globe departed long ago from the fiction of standard economics text books They are the new imperial economic players. Their power and place in the world is ultimately traceable to the military might of their home countries. Once they achieve the dominance of India's industry and financial systems they will buy the appropriate politics[12]."

A greater proportion of profits depend more and more on value additions which are essentially knowledge based.

> "Profit is less and less in manufacturing, and more and more in design, branding , and marketing. Even in a complex product like a car it is only around 60 %, and falling. The manufacturing cost of a product like a CD is less than one twentieth of the retail selling price[13]."

Unrestricted transportation of oil and other products, in various stages of production, uninhibited travel without hazards across the globe, and the C four and intelligence net-work that underpins the global structures are sine qua non of NWO. Any obstruction or disruption will looked upon as a threat

Technology denial is part of the disarming process, and developments in the third world are watched carefully for infringements. At one time the Soviet Union was persuaded not to part with cryogenic motors that propel the rockets. Later, activities of Bharat Dynamics drew fire.

> " The Clinton administration has formally imposed export curbs on India's Bharat Electronics Ltd (BEL), Bangalore, suspected of contributing to the country's missile development.First on the list is Ben-Gurion University in Israel.and the second is the Bharat Electronics for which all US exporters require a commerce licence application[14]."

Means adopted by the Super Power to carry out international policing may not stand the scrutiny of international law. In fact that may not be very relevant to the ends and means equation. Sovereignty of lesser states may not enter into the calculus.

> "The United States is reported to have spent nearly 3.5 million US dollars to capture Pakistan national Mir Aimal Kansi, charged with the murder of two CIA officers... Gul [Lt Gen Hamid Gul, a former chief of the military inter-service intelligence] filed a petition in Punjab province' Lahore High Court challenging what he called an unlawful snatch of Kansi in Pakistan by the agents of the US FBI in violation of the Pakistani extradition law...Prime Minister Nawaz Sharif's government has kept silent on the arrest since the FBI announced it in Washington[15] ... "

One of the major consequences of the bipolar arrangement in the Cold War era was an acceptance of the reality of unequal power distribution within the two blocs. The United States on the one hand, and the Soviet Union on the other, led their respective blocs with such great authority, obviously on account of the power they wielded and the resources at their command that, in spite of very real inter-dependence within the blocs, their leadership was never a matter of serious or lasting doubt. In such a situation a hierarchy had to emerge. The blocs, clearly, had a stratified structure — how else did we come to have the Third World ? Non aligned-or not, and in spite of the popularised and largely believed fib of sovereign equality of all nations, the ruling elite in most nations got to know and accept the ranking of their nations on the basis of their power and strength — and not on the basis of their culture, civilization, ideologies, principles, or values — in the hierarchy, even though they waved, or were expected or allowed to wave, their flags at opportune times. Every nation was aware of the possible source of help or succour in distress. Cuba could rely on Soviet missiles, just as India could conclude a treaty of friendship and cooperation with the Soviet Union. Pak could and did successfully befriend the United States and the Soviet Union in the wake of 1971.Bangladesh War, just as India had done it for a length of time in the wake of the 1962 Chinese aggression. But this was rare. Bipolar world meant two hegemonies with their stratified structures, with some differences and exceptions here and there.

The third world seems to be drawing heavily upon the habits of mind formed in the Cold War era: acceptance of hierarchy of nations in a stratified world in return for help and assistance in distress. This comfortable, if somewhat restrictive environment, no longer exists. There is, now, an association of industrialized countries at the top of the heap with common interests and concerns. Third world countries will matter if and when a need to create a new geopolitical balance is felt by main players. The United States strive at present to keep the world unipolar with a mass of industrialized countries forming the pole. It may take the form of a civilizational or European identity. Should this not happen, and Europe, Russia, China, and Japan emerge as competing power centres, there would be a need for the great powers to seek out the countries of the third world in exchange for some prize or the other. Till then, they can continue to remain objects for power projection, that is, exploitation.

The NWO does not hold out any greater hope for the third world nations that did the bi-polar world. In the wake of the Cold War, in some ways, they have lost some of their leverage, and become more vulnerable. In effect, their governments are likely to wield increasingly less power under the NWO, with a shift in favour of financial institutions, industry, and trade. And yet, governments remain responsible for the security of the country with more and more expected of them. An impression has been created that the security of the individual in the third world countries is ill served by the measures adopted for national security, and only if the third world were to concentrate on development, and reap the 'peace-dividend', not only individuals, but the world as a whole would greatly benefit. The faith of the common man in the nation state is being shaken. He is being made to believe that the process of global integration will bring him all the benefits which the nation states have failed to deliver in all these years, and therefore, he should look up to the script-writers of the NWO and not so much to the national leadership. Should this happen, he is unlikely to be a net gainer under the NWO.

Nations of the sub-continent have the choice of operating within the frame work created for the developing nations, or stepping out of it, with all the attendant risks and penalties. They must find solutions to their security problems which do not shut out the long term hopes of realising the geopolitical potential of the sub-continent.

NOTES

1.Henry Kissinger, 'Diplomacy', Simon and Schuster, London, 1994, (p. 805).

2.Alvin and Heidi Toffler, 'War and Anti-War, Survival at Dawn of the 21st Century', Warner Books, London, 1994, (pp. 319-323).

3.Kenichi Ohmae, 'The end of the nation state : the rise of regional economies', The Free Press, Simon Schuster, New York, 1995.(Excerpted in World Executives Digest, May, 1996).

4.ibid.

5.Max Jakobson, [former Finnish ambassador to the UN],'Five Policemen and their own United Nations', Asian Age, by arrangement with the International Herald Tribune, Bombay, 16 March, 1998.

6.Barry Buzan,'People, States & Fear', TransAsia Publishers, New Delhi,1983,(pp.117-118).

7Stephen Peter Rosen, 'Societies and Military Power — India and Its Armies', Oxford University Press, Oxford, 1996, (p 169).

8.W.T.S. Gould and A.M. Findlay (Editors), 'Population Migration and the Changing World Order', John Wiley and Sons, 1994, (pp.279-290).

9.Siddharth Varadarajan, 'Wishful Thinking on Economic Integration', Times of India, Bombay, 13 May , 1996.

10.ibid.

11.Alvin and Heidi Toffler(1993).War and Anti-War,Survival at Dawn of the 21st Century, Warner Books, London.(pp. 319-323)

12.Gautam sen,' Another Raj in the making', Indian Express, Bombay, 7March, 1997.

13.Hamish MacRae, 'The World in 2020, Harper Collins, London, (1994), (pp.150-1).

14.UNI news report datelines Washington, May 24, 1997, Indian Express, Bombay, 25 March, 1997.

15.Reuters news report datelined Islamabad, June 24, 1997, and story filed by TV Parasuram, datelined Washington, June 24, 1997, Indian Express, Bombay, 25 June, 1997.

11

Outlook For Conflict

The New World Order (NWO) is not concerned so much with peace as it is with regulating conflict that threatens it. Causes of strife and conflict are hardly ever likely to be eliminated. It appears that it may not be a good idea for developed nations to begin from that end — elimination of causes of conflict. It is far more practical to maintain law and order in the international arena. To them, peace making initiatives are not anathema, but peace is difficult to attain, more particularly because there is no consensus about what constitutes peace. Those who prefer status quo look upon lack of overt violence as peace, and ignore latent violence. Those who seek revolutionary change look upon exploitation and/or repression as latent violence, while advocating overt violence as a harbinger of better peace. According to Toffler:

> " Making peace cannot depend on the prior solution of all the world's moral, social,and economic ills. Those who tell us that war is a result of poverty, injustice, corruption, overpopulation, and misery may be right, though the formula seems oversimple. But if these must be eliminated before peace is possible, then war prevention or limitation becomes a utopian exercise[1]."

NWO is a catalyst for power projection, and it does not rule out the use of force. Faith in the use of force may be looked upon as a cultural lag by cultural historians who feel that cultural advances have not kept pace with advances in technology.

> "The chief cause of these world revolutions has invariably been a discrepancy or maladjustment between material

and non-material culture. Sociologists and social historians call this "cultural lag," a term which was popularised by William F. Ogburn in his book, Social Change. At the Dawn of History, improvements in tools and weapons upset the simple life of tribal communities and started mankind on the road to conquest and the creation of larger settled societies...In all of the great world revolutions since primitive times cultural lag has been the factor which upset the existing pattern of life. And never before has there been such a gulf between technology and social institutions as exists today. We have an impressive and up-to-date equipment of science and material culture, while our institutions, mental attitudes, and social thinking are an antiquated mosaic of accretions from the Stone Age to the close of the eighteenth century[2]. "

On the one hand, the technology available is not used for the benefit of a substantial proportion of mankind, and on the other hand, mankind remains threatened with the full range of destructive forces. NWO does not greatly feel concerned about destruction provided, (1) direct and indirect benefits to the developed world are substantial, (2) developed world does not suffer directly from the ill effects of the use of force, (3) if it is in defence of vital interests of one or more nations of the industrialised world, and (4), if the victims are unable to retaliate in kind. So much can be deduced from a number of happenings and pronouncements in the context of the Gulf War.

There is no commitment whatsoever by the United States, or any other nuclear power, that the strategic nuclear weapons will be eliminated in any given time frame. The Unite States are on record to say that they back their diplomacy with force. They have used force on a significant scale in the Gulf in 1991, and they were ready to strike again against Iraq in February/March 1998. Of 14 occasions that elicited serious considerations of the nuclear option, according to Luttwak[3], only 4 were close to or near the industrialized nations.

It is highly unlikely that destructive force including the weapons of mass destruction will be used by the nations of the industrialised world against each other because of interdependence on the one hand, and because the prizes sought may not be fully amenable to the use of force, on the other hand.

Industrialized world may not be averse to the use of force to intervene in the third world. It may be a 'police' action against those who have infringed some international convention or law, or reneged on their own commitment under some treaty obligation or convention to which they are a signatory. The force used may be of constraining or restraining kind, or of the destructive kind. Forces of intervention may deploy screens of highly mobile conventional forces to establish a bridge head for a somewhat larger build up of 'friends and allies' to establish a new front in the Second World War fashion, to take possession of land and to establish 'legitimate' and friendly governments in disputed areas. Or they may land special forces teams, and carry out the necessary missions, or they may strike from a distance. This kind of intervention would be a possibility in respect of land assets which are internationally vital, if and when there is a possibility of their becoming inaccessible : oil fields, choke points and straits, like the Suez Canal, or the Panama Canal, or the Malacca Straits, and so on. Blockades to back sanctions would be a far more feasible option. Revolutionary or peoples' war techniques could be used as was done in Afghanistan or Vietnam, if it is desired to deny political and/or economic space to a potential adversary, till such time as favourable and more propitious conditions obtain. If oil from Central Asian Republics (CAR) has to flow out of the area into safe ports in the Arabian Sea, a friendly Afghanistan is vital, but if that is not feasible, that space may be denied to potential adversaries like Iran, and CAR themselves. Toffler visualizes the possibility of the creation of professional mercenary forces to be used for policing by the United Nations.

> "Why not, when nations have already lost the monopoly of violence, consider creating volunteer mercenary forces organized by private corporations to fight wars on contract-fee basis for the United Nations—the condottieri

> of yesterday armed with some of the weapons, including non-lethal weapons of tomorrow[4]? "

The people in the sub-continent are already aware of this model. The East India Company raised its own army to protect and promote its interest although it was only a commercial concern.

Gulf War in 1991 shifted the focus onto war technologies as very few things did since the advent of the atomic bomb. Ever since then, generally, efficacy of a nation to wage war has been judged by the sole criteria of technologies that it possesses. Modern trends in technology have been equated with trends in warfare. Technology does produce a major impact on warfare, but since it takes at least two to make a war, the kind of warfare that a nation opts for cannot be determined in isolation. Even so there are major pitfalls in assuming that the state of the art war-technology is the sole determinant of the kind of warfare that a nation must opt for. It is the concept of security that a nation seeks that determines the space within which strategies can be evolved, that is, the space within which ends and means both must be located. North Vietnam chose to opt for revolutionary warfare, worked out the strategy accordingly,took the punishment when it could not be escaped, but achieved their security objectives. It is for this reason that Clausewitz emphasizes that the task of a statesman is

> " to determine proper nature of ... war that he has to understand and wage[5]."

Technology only provides the means. It is an important source of strength and power, but its availability, by itself, or lack of it, should not be allowed to determine the strategic doctrine, much less, the security paradigm. Technology considerations should not be allowed to overshadow strategic considerations.

> " While battles and campaigns have sometimes been won largely with the help of clever technological devices, others have been quite unaffected by considerable technological superiority. We should learn that although technology amounts to very much indeed — it after all is

what separates the rich and powerful from those who are neither — it falls short of being the name of the game which is strategy[6]. "

In the third world though, and particularly in the sub-continent, all the three waves of civilization coexist side by side. The use of force to grab land, using primitive means, is common enough. Even grazing rights give rise to international disputes between India and Bangladesh. The dispute about utilization of water impounded in the barrage on the Ganges appears to have been settled by the two countries but not without difficulties. How the agreement operates, remains to be seen. Basic land hunger, shortage of water and power, movement of refugees across international borders, and so on are disputes which do not preclude the use of force in primitive first wave wars indistinguishable from mass riots, to the wars of destruction and attrition in which industrial power is pitted by the adversaries. Nuclear means, although on a limited scale are well within the ken of the nations of the sub-continent. They have till now been thought of as 'deterrent' in very general terms, without getting rigorously into the calculus of what will prevent whom from doing what in which situation. An unstable situation worries the script writers of NWO because the use of nuclear weapons in the sub-continent will cause upheaval of a kind which cannot but cause global concern. As it happened in the Cold-War, the nuclear capability will keep the violence below a certain threshold, it cannot and will not be eliminated.

The use of force on a regional scale can only make matters worse, particularly if the use of nuclear weapons by the rogue states remains a possibilit. Operative deterrence amongst the mature states is a far greater reality. There is a pointer here for the aspiring nuclear powers : develop a proper C four I net-work and a rational decision making process, and put it on view, so that maturity will entitle them to join the nuclear club.

Industrialized nations themselves may not use force against each other, not unless implacable forces of nationalism or ethnicity in Europe assert themselves. But those who have felt short changed or cheated by the industrialized world may do so.

Revolutionary or people's war uses the same techniques of going for the vitals by exploiting vulnerabilities as does the manoeuvre warfare. The fact that these techniques are also used by criminals and psychopaths does not alter the basic nature of warfare or its characteristics.

The self same sculpted terrain and shaped space which is essential for projection of economic power and influence of the technologically advanced and highly organized industrialized nations—which facilitates secure transportation and communication through out the world — is exploitable by special forces and irregulars. Industrialized countries are devising ways of taking care of themselves, but the third world democracies who lack technology and organization both are even more vulnerable to this kind of warfare.

It is worth recalling that Iraq's ingress into Kuwait may have been seen by the rest of the world as a traditional border war, but the MNF intervention was of its own kind, in aid of NWO.

> "It would long be remembered that during the Gulf War, the infra-structure of Iraq, a third world country, was destroyed by high technology weapons of the advanced countries. The worst legacy of the war would be that the third world countries will conclude that, since they cannot obtain and operate high technology conventional arsenals, their security can only be assured by the acquisition of nuclear weapons[7]."

Chemical weapons were considered a viable option on the scale of ascending violence between conventional and the nuclear weapons. At the time, when chemical weapons were not placed out side the pale by Chemical Weapons Convention — which will eventually come into force — it was possible to indicate to the adversary that the matters had become sufficiently serious or critical by using chemical weapons. The adversary could either draw back, or further escalate, as he wished. But a pause was available. Chemical weapons were usable — that is not to say that they were desirable — in that they could form part of dissuasion. Hereafter, between the conventional dissuasion, and nuclear deterrence, there is no intermediate tool of dissuasion that is accessible to developing countries. To that extent, the warfare has become that much more crisis prone. Additionally, non-nuclear powers have become aware that unless they have a substantial power to hurt, they cannot deter, and without nuclear deterrence, they have the choice of living peacefully within the confines of a structured hegemony, or attracting the kind of punishment that visited Iraq. In spite of the NPT, nuclear devices are available to the terrorists and the like, and there is no knowing, how far the revolutionary war will be carried into the First World.

Except in close combat, it is difficult to distinguish between offensive and defensive weapons or equipment. Weapons are used for offensive or defensive purposes, at a point of time, and in a particular place. It is more helpful to view technology for the impact it produces, on war making potential, nature of warfare, power projection, that is, ability to prosecute war at a distance from the home base, resistance to power projection, organizational structures that are required for prosecuting war, and shifts in power centres.

High explosive remains the main agent that kills. Although nuclear explosives have been on hand for many years, because of their residual effects, and safety of own troops, they have not replaced high explosives. In spite of specialized munitions and variety of fuses that allow a projectile to penetrate a target, the effect produced belies the claims made about the efficiency of explosives as an agent that produces 'just enough' destruction. Accuracy has improved and precision guided munitions (PGMs) deliver the projectile on or near the target, the actual destruction is not minimised at the target end. A total of 350 lbs of explosive was delivered per Iraqi. Devastation caused was substantial; actual damage to the weapons was not so spectacular.

> " The amount of ordnance delivered by American B-52 bombers against Iraqi forward positions equalled explosive power of five 'Hiroshima' bombs[8]."

But according to the Commander Artillery of Iraqi 48 Division, on 16 January 1991, that is at the commencement of the air strike, he had 100 pieces; by 20 February, he still had 90. In the last few days, before ground attack, only 10 were left. The destruction was due mainly to ground artillery and helicopters[9].

Larger the distance from which fires are applied, greater the probable error, and greater has to be the weight of fire applied to make sure that the target is hit.

Destruction multiplies because the target is super-saturated with fires. This is to be traced to a desire to increase the statistical probability of hit.

> "In order to achieve statistical probability of success, an over kill invariably takes place[10]."

Application of fire-power at close ranges allows greater scope for the utilization of acquisition and guidance technologies in various forms. It also reduces cost of missiles which rises steeply with range. And ultimately, the collateral damage at target is reduced.

> " Short range systems also have the advantage of choice of weapons. Short range weapon can be guided by laser, active or passive radar, infra-red, millimetre waves, fibre optics etc. Mines can be fitted with various sensors — seismic, magnetic, acoustic, infra-red, and so on[11]."

Weight of fire delivered per man — as a crew-member of an air craft, gun or a missile battery — has increased so greatly that number of individuals who have to be controlled to deliver a given volume of fire has steadily been declining.

To deliver say one KT of explosive with a 203mm Howitzer around 22 rounds will have to be fired. If the entire explosive power is to be delivered at the same time, 22 gun crews will have to be activated. If a single atomic shell were to be fired from US M 110 203 mm Howitzer, using a single gun crew, several thousand KT of explosive power will be delivered on target.[The exact yield of the atomic shell is not known]. Further, only a single aircraft crew needs to be activated to deliver several mega tons of explosive power, through fewer links of command. The gun crew could get involved in a tactical battle, and their fortunes cannot be controlled with a degree of certainty. Therefore, the commander controlling the conventional or tactical nuclear fires will have to be in the chain of command, and not far removed from the guns, so that the fires of his guns is integrated into the larger picture of battle. Contrast this with a strategic air craft wing held well back and controlled directly by the theatre commander who deals directly with the Commander-in-Chief. The hereto unknown possibility of exercising virtually direct control over very large concentration of forces, and that too from great distances, exerts pulls in following directions, alike on professionals and their political masters.

(1) To concentrate greater and greater force by creating more and more destructive weapons, and further, to concentrate authority and control over major instruments of force in as few hands as possible. This is achievable by reducing decision making centres between the 'crews' who actually position and fire the weapons and those who have the authority to permit or prohibit their use in the chain of command.

(2) A desire to retain full and total control at as high a level as possible, and resistance to delegation of authority till the last possible moment.

(3) Inclination to achieve the desired results through massive destruction rather than controlled and intelligent application of force — manoeuvre and attrition — so that delegation of authority is minimised, and errors of judgement are not allowed to surface.

(4) A feeling that an error of omission or delay can be easily corrected by application of massive force at command.

Compare this to, say, getting a battalion worth, or approximately 400 assaulting soldiers, to deliver small arms fire as they move on to the objective. 400 Soldiers have to be controlled — each one fighting 'everyman's war in his mind.

> " The voice of duty tells him that his own safety must be subordinate ... This struggle in the mind of the sentry is everyman's war, and in that war he that findeth his life shall lose it[12]."

Motivation of men who need to risk their life and limb to deliver fires in a manner that the destruction is no more than minimal remains a major problem. It has not been simplified by advents in technology.

Fires delivered by flying and/or fighting platforms against each others do not admit any intermediate results; it has to be a kill most of the time. Therefore, they too stand off.

The most spectacular advances have been made in the field of acquiring information from great distances. Remote sensing and timely interpretation of what is picked up allows effective surveillance and target identification, in spite of efforts at concealment and deception by the adversary. This capability is only partially degraded by weather or darkness. Object of observation is more easily made out and detected if it is seen against a uniform or undifferentiated background like sky or water. Man made objects against background of other man made objects, or when concealed below the surface of earth or within its folds make things a little more difficult. Human intentions, unless they are directly or indirectly given away, cannot be picked up.

Technologies that allow effective consultations from distances, exchange of information in real time, dissemination of information to all concerned, level jumping, and cutting across organizational boundaries create enough scope for total integration of all available effort for a common purpose. Such systems were being described originally as command, control, communications, and intelligence, that is, 'C 3 I'. With the addition of computers, they have now become, C 4 I. Such a system could help in creating organizational 'intelligence' provided there is a will and a doctrine. This is difficult to achieve though. There is a cultural lag in defence services, in that, the military mind still thinks in organizational terms and cannot as yet focus purely on the national 'mission'. During the Gulf War, according to one analyst, the warfare turned out to be air and land, rather than a air-land battle.

"Ironically, during the actual ground-offensive (Phase IV), little close air support was available[13]."

The most important advances have taken place in creating fighting platforms—crawling, hovering, flying, floating, submerged, or in orbit. They have, inter alia, allowed an appreciable increase in what Simpkin calls 'tempo of warfare'; that is, they have compressed the time between two successive blows that can be delivered, and, at the same time, increased the possibility of delivering those successive blows at places separated by great distances. This creates a tremendous scope for 'manoeuvre' warfare over an expanding battle-field, but not without considerable risks to the manoeuvre forces.

These platforms, without exception, do not have adequate protection against direct hits; they dominate for so long as they move. Their destruction, particularly with their pay load and/or armament can deliver body blows and render the war-machine ineffective very quickly, unless there is a matching capacity to replace them. Together with the capacity to deliver heavy weight of fire in few hands, 'war-platforms concentrate war making potential in fewer and fewer nodal points.

Modern technology also creates, or more correctly, allows, options at the other end of the spectrum : shoulder fired missiles and rocket propelled grenades confer fire power on an individual provided he is willing to take the risks. If he is willing to hold his ground, and fire as late as possible, he may succeed in destroying an air craft or a tank. The impact of shoulder fired missile in the hands of hardy and courageous Pathans was noteworthy.

> " ...[T]echnological evolution of warfare occurred in Afghanistan, where the Soviet army suffered a technical defeat because of the sudden introduction of a new defensive weapon. Until then, the Soviets had enjoyed total control of the air and were becoming increasingly effective in using jet planes and helicopters against the Afghan freedom fighters.
>
> "The picture changed dramatically with the introduction of the shoulder-mounted Stinger missile. A simple

> mujaheddin, after just a few weeks of training, was able to shoot down the latest Soviet jet aircraft. Within several months, Soviets air supremacy was gone — and so were Soviet hopes for a successful, low cost counterinsurgency[14]."

Night vision devices, kalashnikovs, helicopters, para-sails, high-altitude, low-opening parachutes, and so on allow the individual to reach vitals and pressure points, and if he can hide his identity and intent for long, they offer him a good enough chance to cause a disproportionate damage. The theory of special forces is built around the individual as a fighting platform: individual courage, improvisation, commitment, and self reliance. It is not to say that commandos act alone. They also work in teams, they make up units, and formations, but the pivot remains the individual. They open up another option of manoeuvre warfare. Courageous, motivated, and trained individuals can have the capacity not only to resist sheer weight of fire, but also to manoeuvre and hurt the enemy. But they too need appropriate technology. It is not as if industrialized countries are not working in this direction.

> "SIPE - Soldier Integrated Protective Ensemble is a 'suit 'that would offer protection against nuclear, chemical, or virological weapons, provide the soldier with night-vision goggles and a heads-up display. It would also include an aiming system that tracks the eye movements so that it can automatically point the gun at whatever the soldier is looking at... According to Maj. Gen. William Forster, director of combat requirements in the Pentagon, the ultimate object of the work on SIPE is 'to increase the effectiveness of the individual so that you need fewer soldiers. The fewer the soft skin soldiers, the fewer the casualties[15]."

No matter, what the intent, it is clear enough that high technology can be effectively used to create any of the capabilities: massive strike from stand-off distances; manoeuvre and follow up forces mainly dependent on fighting and logistic platforms; manoeuvre and resistance and follow up forces built around human-fighting-platforms; and combinations thereof. Other interpretations of how technology can be exploited to create and equip forces are, of course, possible.

Technology shifts burden of war making onto workshops, factories, and laboratories. This has a dual significance; (1) the number of civilians required to support war machine increases rapidly, as compared to persons in uniform, and (2) there is a demand for reduction in uniformed community because modern technology is expected to economise man-power by producing machines which take on the work of men.

> " 77 Percent of an air force in the UK includes civilians; of the remaining, only 13 percent are combatants.

> "Between 1960 and 1974, in the US, the defence expenditure went up by .8 percent, but man power declined by 340,000[16]."

The general trend in the industrialized countries is most likely to be a shift in favour of force-structure and equipping policy that opts for reduction in man-power in uniform, because the corporate profits go up in proportion to expensive items of equipment bought from the industrial complex. As an example, the comments on the cost — $ 45 billion for 21 bombers — and vulnerabilities — moisture in the air, or rain — are interesting. They may be couched in humorous terms, but the message is clear enough : the military industrial complex and the social structure in the industrialized world favours high technology forces that concentrate on massive hits.

> "Here it is : the B-2 'the Stealth'. The original mission of the B-2 was to fly from overseas bases deep into the Soviet Union and drop nuclear bombs. Of course there is no Soviet Union any more, which means that now the mission of the B-2 Bomber is... the mission is ... hang on, it will ... come to me... So far the B-2 closet has cost us taxpayers $45 billion, which has purchased us 21 bombers, which works out to around $2 billion per bomber. It turns out

> that the secret stealthy materials are sensitive to moisture, which as luck would have it (who could have predicted this ?) is plentiful in the atmosphere, so according to the GAO, after the B-2 flies, it tends to need lots of costly repairs.
>
> "In other words, even our top military experts believe that 21 is a sufficient number of extremely expensive bombers with no apparent function[17]."

When and where the target is distinct, and considerable collateral damage is unlikely to prove counter-productive, high technology forces, based on heavy fires and mobile platforms, can win battles of attrition by inflicting severe damage, and/or by exhausting the industrial capacity and will of the adversary. This is the essence of attrition warfare in our times, in so far as the industrialized world is concerned. It is all but obvious that attrition warfare may be undertaken against the third world countries by the industrialized countries, whenever it is necessary to intervene and 'punish'. It is highly unlikely that one industrialized country would strike another with heavy or regular forces. All the predictions and talk about the irrelevance of regular forces in the 21st century is valid in so far as the industrialized world is concerned.

Manoeuvre, on the other hand, relies on exploiting vulnerabilities of the adversary to reach pressure points with a view to magnifying the effect of force applied. Actual destruction is minimised. This, of course, implies greater risk for manoeuvring forces. A valid conclusion may well be that if there is a political compulsion to reduce the destruction at the target end, or if the capacity to successfully project destructive force is limited, manoeuvre warfare may have to be resorted to.

It is worth recounting that Simpkin views revolutionary warfare and manoeuvre warfare, clubbed together, as the opposite or a countervailing pole of attrition.

> "There remain, then, these three theories of war — attrition theory, manoeuvre theory, and the doctrine of

revolutionary war. All these lie on a continuum ...within the continuum of threat and use of armed force, attrition lies at one pole, while manoeuvre and revolutionary warfare adjoin each other out side the opposite pole[18]. "

He exemplifies this further :

" As I write this, one or two men, some simple electronics, and ten kilograms or so of commercial explosive have just come within a whisker of killing the entire British Cabinet with the stated political aim of getting British troops out of Ulster[19]."

Where, target is human, capable of merging with the background, or with other humans, that is while dealing with insurgencies, attrition oriented forces have problems in achieving their political objectives. Manoeuvre forces have a great advantage, in that, by minimizing damage, they off-set to some extent, the mis-match between ends and means that is intrinsic to the use of force.

Terrorism may well be construed as a sub-set of irregular warfare, that is, insurgencies, or counter-insurgencies aided and abetted by foreign powers. Terrorists use force or threat of force to create the greatest possible impact. It is another matter that innocents are victimised. But then, innocents or no more spared in carpet bombing, or when conventional forces surge back and forth. Covert action by commandos of special forces can be differentiated from terrorism with difficulty. It is the intent and purpose of the individual operators on the one hand, and their amenability to control on the other hand, that assist in establishing the distinction between crime and warfare. Many of the terrorists may not be distinguishable from criminals; indeed, many of the criminals may be part time terrorists. For that reason, it would be a mistake to tackle terrorists and terrorism using the same techniques and the same law of the land that is employed to tackle criminals. If terrorism is recognized and acknowledged as a sub-set of irregular warfare, there may be some progress in dealing with it. The means adopted may include commandos who act like irregulars. But they cannot operate unless the government creates political and legal space for their operations. There is always a possibility of the misuse of the means that the state may create, but for want of them, the state may find it difficult to deal with irregular warfare — including terrorism. In point of fact, there is a need to adopt the most advanced technologies in combating terrorism.

Ways of accessing, transmitting, and processing information have undergone, and are undergoing, major changes. The pace is staggering. It is possible to gain or pick up information without alerting the object. This maybe done from great distances, through uninterrupted surveillance from space, or through intrusive devices planted deep within the target, or even through open sources. This information can be transmitted, almost at the speed of light, to multiple points, where it can be processed and interpreted to determine its relevance, utility and importance. It may be used in real time, say, to track and destroy an incoming missile, or stored away for the future use : signatures of formations and weapon platforms may be kept at hand, with as much care and alacrity as records of indiscretions or secret wealth of important leaders. Information may be used to buy or sell stocks, commodities, or currencies ; it can also be used to engineer or squelch coups or 'popular' uprisings. Lack of information may result in unpleasant surprises.

State of the art technologies for acquiring, exchanging, transmitting, processing, interpreting, and presenting information have become part of every day life in the industrialized world. Professionals, businessmen, and common people alike make very extensive use of these technologies in day to day life. They cannot think of life without products of information technologies. A motorist takes another route when he hears on the traffic net that the route he hand intended to follow heretofore, is blocked, or he may give instructions, while on the move, for sales or purchases of stocks. Information is used, as never before, to seize opportunities, to create wealth, to avoid losses and risks, or to minimise unpleasant consequences on being surprised. It is rightly said that people fight as they work and live. The tools, implements, codes of conduct, and other attitudes that they commonly adopt while working and in social inter-course get reflected in the way they choose to fight, or avoid fighting. Access to cyber-space has revolutionized life, and opened up information highways and byways ; it has also opened up opportunities for cerebral thieving, house-breaking, looting and arson. With this kind of impact on everyday life that 'information' produces, emergence of a phrase like 'information -warfare' is only to be expected.

Information revolution or warfare can hardly be separated from the underlying reality of explosion of knowledge, and its impact on all technologies. It is a revolution which has redefined wealth: the proportion of value that is derived from 'knowledge' in a finished product, or a rendered service is greater today than in any earlier times.

> "First wave sector supplies agriculture and mineral resources, the Second wave sector provides cheap labour and does mass production...Third wave sector rises to dominance based on new ways in which it creates knowledge[20]."

When turned around, this means that the value attributable to raw material, energy, labour, or transportation, is much less. If wealth is the set of prizes, and power is the instrument for acquiring prizes, the part played by knowledge — as a component of strength and power — in the struggle for survival and betterment is much greater today than in any earlier times.

Knowledge — and one of its major derivatives, viz information technologies — are likely to play a far greater and virtually defining role in future warfare. Information can be of great help in acquisition of targets, and their engagement. Information may be of substantial help in merging with the background, or in deceiving the adversary. Information is a force multiplier : it helps to achieve surprise and guard against being surprised. It could be of help in -

Locating vitals and pressure points of the adversary.

Determination of vulnerabilities which are unguarded, or unprotected.

Evaluation of sources of strength and power, and shifts that take place from time to time.

Evaluation of forces and other instruments of power.

Evaluation of sources of strength.

In integration of all the components of power, and their concerted application. Related technologies also help in guarding and protecting own sources of wealth and strength, and vulnerabilities, and in resisting and countering hostile power. They create an unparalleled scope for integrating own effort in space and time, and by bringing together and harmonizing different armed service and their components.

But the advent of information warfare has created its own problems. In the Gulf War, not all the demands for information could be fulfilled[21]; and what was actually available could not be fruitfully utilized within the available time. There is every likelihood that, at critical times, commanders may get inundated by information sent to them by their sources, and disinformation fed to them by the adversary; and beyond that, there is a possibility that their own C four I net-works may be effectively denied to them by the adversary. Development and effective operation of own C four I net-works, and their security will remain one of the prime requirements, and may turn out to be one of the prime determinants of success.

According to Luttwak[22], the direction of future warfare is the information warfare, whereby, due to technological innovations, states will be able to carry out special operations rather than frontal warfare. This type of warfare derives from the basic unwillingness of states and superpowers to tolerate huge casualties. Even while accepting the essential validity of these conclusions, there is no need to lose sight of the fact that information does not kill, except figuratively, but weapons do. Information warfare will supplement other forms of warfare, but it may not replace them.

Information warfare is hard to distinguish from intelligence warfare. Its impact on manoeuvre warfare is greatest of all. Richard Simpkin describes preemptive surprise as a manoeuvre-multiplier[23]. Surprise is hard to achieve without availability of accurate and timely information of and about adversary, and denial of similar information to him.

Reverting back to the Gulf War of 1991, we now know on good authority that many of the claims made regarding effectiveness of high technology weapons were highly exaggerated.

> "A newly declassified report says the Pentagon and the weapon makers overstated the effectiveness of high-technology aircraft, bombs and other systems during the Gulf War.
>
> " The congressional report says laser-guided bombs and Tomahawk missiles were less effective than claimed, aircraft touted as attacking in all conditions had trouble in clouds or dust, and the F-117 stealth fighter may not have been the invulnerable weapon of surprise that its supporters touted . While the report analyses performance in conflict of more than six years ago, its conclusions could weigh on multibillion dollar decisions the Pentagon and Congress will make in the coming months, particularly on the B-2 stealth bomber.
>
> " The report cited " a pattern of overstatement by weapon manufacturers and defence officials in connection with high-tech weapons.
>
> " The gap between what has been claimed for air power in Operation Desert Storm and what actually occurred was sometimes substantial," the report by the general accounting office concluded. " Even under the generally favourable tactical and environmental conditions prevalent during Operation Desert Storm, the effectiveness of air power was more limited than initially expected or subsequently claimed[24]." "

Even so, it was proved beyond doubt that the technology had attained remarkable success in remote sensing, target acquisition, direction of fire, assessment of damage, and application of fire from great distances. Less attractive in the popular imagination, but perhaps far more important, command, control, communications, and intelligence systems were so developed that virtually total integration of joint services planning and operations were made possible. It was proved that helicopter as a tank killer was effective cost-wise and otherwise.

In these circumstances, when technology opens up fresh options and creates new possibilities, the side that fails to evolve its own security policy, or is unable to determine the warfare that it will face, will not be able to select the right technology. Following the Joneses may lead to avoidable waste and a mind-set that determines the war making potential with reference only to technology.

• Modern technology and media net-work built up for commercial purposes creates immense scope for psychological warfare. Most sources of strength and power — and most of all, the ultimate source namely the individual — having become accessible, more or less, it is possible to identify and locate strengths and vulnerabilities — the whole range of them, and in entirety. It is possible to look at and assess strengths and vulnerabilities of nations, alliances like NATO, trade blocks like SAFTA, interest groups like OPEC, international unions like EU, or multinational or transnational corporations. Within nations, scrutiny may be directed at political parties, professional groups, trade associations and guilds, government, or non- governmental organizations. Multiplicity of collective identities and associations may be viewed and assessed to understand and construe power distribution, centres of power and decision making, and their relative importance and weightage in multiple hierarchies. Military Balance may continue to be published using nations as building blocks, but that may only be just one of the ways in which evaluations of strengths and vulnerabilities will be carried out. Forecast of possibilities will almost certainly continue to be carried out with nations as main pivots. But beyond that, opportunities and threats, may be constantly viewed from the stand point(s) of numerous individuals who matter, as also collective identities and associations that they subscribe to.The hitherto familiar nodal points for application of or resistance to power — nations — will remain in reckoning, but other nodal points will be explored and evaluated. Sub-national identities and associations may appear as nodal points, along with multinational associations and identities. The process of evaluating nodal points, other than nation states, may prove to be one of the key factors in assessing the nature of conflict in the future.

Types and kinds of warfare have a great capacity to co-exist, particularly so in the sub-continent, which concurrently contains agrarian, industrial, and the third wave societies. The level of deprivation is high, a stable architecture of collective identities has not yet emerged, and the right balance between cooperation and regulated competition has not been struck. Nuclear deterrence cannot replace conventional forces, any more than tactical nuclear weapons can replace regular forces of dissuasion. Irregular warfare cannot be replaced or eliminated by conventional forces using conventional methods. One kind of warfare has a linkage with another, but preparation for one kind does not preclude the need for preparing for other kinds of warfare.

NOTES

1.Alvin and Heidi Toffler, 'War and Anti-War,Survival at the Dawn of the 21st Century', Warner Books, London, (p.298).

2.Harry Elmer Barnes, 'An Intellectual and Cultural History of the Western World, Volume Three, Dover Publications Inc., New York, 1965, (pp.1321-22).

3.Edward Luttwak, 'Strategy : The Logic of War and Peace', Harvard University Press, 1987, (p. 201).

4.Alvin and Heidi Toffler, op.cit., (p.302).

5.Raymond Aron, 'Clausewitz, Philosopher' of War, Routledge & Kegan Paul, London 1976,(p.347).

6. Bernard Brodie, 'Technology, Politics, and Strategy' Alastair Buchan (foreword), 'Problems of Modern Strategy', Praeger Publishers, New York, 1970.,(p. 175).

7.Frank Barnaby, 'Arms Control after the Gulf War', Conflict Study 240, April, 1991, Research Institute for Study of Conflict and Terrorism (RISCT).

8.Lt Col Jeffrey McCansland, 'The Gulf Conflict; A Military Analysis', Adelphi Paper 282, IISS, London,November, 1993, (p.49).

9.ibid., (p. 31).

10.Richard E. Simpkin, 'Race to the Swift, Thoughts on Twenty-First Century Warfare', Brassey's Defence Publishers, London, 1985, (p.168).

11. Frank Barnaby, op. cit., (p. 26).

12.Lord Moran,'The Anatomy of Courage', Houghton Miffin Company, Boston, 1967.[First published in 1945] (p.38).

13.Lt Col Jeffrey McCansland, op. cit., (p.31).

14.Zbigniew Brzezinsky, National Security Adviser to President Carter, 'Entering the Age of Defence', The Washington Post, 2 Oct 88.

15.Alvin and Heidi Toffler(1993).War and Anti-War,Survival at the Dawn of the 21st Century, Warner Books, London, (p.155).

16.JCT Downey, 'Management in the Armed Forces', McGraw - Hill Book Company, UK, London, 1977, (pp.46-56).

17.Dave Barry, 'Sky shattering news : the B-2 Bomber gets wet', Asian Age, Bombay, 3 Nov 97, by arrangement with Miami Herald.

18.Richard E. Simpkin, op. cit., (p. 319).

19.ibid.,(p. 320).

20.Alvin and Heidi Toffler, op. cit., (p. 25).

21.The demand from troops on ground was of the order of 600 frames of imagery per corps, per day. Adelphi Paper 282, (page 57) refers.

22.Views expressed at an international conference held from 5-7 November ,1996 at the Jaffee Centre for Strategic Studies (JCSS), Tel Aviv, JCSS Bulletins 17-18, March,1997.

23.Richard Simpkin, op. cit., (p. 112).

24.AP news report datelined Washington, June 29, 'Pentagon overstated Gulf War Weapons', Asian Age, Bombay, 30 June 97.

12

System For Management of National Security (SYMANS)

All considerations of and about security commence from a world view and outlook which seeks answers to the following sets of questions :

> What is it that it is intended to preserve, for how long, and for whom.
>
> What is it that needs to change, what change should be brought about, and how soon.
>
> What needs to be done about it, who should be doing it, what means should be used for the purpose, or altogether excluded; and in the process, who should be called upon to bear risks, costs and punishments that may be unavoidable.

Three views of security — individual, national, and international — spring from the centrality of identity which seeks the answers. From such a broad beginning, the scope has to be progressively narrowed down and problems so viewed that they become increasingly more amenable to reasoned and implementable solutions. At the same time, it must also be conceded that a wholly rational or universal solution is highly unlikely to emerge, because considerations of identity are not totally amenable to reason, and the very process of defining the problem in manageable bits, creates the possibilities not only of emergent solutions, but also of new problems. Therefore, most of the solutions are likely to fall well short of being comprehensive, or holistic. Security of individuals and considerations of human rights, if not counter-balanced by the obligations and duties of individuals to the collective enterprise, pose a grave challenge to national well being. This consideration entered the political calculus in India rather late. Article 51A listing the fundamental duties of citizens was incorporated in the Constitution by the Forty-Second Amendment Act of 1976[1], although fundamental rights, and concerns of international peace and security had found a place in Articles 12 to 33, and Article 51 in November, 1949 itself. Fundamental duties, inter alia, require citizens to defend the country and render national service when called upon to do so. Perhaps the best of compromises may emerge by devising systems that do not prevent those, who consider and understand bits, from viewing the whole; and equally, not free those, who break the problem into manageable bits, from the responsibility of fitting the bit-solutions into a workable totality.

Security without strength is unthinkable. Without growth and development, strength may deplete rapidly and security may be reduced to a mirage : (1) there would be no resources to spare for raising and maintaining armed forces, the prime instrument of power; (2) there would be a paucity of means to give incentives/subsidy to fledgling industry striving for international standards and exports, and for building of infrastructure, without which economic power projection cannot be resisted or countered; and, (3) the gap between the expectations and fulfilment may cause not merely a change of government, but beyond that, disaffection with the prevailing order. The last of these can put the clock back, and make the instruments of power, that is the armed forces, ineffective. Growth and development are the life blood of national strength, but there is always a temptation to mistake development for security. Therefore there is a need to arrive at the essence of security and so define its scope that the problem become tractable. Security, essentially, amounts to protection and promotion of national interests at acceptable costs. It also implies effective risk management and avoidance of losses which cannot be made good.

Security concerns, in practical terms, pivot around matters connected with employing, neutralizing, resisting or countering 'force' — physical force — in national interest.

The reasons for emphasizing the centrality of force in the field of security are the following:

(1) Possession of instruments of force confers an autonomy on the possessor, and force can be used suddenly and unilaterally, if need be, in contravention of stated logic, and in disregard of on-going negotiations, or understanding reached elsewhere. Such use of force, may well result in a fait accompli that does not admit of a satisfying redress. Possible use of force against own interests, therefore, is a matter of such seriousness that it must outrank all others for attention.

(2) Power projection in political terms — sanctions — may also be backed by 'enforcement', in one form or another, and enforcement cannot be countered except by force.

(3) Fruits of projection of power by other means — say, a favourable balance of payment created through net excess of exports over imports — can be denied and set to nought quickly, almost in no time: freezing of assets on foreign soil, denial of markets by closing ports, or through non-tariff barriers and so on. A redress is unlikely except through exchange of prizes. The use of force may create opportunities for seizing appropriate prizes which could subsequently be ceded in a favourable exchange.

(4) The lead time required to convert a part of 'strength' into coercive components of power — armed forces — is substantial. If a fresh beginning is to be made, it may well exceed two generations. It is believed that to train a general officer, it does not take less than thirty years, unless of course, he happens to be a Napoleon. Perhaps, creating a tradition of soldiering, which requires a young man to unhesitatingly risk his life, in obedience to orders the reasons for which he only vaguely understands, takes longer. If instruments of force are not created in good time, and maintained with care, opportunities will be irretrievably lost. Decisions concerning creation and maintenance of armed forces, and their use can neither be put off, nor ignored, except at national peril.

Decisions with regard to the creation and maintenance of armed forces have the potential to produce a most profound impact on the nation. Errors may lead either to catastrophic and often irremediable damage, or allow opportunities to slip out of hand, unrecognized and therefore, unutilized. Therefore, matters dealing with the armed forces do have a prime place amongst security considerations.

Most national security issues are weighty, in that they call for national effort and will to tackle them; grave, in that the consequences of decisions are substantial and lasting in their impact which is likely to be felt by most people, although not always immediately ; they are not always easily perceived or in good time, and therefore, crises prone. The decision making is, often, reactive, and consequently impelled more by urgency than considerations of intrinsic importance of concerned issues. Decisions taken to tackle crises, in turn, create their own momentum, burdens and compulsions which compound the original problems.

Apart from the armed Services, a number of security related set-ups, for example Border Security Force, Indo Tibetan Border Police, Research and Analysis Wing and so on are maintained in India; intelligence activity takes place — Pakistani spies are frequently expelled, and not without attracting retaliation by Pakistan — , satellites are launched, and missiles are developed and tested. Security in itself is a comparatively new mental construct. Although many of the organizations that contribute to security have been in existence since Independence from the British rule, an integrated and holistic view of security has not been in evidence. That does not at all mean that none of the security related functions have ever attracted the attention of the leadership in general and that of the government in particular. But the effort shows lack of direction, frequent turns and twists that are more indicative of lack of inner consistency and coherence, rather than deliberate responses to changes in the environment, and lack of coordination. More than any thing else, there seems to have been no consensus on what constitutes national interests, or what means are to be adopted for attaining them. Understandably, there has been no enduring commitment to ends or consistent effort to develop suitable means.

Creation of harmony, often out of apparently irreconcilable opposites is the prerogative and art of political leadership. It is a matter of vision and creativity. The past cannot always be a guide, and the future must never cease to beckon. Critics can benefit from hindsight, but the political leadership has to take decisions every day, perhaps, every hour. In this day and age, they have no reason not to draw upon expertise professional. The present set up does not seem to be able to cope up with the requirements of our times. Futurologists, contingency planners, media watchers and observers, and the like who can help with good anticipation, briefs, and assessments are not to be found by accident; even less will they come together for a common purpose unless suitable organizations and fora are created. Notice the contradictory statements attributed to the Indian side about whether or not the Kashmir issue was actually discussed by the Prime Minister with the US President and the Prime Minister of Pakistan during September 1997 visit of the Indian Prime Minister to the United Nations. In this tumult, the non-aggression pact offer by the Pakistani Prime Minister went unanswered by the Indian side.

The time for decision making is shrinking at a fast pace, and simply the need to react to a news item creates compulsions of crises proportions for political and professional leadership. The cost of acquiring 'capability' has phenomenally increased, particularly when it has a sizeable import content. The decision to opt for production of this or that air craft, or an indigenous carrier entails a substantial long term commitment at the cost of competing demands and, perhaps of development. That apart, the decision has to be taken fifteen to twenty years in advance if an indigenous capability is to be developed. There is no method of coming to objective conclusions in such matters without detailed systems analysis by experts on the basis of criteria acceptable to all competing interests. The present set up does not seem to have this capability. Perhaps there is a case for improving the quality of decision making machinery and implementation processes in respect of national security. This could well be done by concentrating on the following:

Policy making needs to be brought fully into the public domain. It must benefit from national debate, and no secrecy whatsoever must be attached to it. All of the proposed policy objectives may not be stated in precise terms ; specific plans may be kept secret, but national policy cannot be a product of secret conclaves. Policies, shrouded in secrecy, are unlikely to draw on national wisdom, or consensus, and may end up being much too short-lived, or down right confusing. India had the peaceful nuclear explosion (PNE) in 1974, but the thrust of the policy was kept hidden from the nation. There was no national debate about whether or not India was preparing itself for developing nuclear weapons. People at large were unaware of the direction in which they were being propelled. The question of creating and evaluating options just did not arise. The senior most scientist associated with the PNE indicated in October, 1996 that India had a deterrent capability, but there was a need to work out a defence policy.

> "India's present nuclear capability is sufficient enough to act as a 'deterrence 'and there is no need to conduct further nuclear tests", says eminent nuclear scientist Raja Ramanna.
> "The use of a plutonium bomb is sufficient enough to act as a deterrent and we have that capability. At the same time we should also determine the philosophy of defence," says Dr Ramanna, who played a key role in India's peaceful nuclear experiment(PNE) at Pokharan[2]. "

It would appear that India has had a nuclear capability, but no philosophy of deterrence and/or defence that incorporated the nuclear capability.

1. Government of India released a draft nuclear doctrine on 17 August 1999. This was in isolation and not within an over all framework of security doctrine. On what basis, then, was the deterrence expected to be effective. If the report of above interview is to be believed, only political leadership and a few selected scientists were in full picture. But there was no stated policy or doctrine, and therefore, the nuclear-deterrence might truly have turned out to be a paper-tiger.

2. Enlarging the base of consultation by incorporating in the decision making apparatus experts and professionals.

3. Insulating the matters of national security from considerations of internal politics within the country —party, elections, retention of power, improving chances of succession, division of spoils, and so on — to the extent possible.

4. Increasing the accountability of decision makers, and those who implement them, to the Parliament, and beyond the Parliament, to the common citizens in whom the sovereignty ultimately resides; and to the generations unborn.

5. Better mobilization, caring, and optimum application of resources.

6. Sensitizing the nation to the national security concerns.

System for Management of National Security (SYMANS) in India should be treated as no more than a mental construct at present. This mental construct could well be a starting point for conceiving of a possible set-up that would improve upon what exists on ground at present.

The system introduced in India, after independence, was based on recommendations of Lord Ismay who had a first hand experience of managing a war machinery with Prime Minister Churchill at its head through the gravest crisis that Britain had faced in this century. His advice was not only sound, but easy to adopt because India had also opted for the Westminster model of democracy. He had recommended, at the apex, Defence Committee of the Cabinet — all meetings of which were to be attended by the Service Chiefs and the Defence Secretary — and the Defence Minister's Committee of which the Service Chiefs were members along with the Defence Secretary and the Financial Adviser. There was to be the Chiefs of Staff Committee (COSC) with the longest serving Chief of Staff as its Chairman, in rotation. The COSC was to be assisted by several inter-service committees dealing with planning, intelligence, training, and aspects of personnel management and logistics. Recommendations of these committees were to be sent up to the Defence Minister's Committee, approval of which amounted to Government decision. As a system it was workable. It catered for interaction between the elected head and professionals of the armed services at the highest level, and created possibilities of inter-service cooperation. It could have worked, but did not. The reasons are many : the political establishment, which had come up through the freedom movement, looked upon the armed forces as former oppressors.

> "There was nothing common between khadi and khaki[3]."

That apart, the use of force as a means was held in some contempt :

> "Nehru was an idealist. A state may need armed forces ; but they were a necessary evil to be lived with[4]."

There was a virtual conviction that the armed forces needed to be kept in their place in the minds of most law-makers.

> "If members of the three Services in uniform, like the Chiefs of Staff Committee, are permitted to sit side by side with civilian members of the Government and allowed to exercise the power of the state , the theory of the governmental responsibility to the electorate and civilian control over the armed forces is completely thrown out of gear[5]."

> "The conception of responsibility implies that is directed towards one and only one entity... Any decisions taken by the Cabinet in consultation with Service Chiefs as Ministers not responsible to legislature would at once destroy the basic principle on which democracy functions[6]."

Therefore, it was only natural that a gap was created between the political master, and the armed services. The fear of coups made things worse. Dr. Nagendra Singh defines three fundamental problems of defence as integration of armed services, cooperation between the civil and military services in national interest, and -

> "..The state which creates and maintains the armed might is not subjugated by the military element...The problem of military coups de etat in relation to the civil government is of growing importance...Thus in attempting a solution to the first two

problems, one has to be careful not to make solution to the third impossible[7]."

The upshot has been a mechanism which has more checks than balances[8] — a mechanism which lacks a soul.

National Security Council (NSC) has been looked upon as a panacea for ills connected with national security. NSC has been firmly advocated by officers of the armed services and analysts, and has received some support from the political leadership from time to time[9]. The bureaucracy, as a rule, have resisted it, and governments have taken only half-hearted steps to implement decisions announced by them. NSC functions efficiently in a presidential system as a decision making and coordinating body. The President can invest it with commensurate authority. The US model cannot be transplanted to India without major modifications. NSC, by itself, may not bring about major improvements, but it will certainly assist. At this stage, NSC may be looked at as an important component of SYMANS. SYMANS need not necessarily imply creation of a single organization to take care of the national security. Even if one were to conceive of a unitary organization, such an endeavour is never likely to take off, in the first place, because of sheer size, and in the second, because no single entity could possibly cope up with the complexity that such an endeavour would call for. SYMANS is essentially meant to create an institutional frame work that will play a major role in comprehending, defining, and tackling the security problem. In India, at present, there are several organizations — varying in size from a defence planning staff of the Ministry of Defence, not exceeding double figures, to over a million strong Army — who severally carry out various security related functions and operations. All of them are set tasks by those higher in the hierarchy than them; all of them draw sustenance from appropriations made to them, and yet they do not seem to have been integrated to serve the purpose of national security. Depending upon whether or not they receive the right impulse in right time, they will cooperate and act or remain spectators. Depending upon how they perceive the actual, or the operative value system, they may either disregard their domestic organizational concerns and give every thing they have to serve the national cause, or follow the dominant trends and jump in the fray to compete for power, prestige, and resources. They may either choose to cooperate only to the extent and when coordinating instructions are issued down the command channels, or take initiative to seek and find areas of cooperation through deliberate effort and anticipation, and act to achieve the common purpose in a concerted manner . In short, all of the discrete organizational structures could act severally, or respond jointly with all the faculties at their command, like an organic whole. To elicit such organic response two conditions would have to be fulfilled : (1) concerned organizations have to be designed and motivated for the purpose ; and, (2) the ambience in the system has to be supportive, that is, operatives values must place a premium on collective effort. SYMANS, as a mental construct, posits an organic consciousness rather than an overarching organization. It is expected to absorb and modify what is already there, with few additions and modifications, rather than create some totally new set up.

Professor Graham T. Allison, at the end of his study of the Cuban Missile crisis placed decision making during the crisis in a conceptual frame work : he concluded that events that took place were a combined out-come of programmes and standard operating procedures (SOPs) that made up the national government, pursuit of organizational interests by members of those organizations, and their own goals by the key players. What mattered was what those goals and stakes were, the extent of power that was possessed by the key players, and the action channels that were available to them. The classical model which presumes that goals are objectively determined, options are examined in the light of consequences that they may entail, and then rational choices are made, does not realistically reflect what actually happens. He observes that -

> "Many crucial details of implementation followed from organizational routines, rather than from central choice[10]."

> The analogy between nations in international politics and coordinated, intelligent human being is so powerful that we rarely remember we are reasoning by analogy[11]."

Therefore, he concludes, that it may be realistic to shift the attention to organizations and individual actors as determinants :

> "We should ask not what holds account for a nation's choice of an action, but rather what factors determined an out-come[12]."

Allison's observations and conclusions are about reactions and responses of a country which has had NSC in position for many years, does not suffer from shortage of funds or other resources, can call upon the very best of information gathering and processing services, and other aids to decision making. The out-come of this particular crisis for the US was far from unhappy ; even so the decision making processes, on scrutiny, were not found to be particularly reassuring. This should cause NSC advocates and supportes to look beyond NSC. NSC, or any single organizational device, for that matter, is unlikely to bring the desired satisfaction. This, of course, is not to suggest that NSC is not necessary. or it will not prove beneficial. There is, clearly, a need to get over the natural inclination of individuals and organizations to do their own things rather than act in the national interest as intelligent beings. SYMANS should work towards attainment of that goal without underestimating the inherent difficulties of the undertaking.

It is just as well to remember that it was the inability of native potentates of India to convert their intrinsic strengths into instruments of power and employ those instruments of power effectively against the foreign invaders that led to the subjugation and slavery extending over a thousand years. Lack of technology, lack of cohesiveness, and the like deficiencies certainly weighed against the Indian rulers, but it was the incomprehension of the problem in totality, and the lack of organization to address the problem, that hurt them the most. SYMANS is thought of as a structure consisting of several sub-structures, each with its domain and internal organization, that are linked together in a common purpose. It is obvious that such a structure has to be efficiently managed, and more than that, it has to be effectively led at all levels, but more particularly, at the highest. To remain in a vigorous and healthy state, all organizations need a well spelt out doctrine and effective leadership. It is the articulated doctrine which creates conditions in which decentralization without confusion and without loss of direction become a real possibility. A brief explanatory note on doctrine appears at the end of this Chapter, as an annex. For want of effective leadership, a drift away from pursuit of national interests, toward partisan ends, and personal interests, if not toward indifference and lethargy, are only to be expected. Energizing the nation, and creation of stakes in national identity and endeavour remain the abiding challenges to the leadership.

Consideration of SYMANS ought to begin from its role — to assist in safe-guarding of national security — and the functions that it will perform. We have examined, in Chapter 6, the concepts of security in contemporary times and described the ongoing 'security process' in a normative sense. Security is not only about protecting interests, it is also about promoting them. It is about creating and maintaining conditions, capacities, and preparedness, within and without, which facilitate protection and promotion of interests. It is not only about risk avoidance, but also about weighing advantages of available opportunities against penalties of inaction. It is about creating plausible equations between ends and means. Ultimately, it is about employing all the instruments of power optimally, and in harmony.

Peoples and revolutionary wars may aim at creating disorder with a view to establishing a better peace, just as policing—national and international — is intended to support a preferred order. Within these two extremes, there could be a range of other conflicts, each claiming vindication of a just cause, either in support of or against prevailing order and power distribution. Apart from weapons of mass destruction, even conventional armament contains such destructive potential, and is so easily accessible to nations and sub-national groups, that a variety of agreements to restrict the scope of violence, by denying the availability of means to those who are not considered responsible enough, are under consideration of the script writers of current international order. On the contrary, those who are displeased with the national or international order try to gain access to sophisticated armaments so that they may disrupt and terrorize, or withstand such effort by their adversaries, till their point of view prevails. The anarchists and terrorists pursue their causes, with help and support from those states who, even as they support insurrection and rebellion outside, use considerable violence to subdue domestic insurgents. So, state sponsored terrorism has these two dimensions : that which is used against antagonists, and that which is used against own citizens.

Organization for security must take into account these features of the current milieu, and the world order so that it can succeed in protecting and promoting national and supra-national interests. For so long as nation states continue to be the building blocks of the international community, national security ought to give primacy to national interests, without disregarding supra-national concerns. The first and foremost task is to carry out a periodic appraisal of the national identity to determine its dominant character and dimensions, and on that basis, to arrive at the mix of aspirations, apprehensions, and commitments which are the true indicators of the prizes that are actually sought, and the national effort which is likely to be forthcoming. This exercise would also indicate the movements and shifts in moods and feelings with respect to affinities and antipathies that are pivotal in garnering support for policies. This is a part of the political process. Great leaders, even as they take stock of things, create, nurture and modify popular responses and feelings in national interest. But in the rough and tumble of electoral politics, this may not always happen. Most liberals in India, perhaps though not the government, were totally surprised at the lack of popular protest against drive for privatisation inaugurated in 1991 as a part of the new economic policy. Had India ever been committed to 'socialism'? Was socialism truly at the core of Indian identity, as the Constitution had us believe. If not, when did the political leadership become aware of the reality ; was it only when the foreign exchange crisis faced us. What and how do most Indians think about Kashmir, if at all. Do they consider it to be a part of India, for which they would rather go to war a fourth time. Why so. Why do they not show similar feelings against the Chinese occupation of a portion of Indian territory. Perhaps, the answers to some of the questions lie deeply rooted in how most Indians define their collective identity, and which adversarial relationships flow out of it. Since all considerations about security are rooted in the perceptions of collective identity, its periodic evaluation is absolutely necessary. SYMANS ought to assign this task to one of its organs. There is a need for such a body which should check out and validate all assumptions and traditional wisdom in this matter.

Safeguarding of national security could be divided into two compartments: (1)raising and maintenance of armed forces and their direction; (2) and their actual employment. The first of these could be called the security functions, and the second, the security operations. This labelling is no more than a short-hand for facilitating further discussion. It is obvious that the decisions taken to raise and equip armed forces have a very long period of gestation, involves allocation of scarce resources, and exercising of positive and negative options on the basis of political-military considerations. A decision taken in favour of air-craft carrier based navy could well mean a virtual rejection of submarines as the main strike arm, unless of course, resources allow both, or a viable mix of both. Decisions so taken create an envelop of possibilities beyond which the armed forces cannot operate, although vigour and ingenuity could expand the envelop to a small extent. Having taken these decisions, if the direction and control are lacking, the returns on national 'investments' and 'insurance' could be disappointing. The time available for decision making in the arena of security functions is comparatively greater, and the extent of knowledge and judgement that these decisions call for are fundamentally different from those required in security operations. Security operations, on the other hand, call for balanced decision making within a comparatively short period of time. Decisions have to be taken within available time, and often in glare of publicity. If the decision making machinery does not have adequate provisions for automatic delegation of authority in default, very much more than advantage may be lost. Security operations may actually be hindered by too much consultation. You must know your man and trust him is a time tested dictum. The lines of loyalty, command, competence, and trust must coalesce to yield a sub-system for decision making, and for communicating those decisions.

SYMANS needs to carry out the following national security functions in order to keep the security process going:

> First: Preparation of national security agenda, with an indication of relative importance and priorities in short, medium and distant time p3erspectives. Security agenda needs necessarily to be culled from broader considerations mentioned at the beginning of this Chapter. It is part of this function to define the scope of national security considerations in manageable terms without disregarding the linkages and the overall picture.This would very much require travel in uncharted territory, because the generalities of statement of national interests will have to be left behind and specifics, in many cases in quantified terms, will have to be stated. The nature of questions which would have to be considered and answered are likely to be baffling: Is uneven growth in population in surrounding countries, and different regions of the country, likely to lead to migration, which in turn, could become a security problem; if force as an instrument is not to be used to prevent the migration, what measures must be taken now. How does it compare with the likely shortage of energy for the pride of place. Will there be a need to be prepared to escort petroleum carrying vessels from the Gulf. When would such a situation arise, if at all. What is the range

of solutions that is available. Who is likely to use force to deny oil to India. Is the degradation of environment more important than both these. For how many years can we give primacy to development without giving undue importance to environmental issues. Can lack of development in border areas be exploited more easily by hostile powers to encourage separatism. For how long can force be used to contain separatism. What is the time frame in which political solutions have to be found. Will separatism pose a bigger threat than migration. Where does the likely nuclear threat from Pakistan figure. How soon would it materialise. Would it set to nought much of development unless it is effectively countered. What will be the cost of deterrence. To what extent will the cost of deterrence and defence cut back investment and growth. Will a drop in rate of growth and development pose a bigger problem than the Chinese and Pakistani threat put together. When and if at all will any or all these issues acquire crises proportion. Which crisis will be more testing. In case of grave doubt, or in absence of objective criteria for determining priorities, is it a good idea to refrain from determining priorities altogether. Why so. Will it guard against the possible error of excessive allocation of resources to the wrong sector, or will this approach ultimately lead to spreading resources thinly everywhere so much so that virtually nothing worthwhile is achieved. This kind of exercise — SWOT ? — would involve obtaining of views and opinions of a very large number of institutions and persons, who in turn would obtain, study, and use huge quantities of data, and come forward with answers, some times conflicting, often incomplete, and not always fully intelligible to lay men. Framing of security issues for analysis itself involves political insight, sagacity, and vision. Undoubtedly a prime job for political leadership — the supreme generalists. But they would have to draw upon the specialist knowledge of the experts. We have had in India, Planning

Commission chaired by the Prime Minister from early Fifties. We also have Atomic Energy Commission and the Border Roads Development Board (BRDB), who report directly to the Prime Minister. This tradition reflects some of the security concerns of the then Prime Minister, although he is not known to have so described them. The BRDB was especially established in response to the hostile activities on the Northern borders and very much represented a dominant security interest at the time. National Security per se has not figured as an overarching concern that subsumes not only the planning for development, but almost everything. Except in moments of crisis, security has not been high on the national agenda. Preparation of national security agenda would be a herculean task, particularly because such an exercise does not seem to have been formally and comprehensibly attempted in India, although most of the discrete items have been on the agenda, more or less, all the time. Unless they are viewed together, with reference to specific time frames, and in relative terms, a lot must remain unseen and hidden. Though security, in practical terms, may have a great deal to do with the use of force, it must cover a much bigger canvas and consider all uses of power together. SYMANS is not to conduct foreign affairs, any more than it is to decide about foreign trade, or energy policy. But SYMANS must have the capacity to integrate the effort of all the instruments of power on the one hand, and see well in advance, threats that have to be countered by the use of force, and opportunities which can only be availed when force is available at hand for possible use.

Second: Assigning nodal or focal responsibilities for the purpose of policy and planning, in respect of major national security issues, to one of the ministries, departments, agencies, or organizations, so that the principal 'player' is so nominated and recognised by all others. It is obvious that this exercise is far beyond the bureaucratic 'pigeonholing'. An array of means would ultimately have to be employed in tackling every single national security issue. If it was amenable to resolution by exertions of a single agency, it would not, in all probability, have rated as a national security issue in the first place. Assigning a nodal agency would indicate, the preference of particular means in tackling an issue, and not the exclusion of other means or agencies in dealing with a particular problem, or in undertaking of a particular project. A problem area is most likely to straddle many departmental and agency divides, although projects could well lie within the competence of an agency, or an agency could be put together for this purpose. Pushing of a national security issue into a departmental mould with a view to arriving at a clear cut distribution of responsibilities would detract from creation of organizational strength. This is still a province of the generalists in the system, perhaps to be tackled by the political leadership in consultation with the bureaucrats : bureaucrats are specialists in working of the governmental machinery, although many of them have distinguished themselves as generalists.

Third: Definition of the space within which the strategies must operate, evolution of strategies for tackling in concert national security issues, their evaluation in comparative terms, and assessment of time and other resources required for adopting the selected strategies, their attendant advantages, and penalties. This is creative work, in pro-active and re-active modes, which has to take into account the available and potential capabilities, and the time required to create and mobilize the requisite resources, the impact these developments would have on friends, rivals, and foes, and the modifications that would be required to the original strategic thinking. This is essentially the field of specialists, experts, and professionals who can give reliable opinions about what can possibly be done, how, at what cost and punishment, and in how much time. They would have to give major and important inputs. The nodal agency would be expected to draw upon the views and resources of all other connected agencies, and draw up a scheme of linkages and procedures for continued interaction and execution of plans. Allocation of prime and secondary roles, responsibilities, and authority would have to be done, sometimes cutting across the established norms, levels, and lines.

Fourth: Nomination of policy objectives, approval of plans for their accomplishment, creation and allocation of resources, and execution of plans and implementation of policies with the nominated nodal agency in the lead. This ought to result in the creation and maintenance of means or organizations which are to be used on an every day basis, like intelligence, and law and order machinery, as well as the strategic forces which may be employed only in an emergency. The professionals at the executive end, the bureaucracy for coordination and resource management, and the political leadership for allocation of resources, and inspiration would all play their parts.

Fifth: An on going review and evaluation starting from the selection of the national security issues down to the plans under implementation, and the results and the fall-out that they have produced in relation to the resources that they have utilized. The conclusions reached would lead to validation or reframing of national security issues and the endless loop would continue.

The above sounds, more and more, like the business of the executive arm of the government, and so it is, particularly when IS is reckoned as a prime candidate for nomination as a national security issue. The questions of government and governance are well settled by the Constitution, precedent and practice. The main question that then arises is, if at all and why SYMANS is required. SYMANS, in a large measure, has necessarily to be a sub-set of the government and governance. The whole purpose of SYMANS is to attract the necessary attention of the decision makers and enabling resources of the nation as a whole, and not only those which are directly at the disposal of the government. SYMANS as of now must stand in the danger of being dismissed as a redundant addendum at best; and at worst, as an effort to dilute, if not to usurp, the authority of the executive. This reaction to SYMANS could well be anticipated on the basis of the fate of — the already accepted — National Security Council (NSC)

Perhaps, there is a feeling amongst the governing class — the political leadership as well as the bureaucracy — that the demand for the NSC, voiced mostly by senior officers of the armed services, and some defence experts, is born to some extent of a desire to imitate what exists in the US, but more because the armed services wish to play a more active role in policy making and thereby establish closer links with centres of power. Even so, demand for the NSC stands accepted by the government.* It is also noteworthy that, with one or two notable exceptions, former or serving bureaucrats have never expressed their support to the NSC. Perhaps, the main resistance to the idea of the NSC, comes from those who carry on the day to day function of governance: those who head and service government ministries, that is those who exercise executive power of a sovereign government in the name of the President. They infer that, with their work open to scrutiny by officials of SYMANS who are neither their colleagues nor superiors, they would have to give data and information on demand, explain their actions in greater detail than they have been used to, place rationale for decision making within their ambit on record, explain inaction or

*Government of India created NSC with three tiers on November 19, 1998. The reader will notice major differences, in approach and organization both, between what is visualized here, and what has come about.

neglect, and in the process, somehow, their executive power will stand in danger of being abridged. Even those who are very correct, and therefore confident, know that their work load is likely to increase substantially, at least initially, and this it self would create major problems. Apart from the Parliamentary questions, queries from the courts of law, and questions from the increasingly active media, could they not do without an additional irritant — those acting in the name of SYMANS. We are aware that even when an institution like the Prime Minister's office starts exerting, the checks and balances, such as they are, get disturbed with unhappy results. These apprehensions and reservations need to be addressed.

Partly, the root of the problem is in the authoritarian system of governance, which was taken over from a colonial power. It abhors consultation, and equates wisdom with authority. After all, the whole of the Indian Government was subordinate to the Secretary of State for India, at one time. The system has been modified to suit the democratic polity of India, and contemporary times, but the concept of ruling over a fief has not been wholly displaced. A deputy commissioner or a collector is the lord and master of the district. He rules over the experts in his domain: the civil surgeon, the forest officer, the police superintendent, the superintending or executive engineer and so on. The basic system of governance is not on the basis of a consultative council. The experts may give opinions when asked to, but ultimately they would be told what to do. The system has the potential for being effective and responsive in a crisis, but otherwise, it cannot rise above the competence of a single individual or a few persons. Collegiate form of decision making does not find favour even at the highest level.

Even the armed forces are not very different in this regard. They have shown a marked inclination, even after Independence, to continue with the commander-in-chief system in all but name. In the British period, the 'Army in India' was also a part of the imperial system. The Commander-in-Chief in India ruled the Army by himself. He would not tolerate 'meddling' of the military member of the

Viceroy's executive council. He had no peers whose advice he was either required to seek or take in decision making in relation to the Army. The differences between Kitchener and Curzon were not only about the civil control over the military; they were also about total autonomy of the Commander-in-Chief in India. Kitchener had no desire to challenge the civil authority over the military. Kitchener and Curzon both were subordinate to the Secretary of State who was a member of the British cabinet. Kitchener did not ever opt for the Army council or the like. He wanted as much to be a master of his own fief, as the Viceroy was of his.

It must be conceded at once that a consultative decision making, implementation, and monitoring process must be far more complicated, and yet it cannot afford to be slow. The system created for the purpose could not be very simple to work, and personnel manning it would require a totally different mind-set and attitudes which would have to be cultivated for the purpose. And most important of all, dealing with the national security issues, the persons working for the organization will have to take especial care that they do not stray into the field of governance. In the matters of Internal Security (IS), the dividing lines between the territories of the SYMANS and the machinery for the governance of the country would have to be carefully defined, and watched with care.

It is very obvious that decision making of this nature is likely to outstrip the capabilities and talent of a few individuals, no matter how gifted and well meaning. A vast machinery is required for gathering of essential information, processing it into intelligence, its presentation to the decision makers, consultation, actual decision making, issue of instructions on that basis, monitoring of progress as decisions are implemented, and processing of fresh inputs and feedbacks to validate or modify decisions. National security functions are not amenable to being 'departmentalized', not only because the strength of a ministry or department may be inadequate, but also because there is every likelihood of the issues being viewed through the lens and filters of the dominant culture of that ministry or agency. If they were so, there could be a simple answer:

create a new ministry of national security under a minister of cabinet rank. The issues need to be seen in entirety, and all necessary resources need to be optimally used and coordinated.

What has been descirbed as security functions, here, need to be taken on and tackled by men and women who have broad range of interests, substantial knowledge base, comprehension of life in widest sense, managerial skills, and leadership qualities, in short, what one would call 'enlightened' persons. Otherwise, there is every likelihood of skewed policy making and a certain lack of balance and moderation in their implementation. It is futile to look for the renaissance men in our times. There will always be some, but they are not available on order, or in sufficient numbers. In any case, they may not get elected. The next best is to settle for the generalists. There was a time in the nineteenth and early twentieth centuries in colonial India when many of the officers of the famed Indian Civil Service brought with them firsts in classics, and enlarged upon their knowledge base, and honed their skills at work, to emerge as very good generalists who handled their provinces, as lieutenant governors, with distinction. A member of the same Civil Service, developed such insight into the British-Indian Army, that he wrote perhaps the best book about it, showing an unrivalled understanding of the Indian soldiery. One of the Viceroys took the field under his own military subordinate so that he could actually fight in battles. Some soldiers developed on their regimental experience to emerge as outstanding administrators and men of vision; and yet others built canals and bridges. Most of the first generation Indian patriots were outstanding professionals and scholars who never confined themselves exclusively to the domains of their chosen fields, but viewed life in its many splendours.

Is there any thing particular, in contemporary times, that makes it hard to find generalists is a question that arises next. Increasingly, there is a greater and greater need for experts in every conceivable field, from cuisine to advertising. A certain level of expertise is necessary even to survive respectably, that is to compete at the lowest level. For an expert to attain a level where he can perform with a substantive degree of autonomy and responsibility, it takes anywhere between 25 to 30 years of combined education and work under supervision or apprenticeship. Greater the degree of specialization, narrower and deeper the range of skills and knowledge. The system of education is geared towards creating specialists and super-specialists. It must also be conceded that without assiduous study and application in ever narrowing fields, there is no real progress. This has been stated here at some length not to lament the absence of generalists, in our time, although arguably that in itself may be justified, but to point out that the business of making a living respectably — and honourably?— in our times requires a process of education and apprenticeship that takes a person definitely into thirties, if not into middle thirties, and thereafter, rewards lie in further narrowing of the field. So the trend would be for emergence of specialists rather than generalists. Since the demand for well rounded and educated generalists is not large enough — who will pay them, for their sense of balance and wisdom — they have to be brought up 'in house' by the concerned organizations who need them, or the problems need to be differently viewed in the hope that a solution may emerge.

Those who work at the frontiers of knowledge or with the state of the art tools need 'generalists' to facilitate communication with the rest of the world. These 'generalists' would necessarily have to be from the same field and may themselves be specialists to other 'generalists' down stream, and so on, till linkages emerge which allow real experts to work on problems in a holistic manner. Without such linkages, bad communication, wastage, frustration, or all of these would occur, and the system would lose effectiveness and efficiency both. The medical profession provides a good analogy. Experts in medicine form the main stream, and other specialities take off from it. Together they form a unity. Consultation amongst several super-specialists may have to be facilitated by the main branch. This kind of integration is feasible and exists in this field possibly because human body, which is their concern, in itself constitutes a unity. In a diverse and essentially composite field like security, it may not be possible to create a single set of generalists who can deal with all specialists. The diversity of fields involved, and their extent make such an exercise a non-starter. The hope lies in informed consultation being able to create its own situation or function specific 'generalist's expertise'. Such generalist's expertise may be an emergent capability, a facet of their collective out-put. SYMANS must fulfil this purpose of linking specialists with decision makers so that, on the one hand, the talent and capability of specialists and experts can be fully harnessed, and on the other, their concerns, predictions, and fears are fully taken into account while rendering advice to the decision makers. The task of the generalists is indeed to bring to bear the skills, knowledge, and creativity of the experts on problems at hand; and equally, to become aware of the problems that are visible on the horizon, and perhaps, only to the experts in the field. This kind of consultation must help in balanced decision making: balance between long term interests, and immediate compulsions; balance in evaluation of competing demands and claims; and balance in allocation of resources.

Contrary to the conventional wisdom, the number of those who can assist in performance of security functions is surprisingly large: politicians, executives and professionals including the armed services, managers and bureaucrats, philosophers, scientists — in the broadest sense —, technologists, and so on. Something is to be said about the special attributes that they can be expected to bring to bear on performance of security functions.

All discussions and conclusions about security are ultimately related to a vision of what constitutes a better 'peace'—what is desired in the long term, and what is acceptable or even tolerable now. That is the gravamen of questions posed at beginning of this Chapter. For want of such a vision, striving for a 'better peace', or going to war to protect democracy, or some other value-based concept or idea, would have little meaning. This vision could be a mix of pure idealism on the one hand, and on the other hand, a hard headed appraisal of what needs to be done here and now to protect and promote own interest : notice that US finds it convenient to club virtues of market place and competition, with human rights for the under-privileged labour in South Asia; and, in a similar vein, had not India been quite eloquent about not using force in international affairs while forcing the Portuguese out of India? Visions of the world based on universal values have a problem about reconciling them with the reality of nationalism and parochialism. What enthuses common man into action are considerations of personal and collective benefits, risks, or opportunities—considerations which pivot around 'we and they' feelings. Universalism is viewed as an attractive proposition for so long as it postulates acceptance of own leadership and preferences by those outside the periphery. Visions of peace and tranquillity, or better world for everybody, or whatever other chosen expression for the same idea may be, contain assumptions about collective identities which need to be protected and nurtured : preferences about national and international order which are of particular benefit to certain sections of the population, or some core nations, or people. Saints and ideologues do contribute to the creation of vision, but it is the politician who makes the vision attractive to common man. The politician is often the purveyor when he is also not the maker of the vision. It need not be spelt out in any great detail, but it must seem to contain something for everybody. The vision of peace, attractive but somewhat vague to start with, is there to be interpreted in specific terms, to condition the popular feeling about what is, and what is not, acceptable. The vision may be grounded partly in the objective reality, but its subjective content is substantial and not any the less important than the objective considerations which can be discussed in quantified terms, and form the basis for reasoned argument, or compromise. It is the politician who is the 'professional' in the field of shaping and judging the popular reactions and moods. He is better qualified than others in gauging the enthusiasm that can be mustered in support of various issues, or indignation that can manifest in response to perceived slights, or real damage, and more importantly, he has the ability to mobilize the opinion and convert the strength of feeling into commitment. Likely commitment of the population, or lack of it, and the effort that can actually be mustered in aid of national causes is the underpinning of national security. The judgement of the statesmen in these matters is vital. It is in this area that he can make the most vital contribution to the national security functions and processes. The statesman, in this context, may be taken to mean the 'generalist' who shows a comprehensive understanding of life. Since statesman is an epithet that is conferred, mostly in retrospect, more as a mark of appreciation and respect than as description of particular attributes, the word chosen here to describe such a person is 'intellectual'. It has been often said that the time horizon of the politician does not stretch beyond the next election, and except when in wilderness, he can hardly get out of the election calculus. Political survival is his principal value and objective, and the extent of his knowledge and the nature of his skills are defined accordingly. But many politicians have a dazzling range of other skills and accomplishments, but most of all, they may show an uncanny knack for keeping in touch with reality. Therefore, intellectuals could be from politics.

Politicians in power, by virtue of their office, undoubtedly have the prerogative to preside over the security functions. Here, a case is being made out in favour of politicians not in office including those who have chosen to retire from active politics, provided of course, that they are 'intellectuals' as described above, and are in full vigour of life.

Most executives and professionals, including those in services, are mainly concerned with producing results. Their concerns are with actualities, and results. For their prosperity in life, they have to rely a great deal on their personal experience, own judgement, and reputation earned in the field. They may be modern in out-look, but their time horizon does not exceed half the length of their professional life. Their personal skills are in a narrow band, their loyalty to the organization is considerable, and the values which appeal to them most are those derived from their professions and vocations. In comparison, bureaucrats depend for their survival upon their ability to operate levers of power, and retain the confidence of their immediate superiors. Their ability to manage resources and men is substantial. Some of them combine an outstanding knowledge of civil administration with substantial analytical abilities. Those in services depend for their prestige as much on their position in hierarchy as on their personal abilities and reputation, whereas, those in professions, may have no concern with hierarchy. Loyalty to services is natural in their members, and they tend to show a surprising lack of inhibition in supporting causes of the concerned service, or its members. But most of them can and do work in a team. On the other hand, professionals may be highly individualistic and getting them to work in a team, if and when possible, may involve herculean effort.

Scientists and philosophers, as seekers of 'truth' are likely to have an extended time horizon, a capacity to see issues more objectively than others, and the ability to place current trends in proper perspective. They may be from the academia or laboratories, and cover the whole spectrum from physical sciences to abstruse metaphysics. Their insights may prove valuable. They are likely to contain generalists and specialist both, but more of the latter. Their informed guesses about areas of likely break through in coming years would prove invaluable.

The technologists are more like executives and other professionals in attitudes, and like scientists in their areas of interest except that their areas of interest may be more broad based. Some technologists have great administrative skills and an ability to execute very complicated plans involving multiple skills and disciplines.

On the basis of their special attributes, a model could be prepared to indicate their possible contribution in performance of each of the security functions. See the Table on the following page.

	'Intellectuals': those with a fuller compreh-ension of life and vision.	Persons from armed and other services, administrators, and technologists.	Managers and coordinators: bureaucrats and professional managers.	Consultants and Advisors :drawn from academia, scientific community, and professionals
Security Agenda.	40%	20%	10%	30%
Policy objectives and plans.	30%	30%	10%	30%
Organizations and allocation of resources.	30%	30%	30%	10%
Missions and contingencies.	30%	40%	20%	10%
Review, evaluation and modification	40%	30%	20%	10%

POSSIBLE CONTRIBUTION IN PERFORMANCE OF SECURITY FUNCTIONS BY CATEGORIES

The whole purpose of analysing the attributes of various vocations is to highlight that they have the potential to contribute to performance of security functions, and that none of the vocations, by themselves, can do so adequately. This is a marked departure from the assumption that performance of the assigned duties by those so entrusted by statute and convention will take care of the security interests. There is, of course, no alternative to performance of duties by those who have the statutory and assigned responsibilities, but a case for drawing upon national resources and wisdom. SYMANS must consciously create conditions and organization for the purpose.

An organization for the exclusive purpose of dealing with the security related issues has been discussed and debated for many years. The inspiration has come from the US National Security Council (NSC). NSC in the US can issue orders on behalf of the government. This is something that can never happen in India, because of the parliamentary system of the government.

Cabinet Committee on National Security (CCNS), would perhaps be necessary, in addition to and over and above the National Security Council (NSC), for the simple reason that the NSC, as visualized here, would necessarily have to include, as members, those who are not members of the Cabinet. The Prime Minister, or any of the other ministers, may want to go over matters considered by the NSC before they are presented to the Cabinet, or for any other reason; or they may like to go over NSC agenda before the formal meeting. The Prime Minister could well dispense with the CCNS before seriously detracting from the SYMANS envisaged. The crux of the matter is the NSC.

The NSC is conceived as hub of SYMANS. Its role is to -

(1) help the government to focus its attention on the national security affairs, suggest measures to be adopted to promote and protect national security, and to assist in the execution of adopted security policies, that is, perform national security functions;

(2) assist in maintaining balance, harmony, continuity and coherence in security policies; and—

(3) to help in increasing the accountability of all concerned to the Parliament in the interest of national security.

It is expected to act as the ultimate consultative and advisory body of the Government on security matters and audit the performance of all concerned departments and agencies from the security stand point. The advice rendered and decisions taken by the NSC would not be binding on the Cabinet. Perforce, they cannot be so in the Indian Parliamentary system. Ultimately the decisions would have to be approved by the Cabinet as a whole, and executive orders and instructions passed through the executive command channels. But if the NSC is not to become just another forum for voicing opinions, it must have the leadership of the Prime Minister. Otherwise, it is likely to be trivialised. The NSC could consist of a set of permanent members, and special invitees. The NSC is expected to bridge the gap between the decision makers — the political leadership — and those who actually execute the decisions on ground, on the one hand, and the gap between the generalists and specialists on the other hand.

The NSC may be composed of nominated ministers and heads of executive agencies and services as members. Some of the members could be on a permanent basis, whereas others could be invited when required. There is every likelihood of agreement on the ministers who should be permanent members: Ministers in charge of Defence, External Affairs (EA), Finance, and Home. Officials on a permanent basis could be the Cabinet Secretary, the Service Chiefs, Secretaries of Defence, EA, Finance, and Home Ministries, the Chairman Joint Intelligence Committee, the head of the DR&DO, and the Chief of the NSC Staff. Within the NSC, there could be Committees for examination of issues before they are brought before the NSC, for each of the security functions. The NSC is not expected to replace or supplant any of the channels for official business and communications. It should not take over any of the responsibilities or prerogatives of the existing agencies, departments, or ministries.

What will have the greatest impact on the effectiveness of the NSC, in the model visualized here, is the calibre of the NSC Staff (NSCS), the access and facilities given to them, and the quality of their work out-put. It is the NSCS that is expected to cut across the organizational lines and bureaucratic levels to obtain and process information in the desired time frame. NSCS is not expected to have any executive authority, but they are to have priority communications and access to all ministries and departments under them. The NSCS will be a mix of career officials and non-officials on deputation, or permanent secondment, and intellectuals and managers vide table on page 303. Some may be taken on contract. Some could be political appointees. The aim should be to create a mix of generalists and specialists, from various fields and experience, who have the capability to undertake creative, systematic, and complete 'staff work' for the NSC. The Chief of NSCS should be from one of the services, and preferably nominated for a fixed tenure. He should be assisted by a Deputy. Out of the two, one should be from the armed services with experience in working with other armed services.

One of the key elements of the SYMANS should be the way NSC staff is selected. It is obvious that the NSC staff will have a proportion of officials from the armed and other services — some of the slots would be tenable only by officials of a particular service — on a tenure basis, a few appointees on a contract extending from three to five years, and a permanent subordinate staff, for continuity, on deputation. Care would have to be taken that the turn over is so spread that the continuity is not lost. It stands to reason that the NSC staff, in essence, must be drawn principally from generalists, and from amongst those specialists who have a grasp of the whole of the field, that is, specialists tending to be generalists. The body must call for, and access the best available information, estimates, and views no matter where they are available. The NSC staff can, at best, evaluate, the expert and specialist views. Their creative effort must be reserved for drawing upon the available ideas and information to put together viable options for the NSC. They must create a data bank and a system of documentation which facilitates speed in decision making.

SYMANS must include an observation post — an elevated post — that looks near and far, and beyond the horizon, to pick up and track disturbances before they turn into a menace, and even to anticipate events, second guessing them as they emerge in the minds of the main players. Extrapolation of trends and developments in India and abroad is their main concern. They are the ones to spot strengths and vulnerabilities — own and that of rivals and adversaries. Either outright avoidance of crises, or better preparation for them could well be a measure of the efficacy of the SYMANS. NSCS has to constitute the elevated observation post.

NSCS should have the ability to draw upon information, views and opinions within the government — from the organic cells in each of the departments and agencies — and from think tanks, trade, universities, and research bodies. They should have the access, and the authority to seek what they want, and the money to purchase that which is available on payment outside the governmental ambit. They should not necessarily have to follow the normal channels, and be permitted to jump levels to get what they need, or consult who they want.

So far, we have not touched upon, the impact of the advice from NSC. Advice, when accepted by the Cabinet, would have to be converted into executive directions, not an easy task, because many flaws will be found and much inter-ministerial cooperation would have to take place before the plan of action is fully 'de-bugged' and made operational. Should this not occur, and if a reference back is required, great loss of time may take place. Self opinionated experts do not give up any more easily than the seasoned bureaucrats. Something of this kind had been happening in processing the recommendations of the Fifth Pay Commission with very unhappy results. Once the advice is accepted by the Cabinet, it could be made available to the Cabinet Secretariat for processing. Every concerned ministry and department could be asked to prepare draft executive and coordinating instructions, to the extent that the matter concerns them, and these be sent back to the NSCS through the nodal ministry for comments or suggested modifications. Thereafter, the nodal ministry or agency could produce the final draft and issue it under the authority of the government.

It is not intended that NSC should take over command functions; they simply cannot, nor would it be desirable. But they should observe, and advice. They are an important part of checks and balances. Some points of special interest are set out below :

> The threat assessment by the intelligence community, the executive departments, and the armed services should be considered by the NSC. Although the Chief of NSCS should be present, in the matter of security operations, he should play a comparatively dormant role.

> Directives on continuing missions and specific operational instructions to the armed services should be drafted by the concerned executive agencies and coordinated under the orders of the Chiefs of Staff Committee before they are placed before the NSC for consideration.

> Continuing missions and specific instructions to the intelligence agencies should be similarly treated before they are placed before the NSC.

> The responsibility for coordination in the field should be given to the a single nodal agency to be approved by the NSC. The suggestion could well have emanated from any source including the NSCS.

> When there is a need for coopting the state agencies, or when the requirement of the law of the land so require, the Chief Minister of the State , or the Governor as the case may be, should be invited to the meeting of the NSC and coopted in

> nominating the nodal coordinating agency. The committee hierarchy for command,control, and coordination, if and when necessary may be so approved by the NSC. The chain of command should emerge not as a result of public posturing and pressuring, but as a deliberate decision of the NSC. In India, that has so many federal features, this vital trouble spot needs to be taken care of. If consensus eludes, then decisions must be taken in the name of national security. A situation in which one of the state governments does not cooperate with the agencies nominated by the Union Government cannot be allowed to arise.
>
> Papers placed or brought before NSC, and discussions in NSC, including advice rendered, ought to remain on record. It should be available for scrutiny by members of the Parliamentary Committees, specifically authorised to do so, in the course of their periodic reviews. Adequate safeguards for security of information would, of course, have to be brought in place.

This will increase the accountability of all concerned to the Parliament.

National command authority (NCA) would be very necessary, as a part of SYMANS. It should have its own operations rooms manned by persons specifically authorized to exercise authority on behalf of the Prime Minister in his absence. With secure communications and data links to the operations rooms of the armed services and all other security agencies, it should be in a position to give executive commands. The question of NCA being inaccessible to the empowered persons should just not arise. With an alternative and well protected underground set up, it must be such that it can withstand a direct strike.

A notional structure of the SYMANS appears on the following page.

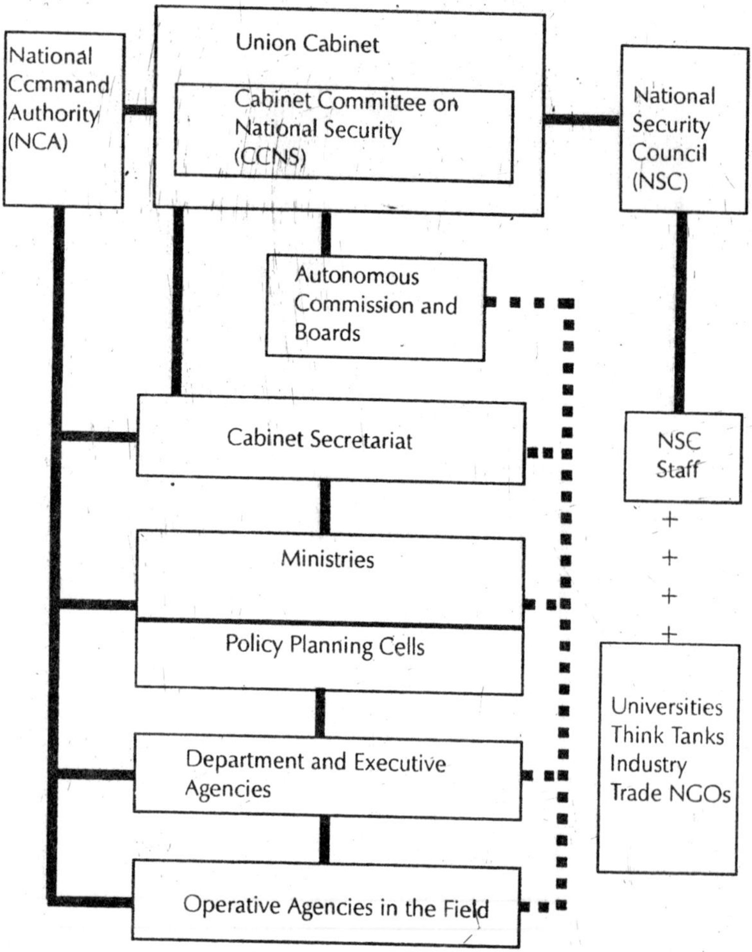

Legend

Channel for communications for exercise of executive authority ▬▬▬▬▬

Channel for formal consultation ■■■■■■■■■■

Channel for informal consultation ++++++

NATIONAL ORGANIZATIONAL STRUCTURE FOR SYMANS

SYMANS, as has been stated earlier, is not expected to be a single organization. Every department and ministry could have certain cells, committees, processes, or functions labelled SYMANS. An official while performing SYMANS tasks or chores, could be expected to show awareness of its importance, inter-act with others, if need be, by jumping levels, or by cutting across the departmental boundaries

Annexure

Tradition and Doctrine

It would appear that, till recently, the word doctrine was neither well received nor popular in India. It remained associated mainly with religion, or a political philosophy to which religion was taboo. Doctrine also, somehow, was not always distinguished from dogma—a word that definitely has had negative connotations. The US preference for 'doctrine' did not seem to make things better in so far as the concepts of doctrine was concerned. Not when they were doling out T 48 tanks and Star Fighters to Pakistan. Perhaps, a secular and democratic people did not favour doctrine, of whatever hue, or doctrine per se. Even so, over a period of time, we have had Indira doctrine, and Gujral doctrine. Both concern security. The late Mrs Indira Gandhi never stated an 'Indira Doctrine'. It is an aposteriori mental construct, something derived from her policies, acts, and their consequences. Gujral doctrine, on the other hand, has been enunciated by him. Whether we like it or not, we at least know what it is. But is it comprehensive enough to fill all the gaps. Perhaps, it was not meant to, be. Then what about the rest of the structure. Should at all there be a national doctrine, what purpose does it serve, and are we likely to fare differently if we had a national doctrine are some of the questions that need to be tackled. A beginning could well be made, by exploring these issues.

Doctrine as positive or prescriptive guidelines for tackling all issues, situations, events, problems et al is a need felt by many who feel comfortable with such dispensations on the one hand, and those who feel even more comfortable with laying down the immutable law. Such efforts are visible since the dawn of history, and have taken various forms. Many of the religions have fulfilled this requirement at one time or the other. Comprehensive and binding guidelines on how to deal with life in this world, and perhaps in the next, have been the staple concern of many sects and cults whose followers exhibit remarkable cohesion and commitment to causes. Doctrines seem to have exerted a substantial influence on their followers, at times baleful. Those in Europe, aspiring to autonomy in the political and scientific fields, even as they sought at least partial freedom from the church, put together a doctrine of their own — secularism. Democracy itself is not without its doctrine — agreement amongst a majority of people is wisdom —, so has Marxism, so has Panchsheel. Philosophies, when operationalized, appear as doctrines, although all of them do not have the same intensity of insistence, pervasiveness, or reach.

Without commonly understood, doctrine — and there need not be a single all encompassing and comprehensive doctrine, but several of them, that add up, each dealing with a specific aspect — the minimum coherence, consistency, and decentralization that are necessary for evolution of policies and their implementation may not be forthcoming. Without coherence in attitudes, thinking, and approach to life a grand design is unlikely to emerge. Without consistency, frequent doubts and changes may result in to make and break sequences, or several new beginnings would be made that do not lead anywhere. Without decentralization, there would be no hope of either popular participation or contribution.

Unless there is a potential, it cannot be harnessed. A brass rod does not get magnetised when placed in a charged solenoid, but an iron rod does. Magnetic properties would not emerge without processing that brings about realignment of and coherence in constituent particles. An articulated doctrine does not create energy or will out of nothing. It reflects back to a people what they already feel and have; it creates awareness of shared interests, ideals, strengths, and capacities. Articulation of doctrine is a function of leadership, particularly when major changes and challenges are on the horizon, and the momentum of the tradition is either dissipating or losing relevance. Mere articulation of doctrine will create no effect whatsoever. Equally, without a well understood doctrine to guide, a people lose heart and energy and opt for inaction. After the death of Chhatrapati Shivaji, the fight against the Mughals continued unabated for nearly forty years; fresh leadership could emerge and carry on where the earlier left off, not only because motivation was there, but also because the sense of direction eliminated doubt and hesitation. Without a general sense of direction, there is no possibility of emergence of a broad and strong current which develops its own momentum. Indian independence movement was informed by a well understood doctrine which reflected the aspirations of the incipient nation. A succession of remarkable and enduring achievements, over a long period of time, could well be attributed to commonly understood and acknowledged sense of direction, or tradition. Articulation of doctrine plays a major part in maintaining that direction, and bringing about those changes in it which help the tradition to evolve with time. Ellora, Ajanta, Rameshwaram or Madurai temples, or TajMahal for that matter are inconceivable without unswerving faith in the undertaking, an unmistakable sense of direction, and commitment of several generations of those who actually worked. Without a living tradition these achievements would have been impossible. This is how tradition manifests: in grand achievements: in space-crafts, mars probes, and also in intercontinental missiles, and neutron bombs. Starting with Washington, many US Presidents have made their major contributions to the prosperity and achievements of the US by clearly articulating the doctrine.

Doctrine often shapes and guides the flow of tradition. Very rarely does it break totally new ground, but it does so now and then: Nazism, or Marxism, for example, did just that. But mostly, what is stated as doctrine of this or that individual is an addendum to a corpus. Doctrine of flexible response is a modification, or a slight swerving. On the other hand, after substantial and major changes, particularly in world order, and or polity, there is a definite need to review and re-articulate the national security doctrine.

Autonomy of individuals cannot be denied any more than the collective need for tradition can be dismissed. Both have ultimately to be reconciled. Weak leadership dithers because it is not sure of itself, or fears being proved wrong. This approach is often justified by pointing out the possibility that the doctrine, once stated, may induce rigidity, may tie decision makers hand and foot, may detract from reacting to new developments in technology, and so on. Perhaps, not so; not if the doctrine reflects realistically the vision, will and aspirations of the nation. The US doctrine of active engagement with the rest of the world was conceived in the midst of tension between two opposite poles: isolation a la Monroe, as against active engagement in the interest of seamless international security. The principle of 'exceptionalism' — that the US are exceptionally well endowed and gifted, and therefore obliged to locate, determine and fight evil in any part of the world, and dispense justice as they deem fit — was accepted and creation of a new world order became the US national doctrine much before the advent of intercontinental rockets, nuclear powered submarines, and satellites. The US preoccupation with the world order predates the actual capacity to dominate it. Their policies and strategies have been guided by the doctrine they have adopted, and they are not merely a by-product of prosperity and technological innovation.

The national doctrine, if it guides the selection of policy objectives and strategies on a consistent basis , over a reasonable time span — say, not less than two generations — may fulfil its purpose. For this to happen, the doctrine may have to build on native and indigenous strengths; otherwise, people will have a reason to wonder one morning about whatever happened to socialism. Without well defined, and generally accepted doctrine, shifts in policies and policy objectives will prove to be to the detriment of all long term pursuits, particularly development and defence both which not only have an unduly long period of gestation, but require participation by all segments of the society. There can be no significant mobilization of national will without national doctrine. National doctrine may then help the professionals, not as a rule, but when unavoidable, to fill the gaps in the political directives. In the absence of both, the national doctrine and specific political direction, the military, like the other professionals, must be left to fill the voids to the best of their ability.

Nations and organizations with long and living tradition that is rooted in an all pervading culture seem to do pretty well with very little by way of formalised doctrine for promoting national interests. Napier conquered Sindh and sent a cryptic message to the Governor General - 'peccavi' i.e. 'I have sinned',in Latin. He had no specific instructions to conquer Sindh. Some belive that the 'peccavi' message is bit of a fib, but that may only was a good story. The point remains that Napies took initiative and did what he wanted to do, and that the Btitish empire enormously benefited from his actions. The living tradition easily served the purpose both of policy direction and doctrine, because the policy objectives ,though unstated, were like writing on the wall. He was aware that the East India Company had created an Empire, if not with guidance from the Crown, then, with its encouragement. Apart from lack of a living tradition of state-craft, India after Independence, has had to face numerous problems associated with nation-building. Commonality of understanding as regards the nature of state, its purpose, what demands it has a right to make on the individual, and what, in return, it promises the individual, needs to be arrived at as yet. A written constitution fulfils this purpose to a certain extent. The need to cultivate specific institutions that will make national security their prime focus of attention, and provide the Government with an analysis of and prescription for national security, does not seem to have attracted any meaningful attention of either the founding fathers, or of the Government(s) thereafter. Even if such institutions were to exist and function in a substantive manner their effectiveness will be less than optimum unless they formulate and disseminate national security doctrine.

Although the Armed forces were extensively employed starting with Kashmir operations in October 1947, each event was treated ad hoc, and the basic and fundamental matters concerning the nations security remained unresolved. Perhaps because of numerous coups in neighbouring Pakistan, it was felt that it was more important to keep armed forces in their place — under civilian control — rather than give detailed thought to creating an all encompassing doctrine for national security. An oft repeated truism about the need for the military establishment to be subordinate to the government — which nobody in India ever doubted, seriously or otherwise — seemed to suffice, at once as the articulated response to many questions regarding the structure of the security apparatus, and a warning to the military. In the wake of the humiliation of India at the hands of the Chinese in 1962, and the arming of Pakistan by the US, resources were released to the Defence forces on a more generous scale. In the wake of conflict with Pakistan in 1965 and 1971, the prestige of the Services went up a few notches, they were listened to a little more seriously; when Pakistan became a front line state after the Soviet intervention in 1979 and rapidly grew in strength, some more resources were released to the Armed forces. But no significant change whatsoever was brought about in the institutions and structures that deal with national security.

Doctrine is meant to answer what, when and how questions to the extent that it is desirable and possible to do so. Large and complex structures which comprise many organizations cannot function efficiently — if they at all fully function — without guide lines on decision making, and their implementation. But for these, decentralization would mean loss of control and lack of co-ordination, apart from loss of valuable time, and a tremendous increase in intra and inter-organizational friction. No large organization functions without some prevailing doctrine, some of it formally laid down, and the rest derived from the common understanding that arises out of shared experience and tradition. Except for the highest in the structure, others must have some guide-lines on how to go about promoting and protecting the organizational interest while carrying out their assigned duties, allotted tasks, and while fulfilling the role for which the organization exists. The services must take care of themselves, even as they fulfil their role. There is scope for and indeed a space for healthy competition but for which individual services will lose their elan. None of the organizations must upset the balance. They must function optimally, work in their ambit, and cooperate. When their roles are defined, likely tasks visualised, and their space clearly delineated, the scope for synergy will increase.

Doctrine creates the scope for decentralisation without the fear of losing coherence, efficiency, or co-ordination. If it achieves rigidity or uniformity, and inhibits initiative, originality, or creativity, it would have sacrificed much and gained very little. That very little may only be the possible survival of the nation, much in need of fresh transfusion, and no more. Properly evolved and disseminated doctrine has the potential to elicit a quick, intelligent, and effective response from a healthy nation. To a certain extent, it also contributes to the health of the constituent institutions and organizations by creating order, minimising doubts, and by inculcating a sense of self-esteem that comes from knowing what to do, and doing it well.

The concept of national security in itself needs to be reviewed since it remains largely undefined for want of national security doctrine. Sooner than later, such an exercise will have to be carried out, and an agreed concept of national security will have to emerge.'

Doctrine could have a broad scope which could be divided in four segments: descriptive, exploratory, prescriptive and binding. Descriptive segment is meant to give a world view and create a perspective within which the national policy objectives, organizational role, tasks, and thrust-lines should be placed. It ought to indicate the environment in which the organization or the sub-system is to function within the system, not excluding vagaries and uncertainties. It should explain the system-structure, motivation,inter-relationships, responsibilities of other organizations and sub-systems,the extent of autonomy enjoyed by each part, predominant compulsions, problems, and the limitations of resources, and compulsions of time. Availability of infrastructure and resources and methods of mobilizing them in critical situations should be included. The corpus of rules, regulations, and law of the land ,as well as international conventions, and international law that have a bearing on the organizational aims and objectives should be included in the knowledge base.

Exploratory portion should aim at evolving operational philosophy,techniques,and practices on the basis of which the organization could achieve the given and/or derived ends by utilizing the available, or possibly available, means. Rather than concentrating on a narrow set of ends or means — as currently defined — it would be advisable to visualise a broad range of possibilities. Guidelines on fashioning of resources into usable tools, or modification of what is already available should receive as much attention. Imparting of knowledge and skills, their continued retention, and moulding of attitudes which are a pre-requisite for achieving the organizational ends is a matter of grave importance because, but for it, the whole edifice will crumble. This would necessarily encompass the whole range of personnel, and logistics fields.Perhaps the most important part is for the organization to indicate the strategic options which it is willing to consider.

The prescriptive part should show organizational preferences,if any, in strategies to be adopted, approach to problem solving, process of planning and co-ordination. It ougnt also to clearly indicate what is anathema. This part of the doctrine — that which prescribes and proscribes — needs to be the most detailed of all. It must cover all significant areas and subjects with which the organization is concerned. It should cover all organizational divisions and functional entities that are expected to act, or render support or service, in achieving the organizational goals. All levels must be included and the extent or autonomy, responsibility, accountability, and authority at each level, that resides as a matter of rule,.and in exceptional circumstances, should be especially stated.

The binding part of the doctrine is basically there to clearly show what has to be inescapably done, and what is forbidden, with appropriate rewards and penalties. It certainly includes the acts and statutes that set the limits of acceptable or unacceptable organizational and individual behaviour; but beyond that, this portion of the doctrine must indicate the essence of what must percolate down to every single man so that an organizational consciousness fully and conclusively supports the actions,behaviour, and attitudes that are in organizational interest.

NOTES

1.P. M. Bakshi (compiler and editor), ' The Constitution of India', Universal Book Traders, Delhi, 1991.

2.News report of an interview with Dr. Ramanna, titled 'N-capability of India enough for deterrence.' Times Of India, Bombay, 28 October,1996.

3.P.V.R.Rao, 'Defence Without Drift', Popular Prakashan, Bombay, 1970, (p.3).

4.ibid., (p.4)

5.Nagendra Singh, 'Defence Mechanism of the Modern State', Asia Publishing House, Bombay, 1964,(p.411). [Dr. Nagendra Singh was a member of the Constituent Assembly of India]

6.ibid., (p.418).

7.op. cit., (p.423)

8."I remember a knowledgeable Defence Minister once remarked that the existing system has led to a situation where "checks have tended to over-whelm balances."

Air Chief Marshal (Retd) O.P. Mehra, The Impact of Defence Spending on the Indian Armed Forces', USI Journal, New Delhi, January - March, 1997, (p.11)

9." Government led by Shri V. P. Singh had announced formation of NSC in August, 1990. Nothing very much happened; and in any case, the

Government did not last long enough. Later, Prime Minister Narsimha Rao also announced a commitment to form NSC in 1994, but not with very different results. Shri Gujral, even before he had his portfolio announced, talked about NSC.

"Though while talking to this paper in his private capacity, Mr. Gujral, foreign minister in the V. P. Singh regime, was not sure of his portfolio in the present government, he said that, `the importance of the NSC lies in the fact that it can provide varied inputs on the basis of which the most comprehensive picture of the country's security needs could be outlined. And once this is outlined, we will be in exact position to know what should be our endeavour in our foreign policy area, particularly in the fields of the economic and nuclear diplomacy.'

" `For instance, whether India should have a nuclear deterrent or not is to be based on the most scientific and systematic assessment of the country's security environment. This task can be best done by an agency like the NSC,' Mr. Gujral argues. `The point is that there should be no ambiguity in the minds of our people about the steps we are going to take to safeguard our security.'

" He, however, avoided, specifying what should be the composition of the NSC, saying, more important is the idea itself. `The details can always be worked out through discussions and consultations at the appropriate level.' However, he hinted that top-level expertise from all the available sources in the country could be associated with the functioning of the NSC with the necessary institutional arrangements and adequate resources."

Prakash Nanda, 'Priority for establishment of Security Council :Gujral', the Times of India, 2 Jun 96."

The present Government (June, 1998), are committed to form NSC, and have formed a task force to that effect.

10.Graham T. Allison, 'Essence of Decision', Little Brown and Company, Boston, 1971, (p.246).

11.ibid., (p.252).

12.ibid.,(p.255).

13

Organizational Imperatives For Armed Forces

It would appear that the nation state is likely to be the basic building block of the international system. This assumption is predicated upon two basic ideas :

(1) The nation state will continue to be the organizational level at which the drive for collective identities to endure and prevail on the one hand, and to progress and prosper on the other hand, stands the best chance of being integrated. Considerations of survival and prosperity both are not without linkages with cooperation at one extreme of the spectrum of interaction, and conflict at the other. That is to say, that a majority of ventures in international cooperation and conflict are likely to be informed by interests of nation states. Nation states are more likely to form alliances and associations than ever before.

(2) This is also the level at which there is the greatest likelihood of the individual being able to reconcile his drive for personal survival and prosperity with the demands made on him by higher organizations. Nation states may vie with each other in forming associations — trade blocs and protocols — which have a prospect of substantial gains without correspondingly high risks. On the other hand, defence and security alliances which aim at controlling and managing risks will also proliferate, so that stability may be achieved through balance of power equilibrium, and conflicts may not be allowed to get out of hand.

Nation states will turn to being more outward looking than ever before. Avoidance of isolation will be a major security objective of most nations. Strength and support of world bodies will be sought in furthering national causes with increasing frequency, and collection and processing of information into useful intelligence will be the dominant activity both in interest of security and promotion of national interests. Extraction of intelligence after processing an almost impossible volume of information and data would pose as much of a challenge to the intelligence professional as the mounting of deliberate intelligence operations for obtaining the desired information using all available means — from humans to space sensors. To spot the trends just as they are beginning to emerge, and to take note of major changes and transitions before they actually occur will be a vital function of the combined intelligence.

All segments of the power structure of the nation state will have relevance in active engagement with the world outside. Contingents from armed forces may participate in the UN operations—peace keeping and peace enforcement—more frequently, or on a larger scale. It is quite likely that the UN may agree to standing contingents being held in readiness in home countries on behalf of the UN. Anticipated and actual performance will determine which contingents get selected in the first instance, and repeatedly. If and when India decides upon an arrangement for the defence of the sub-continent, armed forces may get involved in combined operations. Military missions and teams may well become no less common than trade missions and delegations. Professional competence will be prized, more so, at the international fora. Sub-standard professionals will not be able to take care either of national security or prosperity. At a superficial level, professionalism will get associated, at least in popular perception, mainly with being equipped with the state of the art technology ; but more meaningfully, professionals will be called upon to select the most appropriate technology in given circumstances, and to produce the most effective man-machine mix for their purpose at an acceptable cost.

The foreign policy—its formulation and implementation—will become as important as domestic governance and its scope will enlarge to encompass many of the limbs and agencies of the government who till now have had little to do with what happened outside the country. Professional diplomats may have more to do with the conduct of foreign policy, rather than its formulation, which will increasingly have to draw upon inputs from many fields. As the need for professionalism in their own fields increases, the demand for professionals who can synthesize, harmonize, and assist in decision making at the national and international levels will go up. The senior decision makers and functionaries in all the fields of endeavour, but more particularly in those connected with national security, will have to be from amongst those who have a good grasp of national and international politics, and institutions. The leadership of the elected representatives will continue to be accepted, their views as generalists will matter, but they will be forced to draw upon the views and opinions of the professionals.

> "The greater the interdependence, the more countries are involved and the more complex and ramified the consequences, Yet interrelationships are already so tangled and complex that it is nearly impossible for even the brightest politicians and experts to grasp the first-or second -order consequences of their own decisions... This is another way of saying that, except in the most immediate sense, our decision makers no longer really understand what they are doing[1]."

Therefore, one of the organizational imperatives of our times is to depend upon the collegiate wisdom without losing out on accountability and decisiveness.

> "This new organizational form requires a modification of rigid or narrow views of autonomy, as well as changing attitudes toward incentives systems and toward the role of group and sector executives. Instead of seeking autonomy and viewing committees and other joint efforts as a waste of time, business unit managers will have to modify their conception of what 'managing their own business' means.

> The new requirements of the diversified firm will involve a price in terms of less simplicity, greater ambiguity, more subjectivity, and potentially more conflict. However diversified firms that can successfully negotiate this transition will reap rewards in terms of competitive advantage[2]."

The above applies not only to business but also, with even greater force, to governance and security. Regulatory and administrative skills of professional bureaucrats would be in ever increasing demand, but their views and opinions may no longer count as wisdom.

The individual may best respond to demands for sacrifice and privation when these are made in the name of nation state, but not without a serious examination of credibility, motives, and competence of those who make these demands. As he is called upon to respond to demands made on him in the name of nation state, he will carry out his own cost benefit analysis without trusting the leadership or placing excessive faith in it. He is likely to examine, critically, comparative gains that are likely to be made from policies of appeasement vis a vis confrontation and conflict. He is also likely to stake his claim for his share of the spoils in a more determined manner than ever before. He is likely to demand greater efficiency and accountability from the government who in their own interest would have to explain things to him in a direct and clear manner, and state the assumptions and hopes that underpin the policies, so that he can judge for himself the quality of decision making and its implementation.

Mobilization of the people in national causes is going to be that much more difficult except in emergencies, and when there are chances of reasonable gains to be made at a personal level. National service and the like is likely to elicit poor response in terms of actual utility and productivity unless the compensation provided makes it attractive enough. National service, unlike conscription in the past, may not prove to be an economically viable proposition. Only the unemployed may respond with alacrity, but their fitness, and therefore, their actual utility may be doubtful. The organizational imperatives for security that emerge from the above are as follows : need for an intelligence organization that caters to all segments of the power structure; increased participation by all professionals in foreign policy formulation ; need for thorough education of professionals so that they can assist the country in cooperative and competitive ventures at regional and international levels ; a structure for decision making on security related issues at the national level that draws on the prognostication and advice of the professional elites and indicates to the common man the manner and method in which the political leadership discharges its responsibility, and further, convinces him that demands made on him are just and bonafide. None of the above admits of a simple and prescriptive answer about an organizational structure which would answer to the security needs. Even if such an answer were to be found, it would not hold good for all the times to come. Only institutions, approaches, and processes can be thought of.

Answers to two main questions are relevant in arriving at some of the organizational imperatives with respect to the armed forces :

(1) What role needs to be assigned to the armed forces, so that their natural characteristics are fully utilized in the national cause.

(2) How should they be organizationally structured within the state so that they are enabled to carry out their assigned role without jeopardising national security.

Armed forces are an instrument of national power. It is an instrument that specialises in the use of force. Armed forces create an influence, which is at the disposal of the nation, to be used in pursuit of its policy objectives. Their state of readiness and location, in proximity of the international borders, or on high seas, or on foreign soil, are all relevant to the influence they can actually produce or exert. Most nations profess to maintain their armed forces only for the protection of their vital interests including territorial integrity.

Therefore, they are styled defence forces. But in reality influence created by the armed forces is put to deliberate use to create and maintain conditions outside the national borders in which national interests can not only be protected, but also promoted. Depending upon the reach and policy objectives, the threat of armed intervention in any part of the globe may be justified as defence of vital interests of some ally or the other, or of the whole of mankind. The threat may not always be explicit, nor sufficient, but the impact produced by the capability is never without effect. Ignoring for the moment the actual use of force by the armed forces, even the exploitation of their influence is essentially in the international arena. And even when a nation chooses not to exploit the influence of its armed capability, or even disclaims the intentions of its use except in close proximity of its national borders, the influence is not wished away. It is interpreted as a threat, subject to changes in intentions or inclinations, and invites reactions from those likely to be affected. Influence of armed forces primarily operates in the international arena and is an important ingredient of a nation's foreign policy formulations. When armed forces are actually employed, and they use force in discharge of their missions, they operate in a sphere in which concepts concerning the rule of law are not meaningful or relevant. Fortunes of nations using force outside of their borders are not determined by any moral or international laws or the justness of the cause. Competence and capability matter, with some element of chance. The outcome of serious armed conflict between nations has the potential to produce long lasting consequences, verging on finality in many respects. All major decisions in respect of the armed forces, leading to action or inaction, and their implementation is linked directly to the well being of the nation. The fact that the armed forces are meant to use force — which is the monopoly of the state — on its behalf, and operate in the international arena, beyond the reach of the law of the land, make them more an instrument of the state — and a unique one at that — rather than that of the ruling government.

Police organizations too use force on behalf of the state, but they are required to act within the dictates of the law of the land. Their work is supervised by the judiciary, and though they report to and take orders from the government — executive arm of the government — the government does not enjoy complete autonomy with regard to their employment. Checks and balances of democratic polity are adequate to deal with acts of omission and commission of the government with regard to the maintenance and operation of the police forces. Besides, except in cases of very gross mismanagement over a very prolonged time, the negative impact cannot be anywhere as severe as in case of the failure of the armed forces. Diplomacy too takes the foreign service officers into the uncharted terrain of international relations. Their decisions and advice too produce a substantial impact on the fortunes of the nation, but perhaps with not as great a severity or brutality as those produced by the failure or inadequacy of the armed forces. Diplomats make use of influence – economic and military — but they do not create it. Their actions are subject to continuing and continuous oversight by the government in power; besides, diplomatic errors could be corrected on detection. Even so, in many ways, foreign service too is an instrument of the state.

In very general terms , the role of the armed forces is stated to be the protection of the country from external aggression, and assistance to the civil power in maintenance of internal security. There has been some debate about the primary and the secondary roles of the armed forces, and it has been well founded. The armed forced are equipped, trained, and motivated so that they can use force at their disposal, unhindered by any extraneous considerations, with an eye only on effectiveness. An external adversary using force must not be allowed to have his way. Ethical, legal, and humanitarian considerations, if any, come later. It could not be the purpose of any government to utilize such a force for internal security purposes except rarely. A distinction between the primary and other roles is unavoidable in such a situation. But subsequently, a line of thinking was advanced that the armed forces, the army in particular, must guard the country against all forms of threats and aggressions, no matter whether external, internal, or environmental. The actual tasks carried out will depend upon how the threats materialize. It was also stated by one of the Chiefs of Army Staff that the Army did not distinguish between the primary and secondary roles[180]. This may be good for motivating an Army embroiled in counter-insurgency and proxy war, but tends to confuse the issue. It stands to reason that the Army should carry out whichever tasks that it is legitimately assigned in an emergency, provided it is capable of carrying them out. The concern in this argument is with legitimacy and compulsion produced by circumstances; not about priority of tasks on the basis of the assigned role. Army's organizational strengths may be, and are, used in flood control, or Indian Air Force is tasked to drop food packets to flood victim, but neither organizations are equipped or trained for this purpose. The role of the armed services needs to be defined with clarity. Do all the armed services in India have the same role, or do they have different roles? There is, of course, a common understanding amongst those who constitute the armed forces and those who control them, like an unwritten constitution, and it does seem to serve the purpose, but perhaps, not well enough. How come the Army and the Air Force do not share an understanding about the primacy of tasks that the Air Force should be doing. It is presumed that the appropriate role for the armed services is to protect and promote national interests, mainly through the use of force, by operating in conjunction and cooperation with 'others', as and when ordered to do so by the Union Government. There is a need to acknowledge that the armed forces, as a national instrument of power, must be optimally exploited in national interest without self imposed inhibitions. The United Kingdom define the role(s) of their armed forces with great clarity :

> " The UK has, since 1993, publicly expressed Britain's defence policy in terms of three overlapping defence roles:

- first, to ensure protection and security of the United Kingdom and our dependent territories even when there is not major external threat;

- second, to insure against any major external threat to the United Kingdom and our allies;

- and third, to contribute to promoting the United Kingdom's wider security interests through maintenance of international peace and stability."

Our armed forces were surely not defending Indian territorial integrity in Male when they were employed by the government, at the invitation of Maldives, to put down a coup in that country, or when they were asked to do peace keeping in Sri Lanka. They were employed to protect our interests. Our contingents in UN peace keeping missions, while executing the allotted tasks, as a natural consequence, enhance the prestige of the country, which in turn helps the country in acquiring a little bit of additional influence. Armed forces are so employed to promote our interests. Why not so define the role of the armed forces. It will bring clarity in thinking and give impetus to the armed forces to do their contingency planning. Armed forces cannot and do not act alone. When employed on international missions, they must act in conjunction with contingents from other countries. Should India ever put together a sub-continental security alliance, armed forces will be required to cooperate with alliance partners. Within the country, they cooperate on a day today basis with the para-military forces who manage international border, and they work and cooperate with central and state police forces in the internal security duties. It would appear, from the accounts of peace keeping missions in Sri Lanka, that had they been aware of the intent and actions of some of the other agencies of the government, things would have been less messy. Of course, had their charter and role included a requirement to cooperate with those agencies, things would have been very much better. Cooperating with the state governments is integral to the internal security role of the armed forces. This is common sense, but because it is not explicitly stated in defining the role of the armed forces, not enough thought gets channelised in this direction with the result that organizational mechanisms for regular exchange of views and liaison do not get built, and the essential infrastructure does not remain in place, and even elementary things like channels for intercommunication are seen to be wanting when the crunch comes. But this is not as important as the damage that this state of affairs does due to lack of clarity and suspicions which fuel turf wars and encourage one-up-manship. The point is that the role must be comprehensively and realistically stated for the armed forces. 'Others' in conjunction with whom they are required to work also need to be equally made aware of their obligations, commitments and prerogatives. The list of 'others' is substantially long, and is likely to get longer as organizations get more sophisticated, and the need for effective integration increases.

Mere acknowledgement that the armed forces are an instrument of state would itself suggest some imperatives about how they need to be integrated into the organizational structure of the nation state : links must be established between the armed forces and the State so that the armed forces, on the one hand, can draw upon readily proffered support and resources of the nation, and on the other hand, they feel directly responsible for their performance to the nation. The President of the Union, who personifies the State, is the supreme commander of the armed forces in India. This link serves the purpose stated above in ceremonial matters, but no better. This is not surprising because the relationship was not perceived by the makers of our Constitution to signify that the armed forces are headed by the President to demonstrate that they derive their charter from a symbol that signifies the state[5]. There has been one odd example of an appeal to the President by the head of the armed forces in security interest, but otherwise, neither the armed forces nor the government seem to show a conscious awareness of the armed forces being an institution of the state and not merely an instrument of the government. The executive authority must rest where it is, that is with the government, in our parliamentary system, but the responsibility for approving of all major policy decisions in respect of the armed force needs to be unavoidably transferred to the Parliament in whom the sovereignty of the nation rests. The aim should be to make the government amenable to professional advice and specifically accountable, in matters of security, to the Parliament. Advice on policy regarding the raising and maintenance of the armed forces and their employment could emanate from a statutory body, with a dedicated staff of professionals, created for the purpose. The body so created — NSC — must be such that it takes an integrated view of all the instruments of the state. The government should be required to explain their reactions to the advice, particularly when they reject it, to the nation at large, when the budgetary demands of various ministries are considered. It should be customary to publish a white paper annually for this purpose. Sensitive issues and classified matter could be brought to the notice of the oversight committees of the parliament, when it cannot be included in the white paper.

Now coming to the second of the questions raised about the structuring of the armed forces within the state : The defence forces are meant primarily to protect the country against external aggression, which, when it is of a serious nature, threatens not only the government but the state itself: its constitution, assets, and population. And it is the state which has to be defended in circumstances when many of laws, statutes, and conventions stand devalued, and force holds most trumps. The very existence and survival of the state may be at stake, perhaps with no likelihood of a second chance. The response of the armed forces will depend, inter alia, on the state of their preparedness, morale, and leadership. No evidence including alibis of denial of budgetary or other support to them in preceding years, or weakening of their fabric by malafide interference, or lack of intelligence would be of any significance or avail. The defence forces would be expected to perform with what they have, and succeed. If not, the consequences would be dire, and the losses, irremediable. Failure of the armed forces hold a finality which does not brook any partisan approach. When faced with great danger, national governments are formed, so that ranks are closed and the gap between the ruling party and the state polity is bridged, and the state as a whole reacts to the impending danger. Not only the resources of the armed forces, or the government, but also of the citizens — including their private resources — are mobilized by the state in a life and death struggle. If that is the environment in which the defence forces are meant ultimately to perform, they cannot but be an instrument of the state. State is the stake that they fight for, and they need to draw on resources, good will, and support of the entire state. It is perhaps for this reason, that the defence forces have as their supreme commander, not the head of the government, but the head of the state. Generally, the approach has been to assert that the civil authority is supreme, and that the defence forces must carry out the tasks which are allotted to them by the government. This is indeed self evident, and not open to challenge. What is of interest are the relationships, obligations, and commitments that bind the defence forces to the state, how these are wrought or brought about, and how the purpose that causes the state to raise and maintain the armed forces is realised.

Armed forces being not just one of the instruments, but the ultimate instrument of the state, should remain outside of the government, as far as possible, so that its employment in the interest of the ruling government, rather than in the interest of the state proper, when there is such a divergence in interests, should be prevented through a system of checks and balances. In the early days of democratic India, particularly because of the experience in Pakistan, checks and balances in relation to the armed forces had one specific connotation: prevention of coups, and keeping the armed forces in their place. But after the emergency regime of 1975, and subsequent to operation Blue Star, public opinion became sensitised to the possibility of the ruling government making use of the armed forces to fulfil its own purpose. Inappropriate use of the armed forces poses a threat to the state which is no less pernicious than that of possible coups.

The 'mantra' of civil power being supreme does not address this threat.

It must at once be conceded that India has held its own in three major conflicts since 1947, and do have a system in place. But it certainly needs to be modified so that it takes into account the post cold war world and other changes in the offing at the turn of this century. Some thoughts about a 'System for management for national security' have been presented in Chapter 12. Here it is intended to follow the organizational imperatives in so far as they relate to the Defence Services.

The armed services have no clientele except for enlightened national leadership and public opinion. In the absence of both they must plead for resources for national security as 'their' requirement. This is particularly so in times of peace, or whenever the political leadership 'feel' that the armed forces would have no special or significant part to play in 'their' time, and other means would suffice to fulfil 'their' ends. This was so during the decade preceding the Second World War in Britain. The reality of Hitler's Germany did not seem to make much difference, and in the teeth of Churchill's relentless urging, the armed forces were starved of resources. Britain ended up paying a very heavy price for the neglect. In industrialised democracies, when arms industry can make significant profits out of sales to armed forces, in their own or other, countries turn into clients of armed forces, and create pressure groups and think tanks, who will lobby for higher allocation of resources to the armed forces. Perhaps, that is how military-industrial linkages get established. Perhaps there is a need for privatization of production of a large segment of defence oriented goods, and decidedly those of common user items. Export promotion of war-like and other stores required by the armed forces will be facilitated if these are produced in the private sector. Heavy armament items which require substantial capital outlay could be retained in the domain of the public sector. But regulatory mechanisms and procedures which enable contracting out of war-like goods to the private sector need to be refined. But for them, mobilization is likely to be hindered.

Armed forces must not be starved of support that they need from the society in general and the government in particular. The creation of public awareness through media, purposive and detailed discussions in the Parliament, at least when the defence budget is considered are the obvious means, and they must be pursued. But beyond that, it is through direct contact between the public at large and the armed forces that awareness is likely to spread more rapidly, and make a lasting impact.

As a part of the exercise to increase the contact between the armed forces and the people at large, individuals in all walks of life whether in government service, or self-employed, should be encouraged to join 'reserves' with limited commitment and liability, in return for limited remuneration. The ideas about contributions that can possibly be expected from reserves, the situations in which they can be called out, and the modes and methods of utilizing their services need to be reviewed and recast. Militia, a significant part of any resistance oriented force, has to be put together from reserve units. A great deal of enthusiasm and desire to help, that many well meaning citizens harbour, remain untapped because there is no organizational effort in this direction from the armed forces themselves. India having decided to opt for nuclear weapons, civil defence in and around major centres of population close to border, and in metropolitan cities, must assume serious proportions in years to come. The question of armed forces active units being made available for crisis management should make way for reserve units taking on these tasks, and further extending a helping hand to the front line soldiers.

National Cadet Corps also serves a useful purpose, and may become the nucleus of a university reserve programme. Departmentally organized Territorial army units on the lines of Railway units, if encouraged, would serve the purpose of reducing the army's burden of running essential services in emergencies. Militia — home guards — and civil defence units could also be added to the territorial army. This movement could also be carried forward into the road transport sector. This is an area where the purpose of a young service, reserve for expansion, and creation of awareness converge. The armed forces would necessarily have to create training facilities and mechanisms for the purpose. This should not, of course, be looked upon as an economy measure or an employment oriented exercise. Considerable organizational and motivational skills will be required to derive the necessary benefits. Armed forces, for many years, and very unsuccessfully, pleaded for lateral induction of soldiers who were retired from the armed service at an early age, into other government jobs. This has been looked upon by the receiving ministries and departments as a plea for reemployment opportunity. The positive side of the proposal has invariably been discounted. Attitudes and experience that the personnel of the armed forces bring with them cannot but be a source of benefit to the recipient organizations.

Although there are situations in which single services may act entirely on their own — aerial combat, aerial bombing, engagements at sea, and so on — the possibility of a single service successfully concluding a conflict by carrying out tasks independently and on its own is very small. Such claims were made on behalf of the air power before the Second World War. With major advances in nuclear, rocket, space communication, and air technologies such claims are reiterated with renewed vigour For so long as mankind lives on land, such claims must be examined with great care, and reliance placed on conventional wisdom that all means need to be used to locate and exploit vulnerabilities with a view to securing the best advantage. Faith, ability and skill in the purposeful use of force, as the prime means, in the interest of the nation is what distinguishes the armed forces from the rest, and should bind them together. The tasks that they carry out will depend upon the environment in which they operate, and their capabilities in terms of equipment and training but their role cannot but be identical. The need for the armed forces to work and act as an integrard system, and not as individual services cannot be over emphasized. This is not to question the need for the existence of independent armed services—army, navy, air force—but a plea for some functional restructuring.

Fighting on land is essentially different from fighting on sea or in air. It is possible to fight on land by making skilful use of ground and cover it affords. Although fighting platforms are extensively used to fight on ground, in the ultimate analysis, ground can best be defended, or held after it is captured, by men on ground. They can resist, and they can actually obtain compliance of the adversary, because of their ability to hold together in adversity, take punishment, renew themselves and subsist on little, and ultimately prevail through sheer perseverance and will — collective will. Of course technology matters, and admittedly, men in trenches cannot survive nuclear or even precise conventional strikes, but the part that hardihood, faith in leadership, cohesion, and the will to persist collectively play in land warfare are likely to retain their significance even in our own time, and are likely to do so in the future also. Professional values that are essential for fighting on land are derived from these primary considerations, and the basic organizational philosophy reflects them. Experience of the British Indian Army indicated that a single person could not possibly exercise direct command over more than 800 to 1000 soldiers, that is, knit them into a cohesive and coherent unit that will perform and hold under all circumstances. A single human being, so fragile in a sense, is collectively strong, and performs best in adversity by being a part of a larger collective identity. This is the basic unit of 'strength' which can be turned into an instrument of 'power' by equipping and training it. The unit is the matrix in which the equipment is embedded, to obtain the best of man machine mix. These building blocks are used to create the fighting potential of land armies by training them to interact and cooperate. Of course there are variations. With man-power having become expensive and scarce, it is reduced so that no more than what is necessary to fight with, or use the main equipment of the unit, is retained. Of course, surplus manpower can be an embarrassment, where it is essentially not required, because destructive potential of strike weapons has gone up so high. The methods of recruitment, training, motivation, and techniques of leadership are based on creation of strong and nesting collective identities which will perform under conditions of terrain and development that actually obtain on ground. Most units meant for prosecuting land warfare, including those meant for combat support and service, have often to work in primitive conditions where substantial hardship is unavoidable irrespective of and apart from the actions of the adversary.

Organizations of the navy and air forces are built around fighting platforms with human being superimposed on or in them. Keeping the platforms afloat or in the air is the minimum precondition for operational viability. Living and fighting must be carried out from within the confines of the fighting platforms. If training and motivation of contestants is comparable, technology used is by far the most important determinant of who will win or lose in a fire fight. Results of a single direct hit can be near final with no chances for survival and renewal. Individual's skill and courage matter a great deal, particularly so as the size of the crew decreases. Each of the organizations is tailored to the requirement of the craft. Individuals have very limited freedom to act. Their duties in the ship or aircraft are precisely defined, and do not change in response to the environment as much as they do in the case of the army. The emphasis is on imparting of precise skills. An individual has to be fitted out to work in a particular craft. The training and motivating philosophy must perforce be different.

It is difficult to think of a single unified armed service. Such a venture, if attempted may become unmanageably complicated, with no advantage to show for it except some economy in financial terms.

> " It is that, in the ultimate, defence organization requires that men should fight; that men can be ordered to risk, and indeed lose , their lives without the option of lawful refusal. It is this characteristic that makes career in the Services not just another job It is this characteristic, so it is argued, that demands an unbroken chain of single service command from the lowest to the highest level in order that those who lead should have the necessary legal and moral authority to give such order, and maintain the trust and confidence of those to whom orders are given[6]."

Each of the armed service has a proud tradition which is a source of inspiration. It needs to be preserved. The most admirable goal of operational integration of the armed services must be achieved through other means : unification of services may not be the answer. In fact unification may prove to be counter productive. Even some of the single service organizations are very large — particularly those of the army — and integration, if attempted, may not be really viable. Canada attempted such an exercise, perhaps with not too great a success, because there has been no emulation of it by others on any scale.

What has necessarily to be done is the integration of operations. More easily said than done, it would create new problems: some additional organizations would have to come into being; organizations which have had an uncluttered field to themselves would have to work together, in restricted space and constricted time frames, and achieve synergy. Individual services must not lose their agility, effectiveness or elan must not take friends for foes or vice versa ; fully discharge the responsibilities assigned to them ; and yet contribute effectively to achievement of the combined goals so that the totality of achievement exceeds the sum of achievements of individual single services. These ideas are not new. All along, this has been the general thrust. But the compulsions to act together were not so great, and problems associated with integration were considered insurmountable ; or to put it in another way, the penalty for not operating together was not so excessive, and it was possible to achieve success largely by going it alone. Computer backed communications and broad band remote sensing and interpretation facilities make operational integration possible without giving rise to additional 'friction'. The only limitation is the human factor. Getting people to accept that they have to learn to work in more complex organizational structures, and within the 'space' and opening allotted to them. If the adversary achieves such an integration more satisfactorily or earlier, the power differential would be in his favour, because organizational strength is a source of power.

We have the model of the United States with operational commands with theatre and functional responsibilities : for instance, the US Pacific Command is a command with a territorial responsibility, but the US Special Operations Command has a functional responsibility dealing with special operations of all the four services. If special operations were to be conducted, say, by the US in the Pacific theatre, it would call for close coordination between the two theatre commanders, and the sharing of responsibilities, and authority that goes with it, would have had to be decided with reference to generic and specific criteria, and in close consultation with each other, at every step. Communications have to cater for this so that rapid grouping and regrouping is possible and teams can move in and out of operational chain of command swiftly with all the necessary logistics and intelligence back up. That indeed is asking for a great deal. The detail that would have to be taken care of would be substantial, and the commitment would have to be to the task at hand. The centres of professional single service pride would have to be relocated, and individuals will have to be differently sensitised. This is not easily achieved. It is not easy to convince those who are used to clear cut single service and territorial commands that have clearly defined boundaries and responsibilities that there is a need for a switch over to a more complex system.

The system in India has been tried and tested, and has the advantage of simplicity. But it has worked only indifferently in the past. The Air Force in 1971 operations blamed the then Army Chief for poor coordination and utilization of resources But similar charges were also levied on the other side of the hill, that is in Pakistan, where the Pak Air Force and Navy felt left out and under utilized in 1965 and in 1971. Both the nations have generally followed comparable systems except that Pakistan have a Chairman Joint Chiefs of Staff, a job no body seems to want because it commands no power. Pakistan appears to have made some cosmetic changes, but does not seem to have touched the core. The systems which were found wanting by the end of the Second World War cannot be continued indefinitely. Not in the age of satellites and ballistic missiles. By closing years, the Supreme Commander system had gradually replaced the system of having independent single service theatre commanders, that the British had followed at the beginning of the Second World War. The Indian system is in need of a change. There is a strong case for introducing integrated operational commands on territorial and functional basis. It does require a lot of care in actually designating the territorial commands with their boundaries and allocating resources to them, but conceptually, it is easy to see that India could be divided into, say, six territorial commands north, north-east, south-east, south west, west, and north-west commands, with suitable elements from the three services, with their unified theatre commanders. It is very obvious that every unified command is unlikely to have elements from all the services; in fact, the army element in most commands will be disproportionately greater. Unified functional commands could include the 'strategic forces' command and 'strategic movement' command, once again with complements from single services. Every unified command would necessarily have to have single service advisers with certain allocated functions. These two functional commands have been mentioned because they are the most obvious ones. It would make good sense to bring under a unified commander deep penetration strike capability and Prithvi missiles. Similarly Indian experience in Sri Lanka has convinced many that strategic movement can only be undertaken nationally and on a tri-service basis. Even the railways would like to deal with a single nodal contact. Other functional unified commands could be thought of later, and they would emerge. Some may not deserve the grand title of the command, and a modest 'agency' would do just as well as in the US. What is important is the principle that such integration has to take place. The brigade commander fighting a battle north of Pathankot should not have to worry about whether or not the fighters will appear on the scene to beat off the tanks, in time, and without the intervention of the Air Headquarters, any more than the air base commander should have to worry about dealing with aerially delivered mines, deep penetration bombs, or an air drop by Pakistani commandos. If air force or army units have to move from Western to South Eastern theatre in an emergency, it should be possible at the national level to deal with a single unified command as a nodal agency. It is only to be expected that the idea of unified commands is likely to be resisted because it involves integration.

> "... Organizational change is disruptive. It cuts across old loyalties, requires new ways of working and offers benefits that are uncertain and unproven. Of all the organizational changes those that involve the integration in some form or another of the individual armed services are the most fiercely resisted and the most controversial[7]."

Insufficiency of air force and naval resources is cited as the principle reason against creation of combined commands. General V N Sharma, one of the former Chiefs of the Army Staff, holds this view[8]. Indian Air Force (IAF) doctrine strenuously advises against such integration.

> "On the question of jointmanship while the doctrine declares that a future conflict for the Indian armed forces will almost certainly involve joint operations, it does not, however, look at the unified command to realise this objective. Acknowledging the resistance of the IAF on that point, the doctrine proclaims that, 'Air assets should never be parcelled out. If India is to achieve maximum military effectiveness with its limited resources, we must be fully aware of the dangers of dividing the asset of a potent instrument of national power — air power[9]."

Valid as these arguments are, they opt for status quo which has created a situation which prevents effective integration and utilization. One of the US studies — a study sponsored by the U.S. Army's Deputy Chief of Staff, Intelligence, and conducted in the Strategy and Doctrine Program of RAND's Arroyo Centre[10] — paints a particularly unflattering picture of Indian armed forces and points out lack of agility and integration as the main culprits.

"Indian army is unlikely to perform operationally within a given time frame. IAF does not contribute operationally, and the Indian Navy is irrelevant."

Organizational integration should certainly be possible, given the current state of command, control, communications, and intelligence technology. Without an integrated organization, efficient utilization of the armed forces will be that much more difficult.

The composition of each of the territorial and functional commands would have to reflect the underlying purpose that each of the commands would be required to serve. The design should be derived from the anticipated types of warfare and war aims. (A reference may be made to Chapter 8). The linkage is vital. It took the US the worst of Vietnam years to conclude that the war aims were not being progressed by using forces which were not structured, trained, or equipped to combat the Vietnamese who used a mix of irregular and regular warfare with emphasis on resistance and manoeuvre. Forces which had been designed to prevail against other conventional forces in warfare involving attrition, could not find ways and means to convert what they considered to be their victories in battles, into a favourable outcome of war that the Vietnamese were fighting.

Strategic forces command would primarily have to rely on deterrence. Dissuasive elements will have to go to territorial commands. Each of the commands would have to have a mix of forces that enable it to prevail in warfare that it may either select or which may be forced upon it. Elements may have to come from one or more, or all the services as the case may be. The mix would have to include not only regulars, but also reservists.

It is obvious that unification of the operational and functional commands cannot take place without the unification at the top. The unified commanders can only report to and take orders from a unified command authority. It could be chairman of the chiefs of staff committee ('COSC) or the chief of defence staff (CDS) who, in turn, would be accountable to the defence minister for all military operations. CDS has been a very sensitive issue in India, advocated by the army, and generally not supported by the other two services for the obvious reason that the appointment is likely to be occupied more often by an army man, being the largest service. In any case, the benefits may not be as great as made out by those who support it. The idea that CDS will be able to over-rule a service chief in his own domain is not convincing; in any case, the service chief will have the right to make his dissent known to the Defence Minister. Ultimately, a consensus would have to work. A full time Chairman COSC would do as well[11], except that the position in reality would be much less influential than that of any of the service chiefs whose nominal superior he would be.

A unified command structure for operations is predicated upon the existence of a joint doctrine and joint staff. The joint staff would have to function mostly at the national, theatre, and functional command levels, and perhaps even at the level of joint task forces, as and when they are put together. It may not be easy to formulate a joint doctrine, or joint staff procedures, but that would not be anywhere as arduous or as problematic as training officers in joint operations and joint staff work. Joint staff work, which would include operational plans and their execution, would call for skills, knowledge-base, and experience which would have to be built up gradually and painfully, from scratch. In concept, it would have to be general-general-staff, so to say. Rewards for the labour would be few, because the opportunities for promotion would be few, and there would not be many takers. This problem was also faced in the United States, and a time worn algorithm was employed to deal with it : no promotion to the next rank — above a certain level — without a ticket punched in a joint slot. It would work mechanically ; it is a mechanical solution. But the main purpose of inspiring officers to take pride in joint staff work and cultivating skills in it will not be met in this manner. Joint operations will have to be acknowledged by the military as the acme of professional achievement, and not merely tolerated because they are ineluctable. For effective joint staff work, there would have to be uniformity in the staff procedures, and, if possible, in branches of the staff in all the three services. This is not at all as difficult to achieve, but for the desire to continue with what one has been doing in the past.

Operational directives and orders to the unified commands could be sent by the chairman chiefs of staff committee, after obtaining concurrence of the minister of defence, or on his instructions. The issues would have been discussed and analyzed in the National Security Council, and in chiefs of staff committee, and in single service headquarters. The draft directives would have been prepared by the joint staff and scrutinised by the single service headquarters too. As in any complex system procedures would indeed take a lot of coordination. Since time would be of essence, a single operational headquarters, co-locating joint and single service operational and intelligence staffs would be necessary. The national command centre could be superimposed on this joint services operational and intelligence headquarters with complete live-in facilities for essential personnel. Very obviously, such a headquarters would be amongst the most attractive targets. It would have to be well protected, with one, or even two, alternative sites, equally prepared and connected, to which a shift can be made at short notice.

The main issue does not appear to be whether there should be a CDS or not. Of course, CDS would be a better solution ; he would be able to sever his single service loyalty with greater determination in view of his total and singular responsibility and the accountability that goes with it. But this would only happen when a generation of 'general-general' staff comes up for whom joint operations and jointmanship is an article of faith. But till then, even chairman chiefs of staff committee could carry out the task, provided he is also not burdened with conduct of operations as at present. With a joint services operational headquarters and national command centre as visualised, the actual conduct of operations would be the responsibility of theatre commanders or commanders of functional commands, with only the planning and supervisory role with the COSC, something that they would share with the Defence Minister. The chain of command would be from the Prime Minister to the Defence Minister; and from him to the theatre commanders, through the COSC[12].

Perhaps, the necessity to bring about these structural changes, may also be reached by another route. The raising, equipping, and maintenance of the armed forces is quite a distinct function from their actual employment. It stands to reason that the structure and equipment of the armed forces should be derived from their role and tasks and must be compatible with the range of strategic options that they are likely to consider. But in reality, very rarely, those who take the decisions regarding the development of equipment or their acquisition actually use it in war. Conduct of operations is circumscribed by what is available. If need be the ends are adjusted to suit the means. Conduct of successful operations, with all the resources that can be garnered is the quintessence of the task of the armed forces. Raising and equipping of the armed forces is done over a long period of time, with decisions being taken by the political masters on professional advice. Decisions in the field have to be taken by the professionals in the light of political directions, but mainly on the basis of what is possible at the time, and what is likely to be the most advantageous in the best professional judgment. Operations is the area of maximum autonomy, though not total, and their conduct has to be in the hands of the professionals. The reasons for separating the operational functions from the rest are as follows :

(1) A certain advantage is to be gained by creating a degree of competition between those who raise and maintain the forces and those who employ them : operational commanders, being down stream, would be in a position to point out the short-comings and deficiencies. Both together may point out faults in allocation of role and tasks in the national security doctrine or directive. This could result in airing of matters and views, that will ultimately be, to the advantage of national security. If there is a single point

of decision making and responsibility, such criticism may never surface, and many short comings may not get either detected or corrected. It cannot be anyone's case that the proposed arrangement is without faults. Mutual recrimination can lead to unhealthy relationships and worse unless right attitudes are developed. Those who oppose these changes could also point out that the present generation of the operational commanders may be cavilling at those who laid down their jobs 15 or 20 years earlier, because that's how long it takes to get the equipment on ground and issued to units and formations after the decision is taken to introduce the equipment.

(2) Perspective planning is the key to creation and maintenance of forces. Although it takes only a couple of years to get persons from civvy streets into uniform, it takes anything between 7 to 10 years of training for an effective junior NCO or a company commander to emerge. The perspective planner must see at least that much ahead, if not more. The operational commander is concerned with here and now. The qualities required to be an effective perspective planner are those which, in an operational commander, may be undesirable and vice versa. Ability to question basic premises, wait patiently for consensus to emerge, dependence upon hard data, utmost caution, and virtual rejection of intuitive urges are not likely to make good generals in the field; similarly, cutting into margins of safety, reliance on personal judgment, or dependence upon personal ability to inspire subordinates into superhuman effort may not get the perspective planners any where. Technology assessment is a major concern of the perspective planner whereas the use of available technology is the concern of the operational man. The nation may benefit from separating these functions.

(3) Operational command is very much an exclusive function of those in uniform; perspective and proximate

> planning and raising of forces, can admit those who are specialist planners. Personnel from the uniformed cadre would still be required but in fewer numbers. As the cost of training goes up — and it is bound to go up steeply with the rise in equipment prices and their operation and maintenance — there would be a pressure not to use trained operational personnel on the logistics side except where necessary.

Reorganized Ministry of Defence could consist of two main wings : one dealing with the raising, equipping, and maintenance of the armed forces (REM Wing) ; and the other dealing with their role, tasking, and employment (ROTE Wing). The REM Wing could be headed by the Defence Council, and the ROTE Wing could be headed by the Chiefs of Staff Committee, both performing a range of line and staff functions for the Defence Minister. Chart on the following Page shows a notional organization based on the above concept.

The Chart shows each of the departments of the REM Wing headed by a minister, apart from the Defence Minister heading the entire ministry. The presence of these ministers is not crucial to the organization, but these slots can be used for grooming prospective defence ministers, or for utilizing exceptional talent in management or other fields. There has been a wide-spread belief in the Armed Forces, that bureaucrats have driven a wedge between the elected representatives and the armed forces to subserve their own interests. With a single minister dealing with all the issues dealing with the armed forces, he could just not have had enough contact with the armed forces. That apart, with Defence Ministry being the direct charge of the Prime Minister for long periods, the question of meaningful attention to defence and related security issues just did not arise[13]. Deputy ministers and ministers of state in the Defence Ministry, in the past, might have relieved the Defence Minister of some of the less important 'files', but beyond that, their contact with the armed services did not break out of the established mould; if anything, they were even more dependent on bureaucrats. Unless there is a structural

National Organization of Ministry of Defence

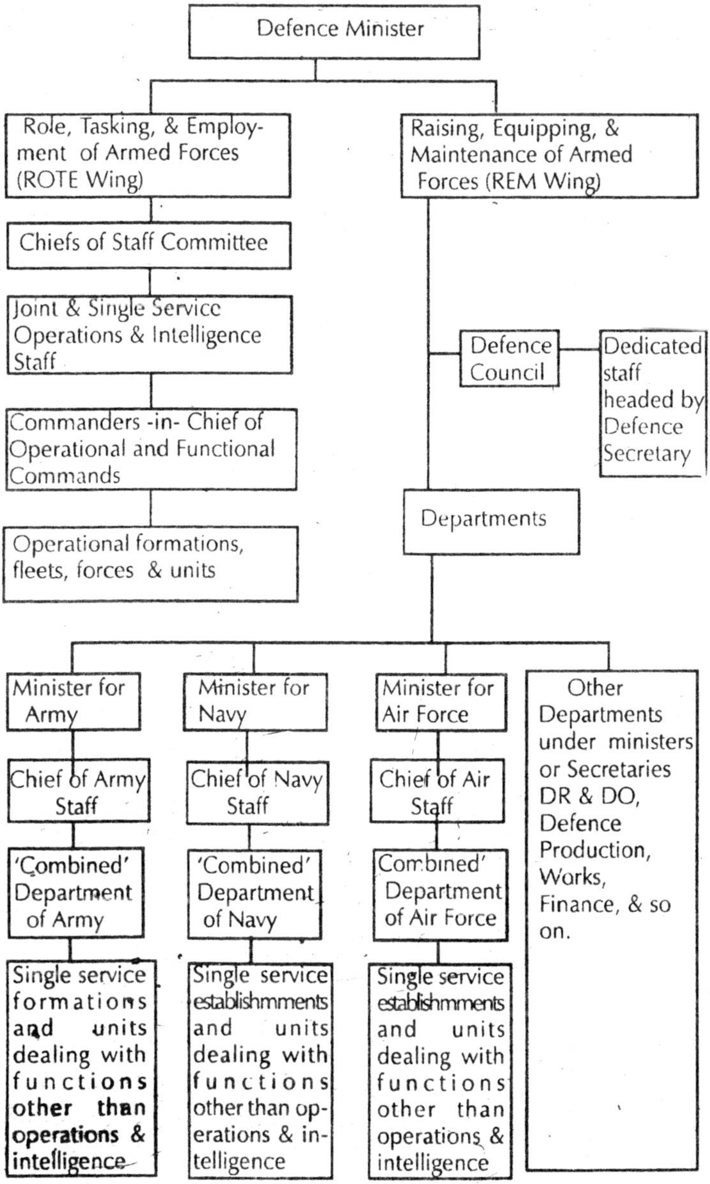

change, as reflected in the Chart, and the ministers are made accountable for their departments, interact directly with those on whose performance they depend, and in the process develop some loyalty to the armed services, the intended purpose may not be served.

A set of 'combined' departments of army, navy, air force, works, procurement, production, R&D, and Finance could be visualised — the list is illustrative, and admittedly incomplete. All the 'departments' come under the purview of the REM Wing. Each of the departments could have a mix of permanent cadre of bureaucrats and professionals, with bureaucrats giving continuity. Departments of the army, navy, and the air force would be headed by their respective Chiefs, and other departments by the civilian secretaries. Even in the armed services departments, some of the slots on the third rung could be filled by the civilians of the Ministry's permanent cadre, with at least one of the Deputy Chief's post — perhaps, that dealing with planning, budget and accounting — being held by one of the civilians. On a reciprocal basis, some of the posts in the Defence Council, and other departments, should be held by officers of the armed services.

The recommendations could be considered by a Defence Council chaired by the Defence Minister, and comprising all other Ministers in the Ministry, the Service Chiefs, the Defence Secretary, the Scientific and Financial Advisers to the Defence Minister, and Secretaries heading other departments. The Defence Council could have a dedicated secretarial staff of their own. Defence Secretary is visualized as the Defence Council Secretary, and one of the Advisers to the Defence Minister.

The Defence Council should also have a dedicated staff drawn from all the streams that make up the Defence Council. All the departments should be responsible for perspective and proximate planning and for mobilization. Defence Council should have the responsibility for integrating and monitoring the effort. The idea that a single set of people can do all the analytical and creative work that is associated with planning and mobilization is not well founded. Each speciality have their own world view by way of trends and prognosis, and what needs to be done in response. Such a view of the specialists may perhaps be narrow and even uni-dimensional; even so it is required to be stated without reservations so that the generalists may then bring in the necessary balance and harmony. Generalists cannot and should not tell specialists how to view the world or on what lines to think, nor think for them. It is for generalists to fully comprehend the viewpoint and advice of the specialist, reconcile the conflicting pulls and pressures and inconsistencies, and then, to arrive at a coherent plan. Resolution of divergence through debate is a democratic process, and it need not be ruled out of interaction between the specialist and the generalist. But retention of internal contradictions in plans is something that has to be avoided. This process has to take place bottom upwards, and specific effort has to be earmarked for it. In small organizations, it may suffice merely to reserve specific slots and ask the concerned officials to place their conclusions on record. In larger organizations, it may be necessary to earmark specific staff for this purpose. Care, of course has to be taken that the planning staff are not treated as laggards not doing any useful work. It is worth considering that much of the so called work — efforts to address and solve actual problems which cannot wait any longer — is really, in many instances, a direct result of failure to anticipate problems before they arise, or inability to resolve them before they assume crisis proportions.

Mobilization of resources is an equally challenging task, and it will become even more challenging as the command economy gradually disappears[14]. Resources required in war, prolonged or otherwise, cannot be kept impounded. Reserves have to be maintained, and yet, reserves which cannot be turned over, and lose their effectiveness with passage of time, partially or totally, without ever being put to any use, is a wastage. There is a need to reduce this wastage. The quantum of reserves can be reduced if procurement or production can catch up with the actual usage—or destruction—in the shortest possible time. One way is to introduce a large proportion of items of common use into the armed services to the extent possible ; another is to modify the existing industrial capacity so that it can manufacture the specific warlike goods, when required, in as short a time as possible ; yet another is to impose on the industry—of course for a compensation to be paid by the government—,a certain holding of materials which they need any way, but in excess of their actual requirements, so that reserves are maintained, at one remove, at a comparatively lesser cost. This approach is applicable to manpower and other services too. The exercise is extremely complex and needs to be initiated by the armed services. For a single aspect, say mobilization of the railway effort, where there is a single point contact like the railway board, things are more manageable. But say if capacity of the automobile industry were to be employed to produce assemblies and spares for products required in bulk by the armed forces in war, the undertaking would be far more difficult and complex with the demands of security having to be taken into account. No single agency of the government may be able to handle it. To generate expertise of this kind the United States have a specific institution — The Industrial College of the Armed Forces. Such a need had not perhaps been felt in India because of the command economy, and partly because of the experience of short conflicts[15]. Some problems, even under a command economy regime, were experienced by the armed forces when even public sector factories could not execute the orders placed on them because they were not supported by the budgetary allocations. Things would be that much more difficult to manage in years to come. The Armed Forces, over a period of time, got used to the idea of fighting from stacked reserves in the hope that the match would be called off, at the instance of the super powers, before they ran out of reserves. Mobilization of material and non-material resources like media in support of armed forces and national cause has to be made a field of conscious activity in every department of defence. Eventually, inputs coming from every department will have to be reconciled and managed by a designated nodal department or a ministry which would, hopefully, not treat its nodal responsibility as an exclusive prerogative for fighting turf battles, but treat it as a mandate for cooperation

Decisions given by the minister in Defence Council could then be carried out, or referred to the cabinet for approval directly or through the National Security Council, as appropriate. Arbitrariness in decision making or evasion of issues, or playing off one service against the other may become that much more difficult. The minister can and will certainly have his way in the end, but he will also have to get used to collegiate decision making as in the case of the Railway Board. It is obvious that all decisions will not be given in council, nor is it necessary. Departmental heads could obtain decisions from the Minister in charge of the department provided the minister is empowered to do so. But for such empowerment, Defence Council is likely to occupy itself with trivialities. Departmental heads must not be denied direct access to the Defence Minister, particularly when there is a disagreement with the minister in charge of the department. In fact, the minister in charge could be asked to bring any dissent that he may have with the departmental head, and jointly refer the matter to the Defence Minister.

The organizational structure suggested above gets over some of the major shortcomings of the present system . At present the services carry out all the creative work about planning and 'submit' it to the defence ministry who, theoretically, are required to evaluate these proposals, express their views, and make recommendations to the minister for his 'orders'. There are several flaws in this approach:

(1) Services are reduced to the status of supplicants who are asking something for themselves. The idea that the armed services have a national role, in performance of which they need to carry out several tasks, and for which purpose, they need resources tends to get forgotten, and what is in essence a national requirement, gets construed as a requirement of the armed services. Under a regime in which neither a security doctrine exists, nor an operational directive stands formally approved, it is quite possible for a bureaucrat to argue that the tasks visualized by the

armed services may not have to be performed. On the basis of that argument or conviction, he may find ways and means of avoiding or evading the requirements projected by the armed services. The system is inertia prone, and rewards inaction.

(2) The 'evaluation' of proposals is done by those who have no first hand experience of the use of force. Their approach is to examine the stated logic, spot some contradiction or the other, and return the proposal. They have no stakes in improving the system because they are not accountable for consequences of their inaction. They are not expected to do any creative work or participate in the process in a constructive manner. Their purpose is to chart a course of least resistance—that which will not bring them into troubled waters. It is not as if uniformed officers, similarly placed, may react differently. The system is weighted in favour of inaction.

At present, with the defence ministry and the services functioning as two separate entities, service headquarters act as an inter-face between the services—which are not a part of the government—and the government. This inter-face has proved less than satisfactory, a few reasons for which have been stated above. A service officer with excellent performance in the field is often posted to the service headquarters only to learn that his skills and attitudes are not of any particular use. After he finishes his tenure, and returns to service headquaters after several years, he makes an effort to re-learn the bureaucratic skills. The system proposed should capitalise on his military experience, with bureaucratic skills being provided by the permanent staff. This argument could only be superficially countered by pointing out that even at present, the service headquarters have a permanent staff, and therefore, the proposed system may fare no better. The proposed 'combined' ministry of defence will, in reality, be a part of the government, with some posts being occupied by uniformed cadre. Presumably, the Defence Council will delegate authority and responsibility to department heads, and at lower levels.

Only some part of the service headquarters would be a part of the ministry — and the government, but rest of the services would not be. That part of the service headquarters which is part of the government would exclude operations and intelligence, and would not have direct operational authority. Single-service-specific demands and requirements of units will be reflected through single service channels to the single service departments in the ministry, through single service commanders up the channel. On the other hand, demands of the formation commanders will travel up the operational channels to the chairman of the chiefs of staff committed or the chief of defence staff, or the chief of the joint staff. The point to note is that the separation of the operational command channel is compatible even with the current chiefs of staff channel, except with one major difference : the single service chiefs would lose total operational authority over the single service commands. The authority would have to be exercised collectively and jointly.

Dispensation of the Defence Council will be implemented through departments, and instructions on matters other than operation and intelligence would go down the single service channels. The Defence Minister and the service chiefs of staff would be the links that would be expected to bind the system together. As professional heads of services they will be advisers to the government, at the level of the National Security Council, and to the Defence Minister as his Chiefs of Staff Committee, and in Defence Council. They will be responsible to the government for implementing its operational directives and plans, making optimum use of resources at their command. They will advise the government on the raising and maintaining the armed forces, but the responsibility for deciding the size of the armed forces, and keeping it supplied with the necessary resources including the manpower, equipment, fiances, and all other resources will rest with the Defence Ministry of which the service headquarters will form a part. The service headquarters will become a part of the government in totality, but the operational and functional commands will remain out side the government, as at present. The armed services and their chiefs must not be seen to be a part of the government in totality, although they take orders from the government. The parliament, the bureaucracy, and people at large must be made consciously aware, that the armed services are apolitical, in that, they do not form a part of the political team of the Prime Minister, which is not expected to keep above the party politics. The proposed system allows only a small proportion of the service headquarters to become a part of the machinery of the government, but keeps the rest out of it[16].

The fear of coups that did crop up from time to time, and which in popular perception, caused the political leadership and bureaucrats to keep the armed forces under strictest of scrutiny and control may be dissipated by the proposed organization. No single service chief of staff will have direct control over any of the operational commanders to whom instructions would only be sent through the national command centre/ joint operations room. Chiefs of staff, will be able to place their views on record in the National Security Council and in Defence Council, where they will be heard directly by the Prime Minister and the minister of defence, without being filtered by the bureaucracy, as at present. In short, the chiefs of staff would lose some of their autonomy, in comparison with the current system, but would have more effective authority, in that they will have direct access to centres of power, not as an exception, but as a matter of routine, and hopefully, this will result in more reasoned decision making, on the one hand, and greater and more positive participation in decision making by the government, on the other hand.

NOTES

1.Alvin and Heidi Toffler, 'War and Anti-War,Survival at the Dawn of the 21st Century', Warner Books, London, 1993, (pp. 279-280).

2.Michael E. Porter, 'Competitive Advantage', The Free Press, New York,1985, (p 415).

3." Yet the erosion of what can be called the cantonment mentality began the other day when the eighteenth army chief General Roy Choudhury, declared that the army's "internal duties are as important as tackling the external aggression" "

N.J.Nanporia, 'Bring Army Out of Its Isolation', The Asian Age, Bombay, 28 May, 1995.

4.Sir Christopher France, 'UK Defence Reorganization', USI Journal, April-June, 1995, New Delhi.

5.Pt. Jawaharlal Nehru, apropos of the report made by the Union Constitution Committee, made the following observations in the Constituent Assembly on July 21, 1947:

" We have given anxious thought to this matter and we came to the very definite conclusion that it would not be desirable, first because we want to emphasize the ministerial character of the government, that power really resided in the Ministry and in the Legislature and not in the President as such. At the same time we did not want to make the President just a mere figurehead like the French President. We did not give him any real power but we have made his position one of great authority and dignity. You will notice from this Draft Constitution that he is also to be Commander -in-Chief of the Defence Forces just as the American President is."

B Shiva Rao,' The Framing of India's Constitution', The Indian Institution of Public Administration, New Delhi, 1968, (p.345).

6.Rear Admiral J.H.T. Eberle, 'The Defence Organization of The Future', Lawrence Martin,(Editor), 'The Management of Defence', NDC (UK), 1976.

7 Sir Christopher France, op. cit., (p. 163).

8.General V N Sharma (Retd), 'India's Defence Forces : Building of the Sinews of a Nation', USI Journal, October-December, 1994, New Delhi, (p.459).

9.Manvendra Singh,'Political will limits the use of IAF against insurgents : IAF Doctrine', The Indian Express, Pune, 1 November, 1997.

10.Ashley J. Tellis, 'Stability in South Asia', Arroyo Centre, Documented Briefing, Rand Research Project, 1997.

11.General V N Sharma has recommended a modified CDS system with a full time Chairman. He feels that the full time Chairman will have the ability to interact with and brief political leadership in crises and thus free the service chiefs to conduct operations. In his scheme of things he does not approve of theatre commanders. op. cit., (p. 463)

12.This is the US model adopted in accordance with Goldwater-Nichols Act of 1986. It places full responsibility for every action of defence forces and orders given to them on the political masters. This should ensure their active involvement and engagement. If and when an active deterrence is in place, no other arrangement is feasible. The idea that there would be a dilution of authority and responsibility at the level of single service chiefs is misplaced. The orders would still be prepared on their professional advice and under their supervision.

13.McCloughry points out the undesirability of the Prime Minister holding the charge of Defence Ministry.

AVM E J Kingston McCloughry, 'The Spectrum of Strategy', Jonathan Cape, (p.139).

14.Air Vice Marshal Samar K. Sen points out that there is an absence of integration even amongst Departments of Production and Supply, and Department of Research and Development.

" The most important aspect is the need for providing a unified organizational structure for the management of India's Defence Technology and Industrial Base."

Air Vice Marshal Samar K. Sen, 'Some Aspects of India's Defence Industrialisation - An Overview', USI Journal, April-June, 1994, New Delhi.

15.According to Major General Pratap Narain, such a suggestion was made in 1969 by Mr. S. Mulgaonkar. He further mentions that the institution was established in the US at the instance of Bernard Baruh, industrialist and statesman. Major General Pratap Narain (Retd), 'Indian Arms Bazaar', Shipra, New Delhi, 1994.

16.David Isenberg, a defence analyst, quotes following comments of General W. Y. Smith, with approval :

" An equally valuable outcome of Goldwater-Nichols [Goldwater-Nichols Department of Defense Reorganization Act of 1986] was what was not done : the JCS chairman was not made a statutory member of the NSC, as had been proposed earlier. To have done so would have violated the tradition that the military be non political."

David Isenberg, ' Missing the Point : Why the Reform of the Joint Chiefs of Staff Won't Improve U. S. Defense Policy', CATO Institute of Policy Analysis, Washington DC, 1988.

Bibliography

* Allison, Graham T., 'Essence of Decision, Explanining the Cuban Missile Crisis', Little Brown and Company, Boston, 1971.

* All India Reporter, Supreme Court Section, AIR Ltd, Nagpur, 1992.

* Aron, Raymond, 'Modern Strategic Thought', Alastair Buchan (foreword), 'Problems of Modern Strategy', Praeger Publishers, New York, 1970.

* Aron, Raymond, Clausewitz, Philosopher of War', Routledge & Kegan Paul, London, 1976.

* Bakshi, P.M. (Compiler and Editor), The Constitution of India', Universal Book Traders, Delhi, 1991.

* Barnaby, Frank, 'Arms Control after the Gulf War', Conflict Study 240, April 1991, Research Institutue for Study of Conflict and Terrorism (RISCT).

* Barnes, Harry Elmer, An Intellectual and Cultural History of the Western World, Volume Three, Dover Publications Inc., New York, 1965.

* Bon, Edward D., 'Conflicts. A Better Way to Resolve Them', Penguin Books, London, 1985

* Beaufre, Andre, General d Armee, 'Strategy of Action', Faber and Faber, London, 1996.

* Brodie, Bernard, 'Technology Politcs, and Stratey', Alastair Buchan (foreword), 'Problems of Modern Strategy', Praeger Publishers, New York, 1970.

* Buzan, Barry, 'People, States & Fear'. Trans Asia Publishers, New Delhi, 1983.

* Calvin, William J., 'The Cerebral Harmony' Bantam Books', 1990.

* Charnwood, Lord, 'Abraham Lincoln'. Pocket Books, USA, 1948.

* Chaudhuri, Nirad, C., 'Thy Hand, Great Anarch', Chatto & Windus, London, 1987,

* Churchill, Winston S., 'A History of English Speaking People, Volume IV, Casell and Company, London, 1957.

* Coblentz, 'Arrow to Atom Bomb', Peter Owen London.

* Dixit, J.N., 'Assignment Colombo', Konark Publishers, New Delhi, 1998.

* Douhet, Giulio, 'The Command of the Air', Faber and Faber Ltd, Mcmxliii.

* Encyclopeadia Britanica, Volumes 4 &11, 1964.

* Downey, JCT, 'Management in the Armed Forces', McGraw- Hill Book Company, UK London, 1977.

* Fuller, J.F.C., Major-General, 'The Conduct of War, 1789-1961', Eyre and Spottiswoode, London, 1961.

* Galbraith, John Kenneth, 'The Anatomy of Power', Hamish Hamilton, London, 1984.

* Gould, W.T.S and Findlay, A.M., (editors), 'Population Migration and the Changing World Order', John Wiley and Sons, 1994.

* Kangle R.P. (translater), 'The Kautilya Arthasastra, Three Parts, Motilal Banarasidass, Delhi, 1992.

* Kaplan, Abraham, 'The Conduct of Inquiry' Sachin Publication, Jaipur, 1980.

* Government of India, 'The Army in India, and its Evolution.' Superintendent, Government Printing, India, Calcutta, 1924.

* Howard, Michael, 'Classical Strategist', Alastair Buchan (foreword), 'Problems of Modern Strategy, Praeger Publisher, New York, 1970.

* Huntington, Samuel P., 'The Clash of Civilization, and the Remaking of the World Order', Viking, New Delhi, 1996.

* Isenberg, David, 'Missing the Ponit: Why the Reform of the Joint Chiefs of Staff Won't Improve U.S. Defence Policy', CATO Institution of Policy Analysis, Washington DC, 1988.

* Khanna, D.D.& Mehrotra, P.N., Defence Versus Development, Indus Publishing Company, New Delhi, 1993.

* Kingston McCloughry, E.J., AVM, 'The Spectrum of Strategy', Jonathan Cape.

* Kissinger, Henry, 'Diplomacy', Simon and Schuster, London, 1995.

* Jalal, Ayesha, 'The State of Martial Rule', Cambridge University Press, 1990.

Lukes, Steven (editor), 'Power', Oxford, England, 1986.

* Luttwak, Edward, 'Strategy : The Logic of War and Peace' Harvard University Press, Cambridge, Massachusetts, 1987.

* McCansland, Jeffrey, Lt Col, 'The Gulf Conflict; A Military Analysis', Adelphi Paper 282, IISS, London, November, 1993.

* MacMunn, Sir George, Lt Col, 'Vignettes From Indian Wars', Sampson Law, Marston & Co., London.

* McNamara, Robert, 'The Essence of Security', Hodder & Stoughen, London, 1968.

* MacRae, Hamish, 'The World in 2020', Harper Collins, London, 1994.

* Malleson, G B Colonel, 'The Decisive Battles of India', Sagar Publication, New Delhi, 1969, [first publihed in 1883].

* Martin, Lawrence, (editor) 'The Managemnt of Defence' Rear Admiral J.H.T. Eberle. The Defence Organization of The Future', NDC (UK), 1976.

* Moran, Lord, 'The Anatomy of Courage', Houghton Miffin Company, Boston, 1967. [First published in 1945].

* Morgenthau, H.J., 'Politics among Nation', New York, 1949.

* Palit, D.K., Major General, Vrc, War in the High Himalaya',Lancer, New Delhi.

* Nye, Joseph S., Jr, 'The Contribution of Strategic Studies', IISS, London. 1989.

* O'Ballance, Edgar, 'Afghan Wars 1839-1992', Brassey's, London, 1992.

* O'Dwyer, Michael, 'India As I Knew It-1885-1925', Mittal Publication, 1988 [originally published circa 1930]

* Osgood, Robert T., 'The Reappraisal of Limited War', Alastair Buchan (foreword), 'Problems of Modern Strategy', Praeger Publishers. New York, 1970.

* Porter, Michael E., 'Competitive Advantage', The Free Press, New York, 1985.

* Pratap Narain, Major General (Retd.), 'Indian Arms Bazaar', Shipra, New Delhi, 1994.

* Rao, P.V.R., 'Defence Without Drift' , Popular Prakashan, Bombay, 1970.

* Raghavan, R.V. Lt. Gen, 'India's Need for Strategic Balance', Delhi Policy Group, Delhi.

* Renn, Ludwig, 'Warfare, The Relationship of War With Society', Faber and Faber, Londen , Mcmxxxix.

* Rosen, Stephen Peter, 'Societies and Military Power---India and Its Armies', Oxford University Press, Oxford, 1996.

* Russell, Bertrand, 'Freedom and Organization--1814-1914', George Allen and Unwin, London, 1934.

* Russell, Bertrand' 'Human Society in Ethics and Politics', Routledge, London, 1954.

* Schelling, Thomas C., 'Arms And Influence', Yale University Press, New Haven, Connecticut, 1966.

* Simpkin, Richard E., 'Race to the Swift, Thoughts on Twenty-First Century Warfare', Brassey's Defence Publishers, London, 1985.

* Shiva Rao, B., 'The Framing of India's Constitution', The Indian Institution of Public Administratrion, New Delhi, 1968.

* Singh, Nagendra, 'Defence Mechanism of the Modern State', Asia Publishing House, Bombay, 1964. [Dr. Nagendra Singh was a member of the Constituent Assembly of India]

* SIPRI YEAR BOOK 1995, Stockholm International Peace Research Institute.

* Smith, Chris, 'India's Adhoc Arsenal, Direction of Drift in Defence Policy?', SIPRI, Oxford University Press, New York, 1994.

* Tellis, Ashley J., 'Stability in South Asia', Arroyo Centre, Documented Briefing, Rand Research Project, 1997.

* Toffer, Alvin and Heidi, War and Anti-War, Survival at the Dawn of the 21st Century', Warner Books, London, 1993.

* Wrong, Dennis H., 'Power', Basil Blackwell, Oxford, 1988.

* Young, Oran R. (editor), 'The Resolution of Conflict', Bargaining, Formal Theories of Negotiations', University of Illinois Press, 1975.

* Venkateswaran, A.I., 'Defence Organization in India', Publications Division, Ministry of Information and Broadcasting, Government of India, New Delhi, 1967.

* Articles & News Reports

* Albright, Madeleine, US Secretary of State, Statement before the Senate Forign Relations Committee, on January 8, 1998, USIS, Mumbai.

* AP news report datelined Washington, June 29, 'Pentagon overstated Gulf War Weapons', Asian Age, Bombay. 30 JUN97.

* Askari, M.H., 'Thought :Let's celebtrate the end of Raj too', Asian Age, Mumbai, (By arrangement with Dawn), May 5, 1997.

* Sharma, Devinder, 'Food for thought from Australia', Indian Express, Pune, 19 July, 1997.

* Barry, Dave, 'Sky shattering news : the B-2 Bomber gets wet', Asian Age, Bombay, 3 Nov 97, by arrangement with Miami Herald.

* Beg, Mirza Aslam, Gen.(Retd), 'Trilateral zone', Asian Age, Bombay, 14 October, 1997. By arrangement with the Dawn.

* France. Christopher, Sir, 'UK Defence Reorganization', USI Journal, April-June, 1995, New Delhi.

* Gupta, Rajan, 'Look West through the East', Indian Express. Pune, 22 August, 1997.

* Jakobson, Max, [former Finnish ambassador to the UN], 'Five Policemen and their own United Nations', Asian Age, By Arrangement with the International Herald Tribune. Bombay, 16 March, 1998.

ICSS Bulletins 17-18. March, 1997, Tel Aviv.

* Kissinger, Henry, 'US needs China for balance of power', Express, Pune, 4 November, 1997, quoting an article by Kissinger in Newsweek.

* Nanda, Prakash, 'Priority for establishment of Security Council: Gujral', the Times of India, 2 Jun 96.

* Nanda, Rajiv, 'Analyst wary of Sharif's peace-intent', Times of India, Bombay, February

* Nanporia, N.J. 'Bring Army Out of Its Isolation', The Asian Age, Bombay, 28 May, 1995.

* News report of an interview with Dr. Ramanna, titled ' N-capability of India enough for deterrence.' Times of India, Bombay, 28 October, 1996.

* Ohmae, Kenichi, 'The end of the nation state : the rise of regional economies'. The Free Press, Simon Schuster, New York, 1995. (Excerpted in World Executives Digest, May, 1996).

* Pike, Francis, 'Mandate from heaven : China will weat the crown', Asian Age. Bombay, 22 July, 1997 By arrangement with The Spectator.

* Sen, Gautom, 'Another raj in the making', Indian Express, Bombay, 7 March, 1997.

* Sen, Gautam, writing on China Indian Express, Pune, 2 November 1996.

* Sen , Samar K., Air Vice Marshal, 'Some Aspects of India's Defence Industrialisation- An Overview', USI Journal, April-June,1994, New Delhi.

* Singh, Manvendra, 'Political will limits the use of IAF against insugents : IAF Doctrine', The Indian Express, Pune, 1 November, 1997.

* Sharme, V. N. General, (Retd.) 'India's Defence Force :, Building of the Sinews of a Nation', USI Journal, October-December, 1994, New Delhi.

* Varadarajan, Siddharth, 'Wishful Thinking on Economic Integration', Times of India, Bombay, 13 May, 1996.

* Brzezinsky, Zbigniew, Nationals Security Adviser to President Carter, 'Entering the Age of Defence', The Washington Post, October 2, 1988.

* Vohra, N.N., former Home Secretary, quoted in the Times of India, Bombay 6, October, 1996.

* Zakaria, Rafiq, 'The price of partition', Indain Express, Pune, 14 August 14, 1997.

* Wyatt, Woodrow, 'Two Fathers with a Mission', The Asian Age, Mumbai, August 14, 1997.

Index